CHAPTER 38

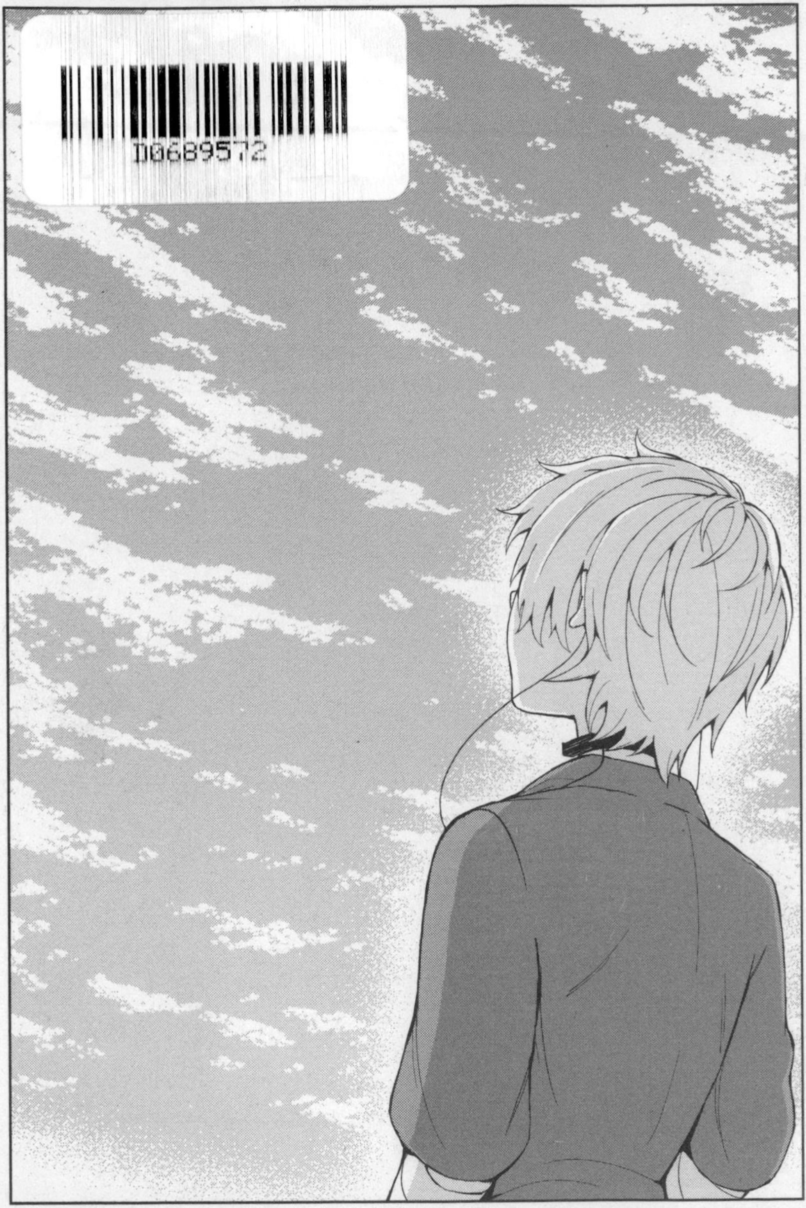

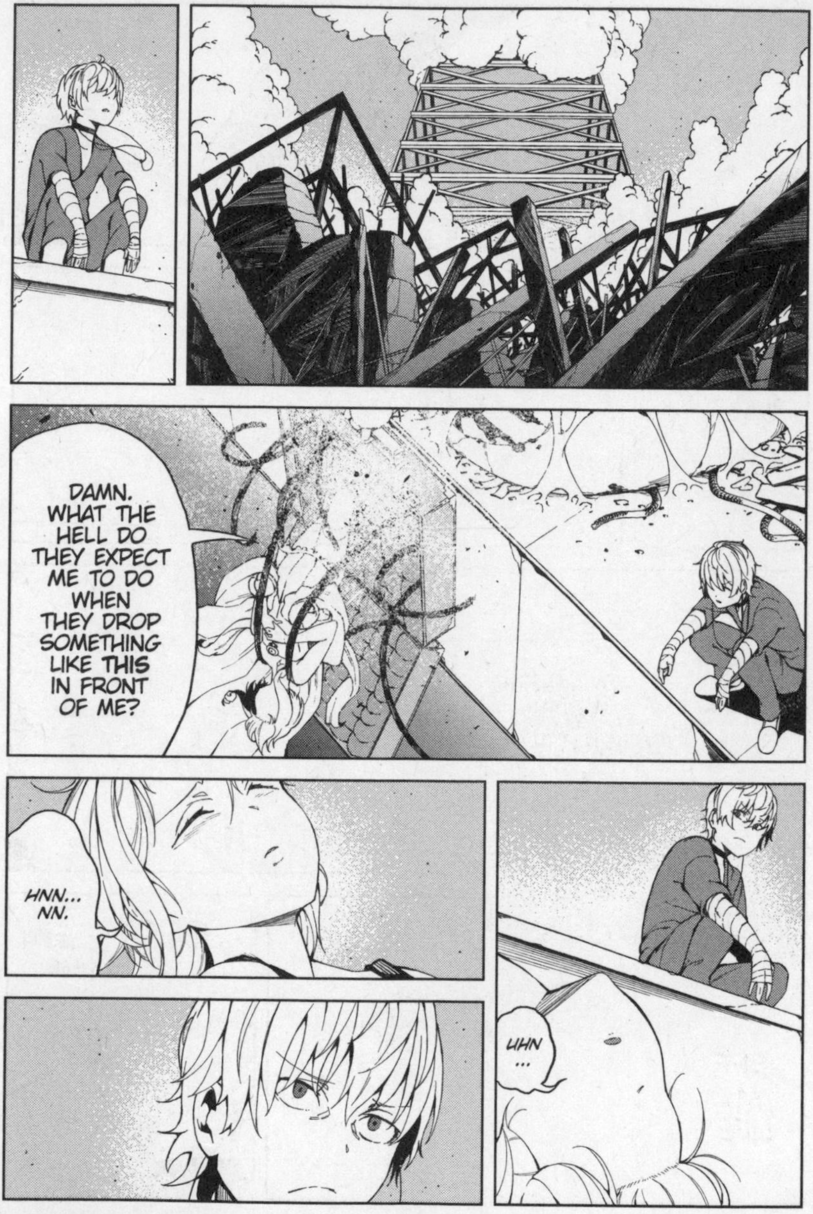
DAMN. WHAT THE HELL DO THEY EXPECT ME TO DO WHEN THEY DROP SOMETHING LIKE THIS IN FRONT OF ME?
UHN ...
HNN... NN.

A Certain Scientific Accelerator 08

STORY BY KAZUMA KAMACHI

ART BY ARATA YAMAJI

CHARACTER DESIGN BY KIYOTAKA HAIMURA & ARATA YAMAJI

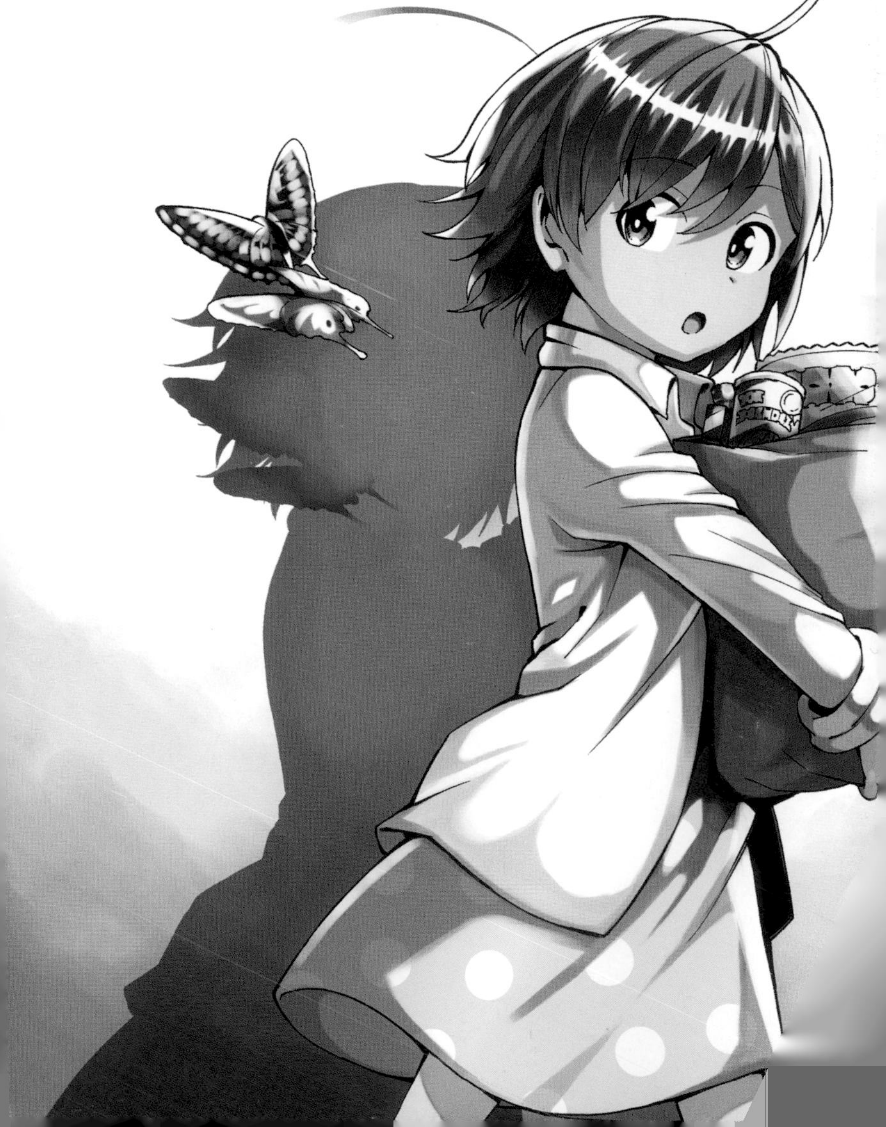

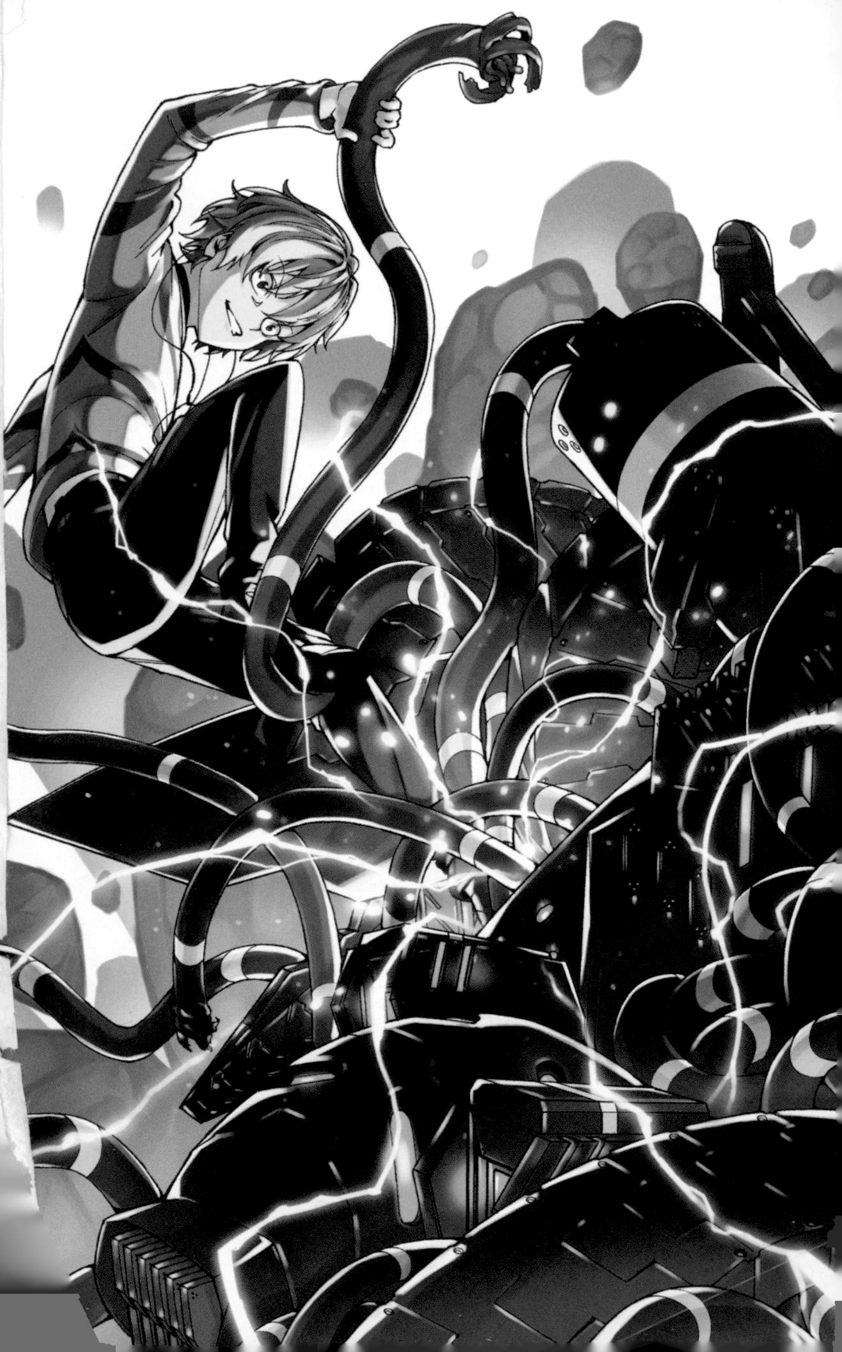

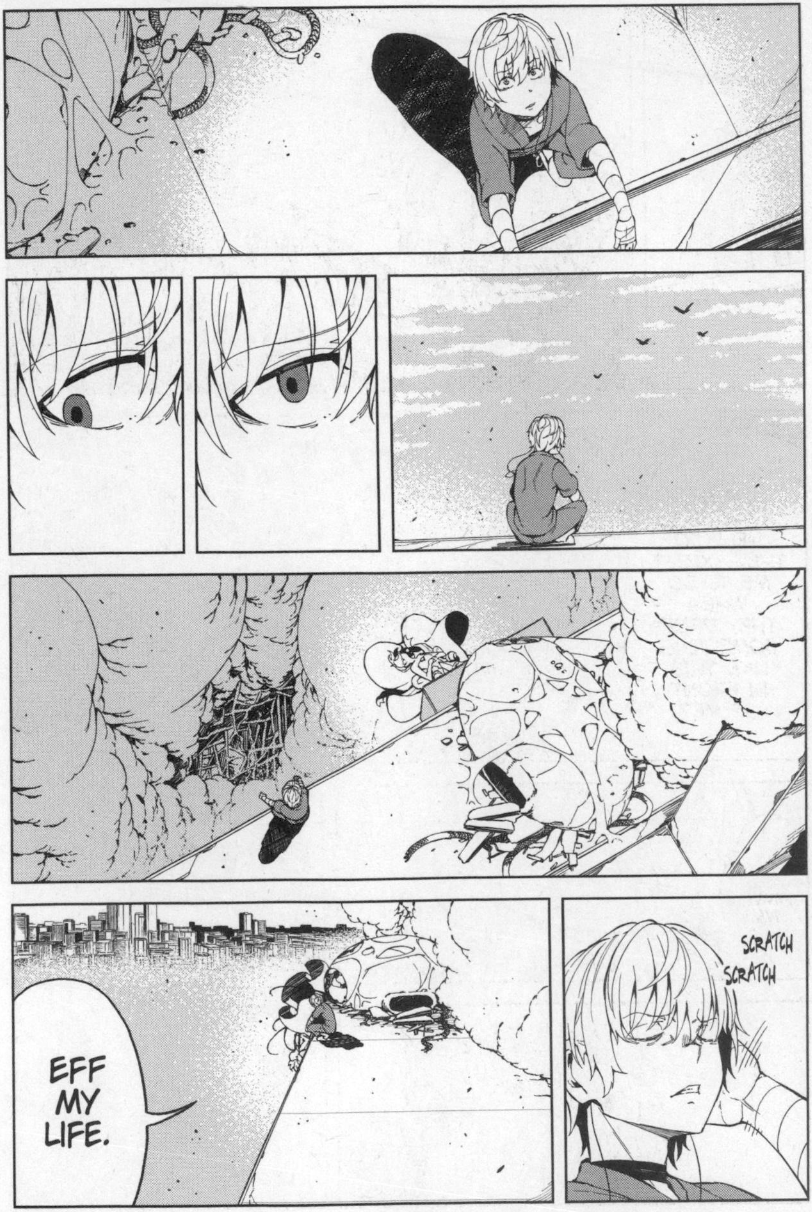
SCRATCH
SCRATCH
EFF MY LIFE.

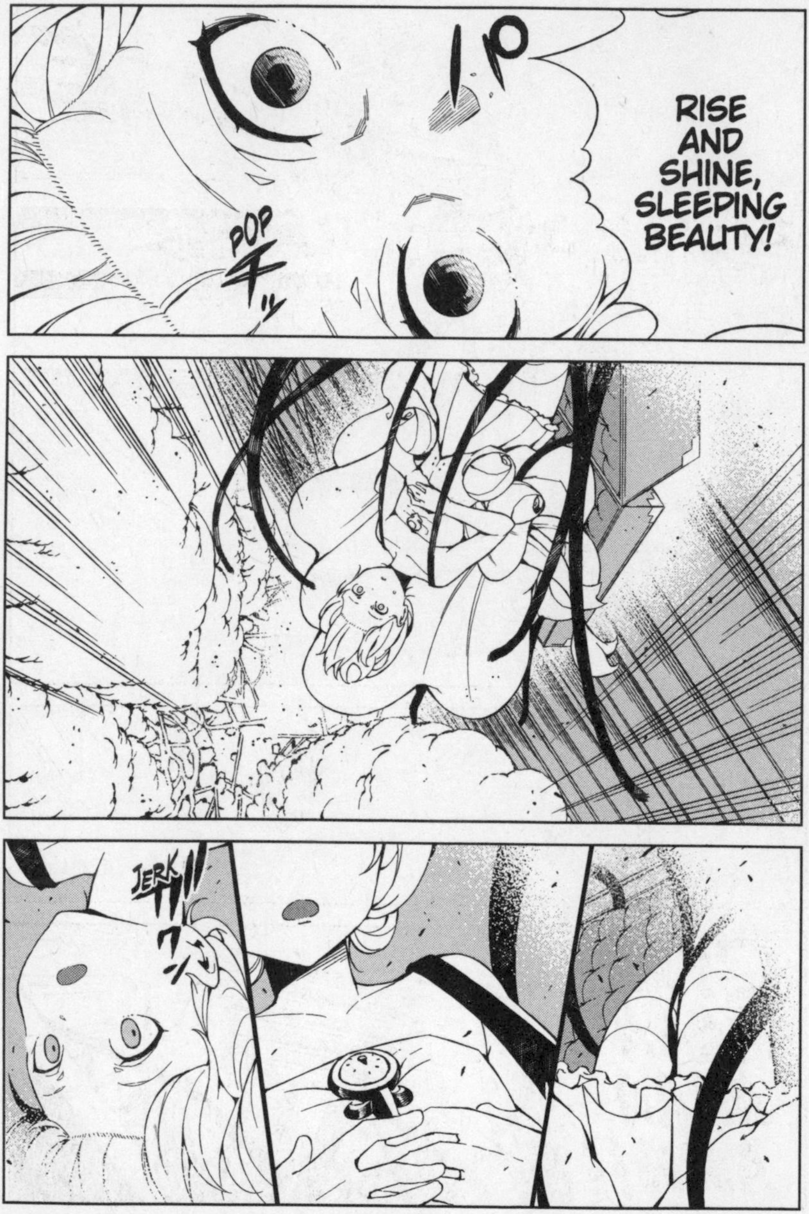
RISE AND SHINE, SLEEPING BEAUTY!
POP
JERK

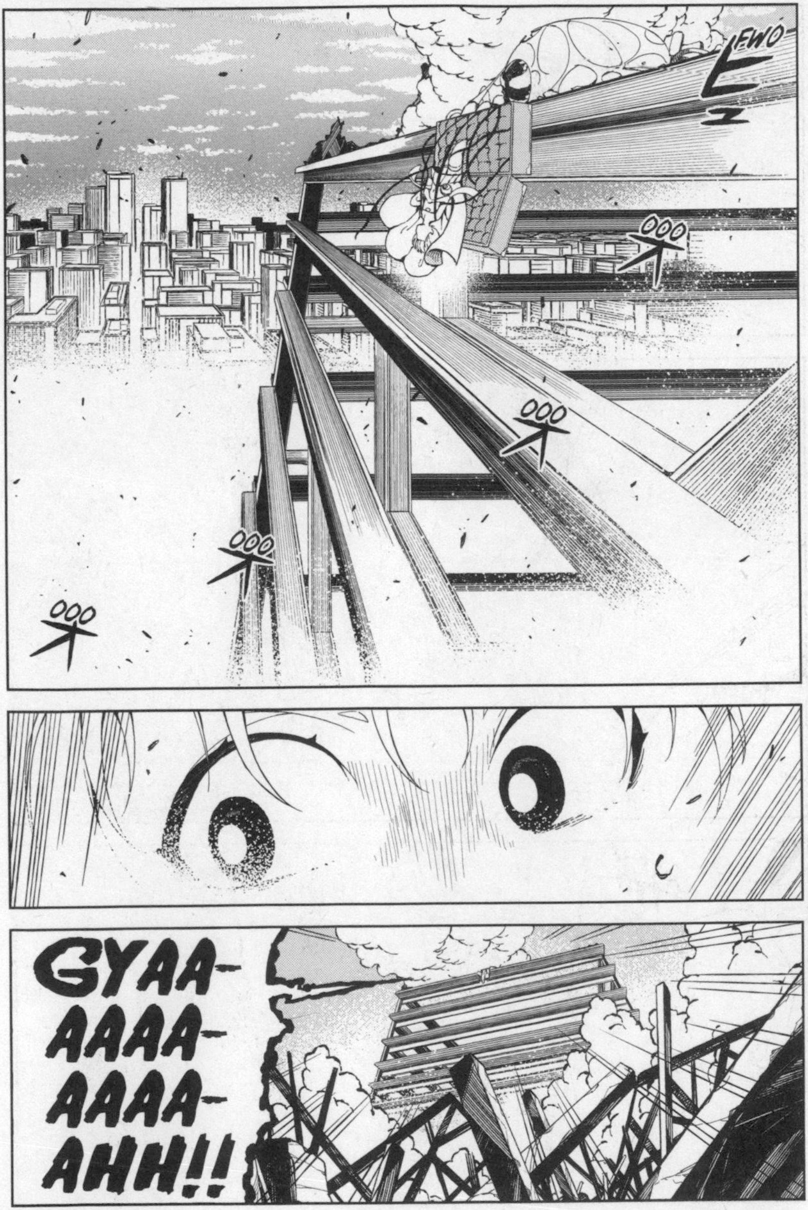
GYAA-
AAAA-
AAAA-
AHH!!

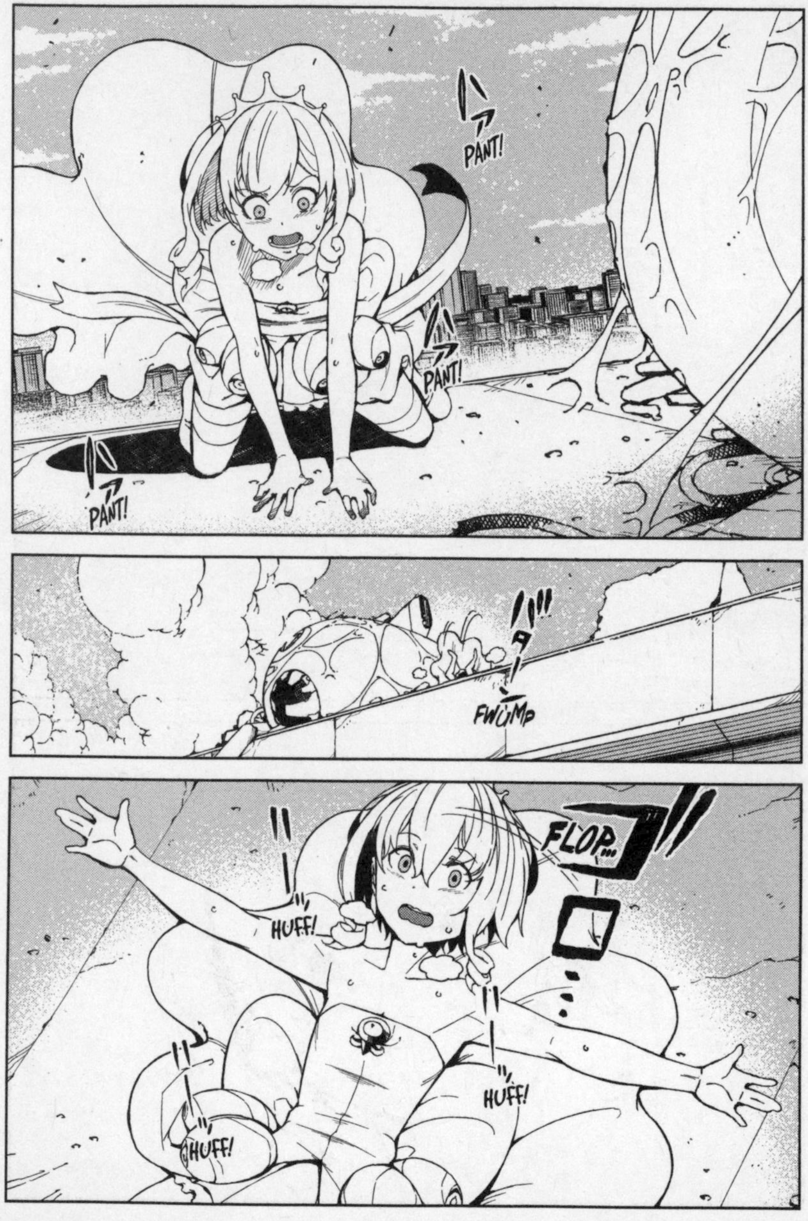
PANT!
PANT!
PANT!
FWUMP
FLOP...
HUFF!
HUFF!
HUFF!

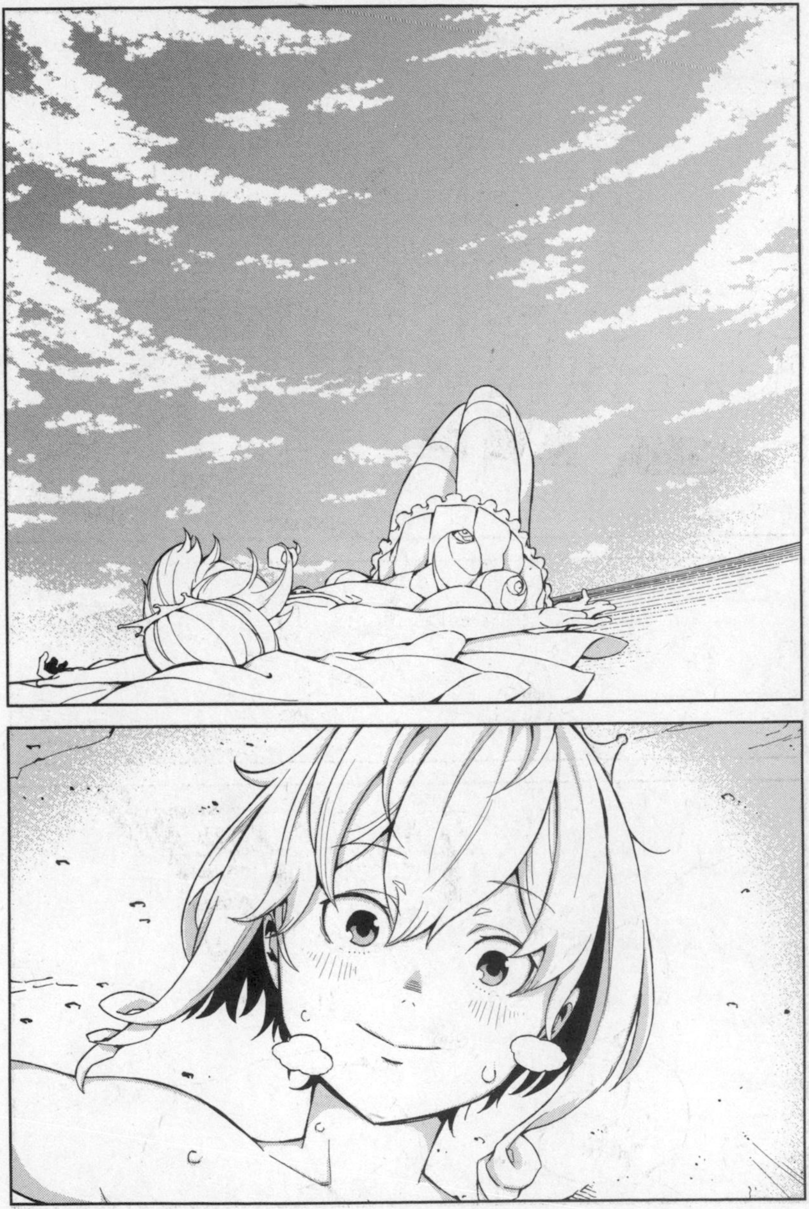

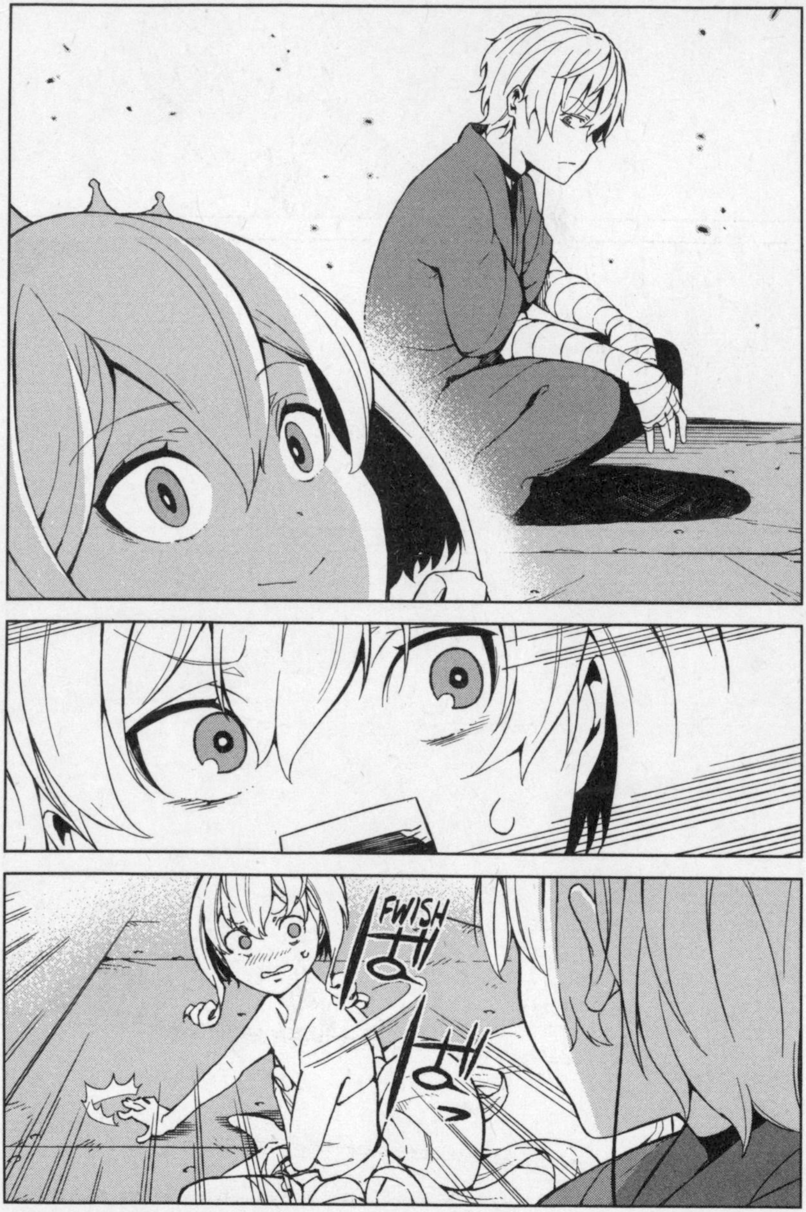
FWISH

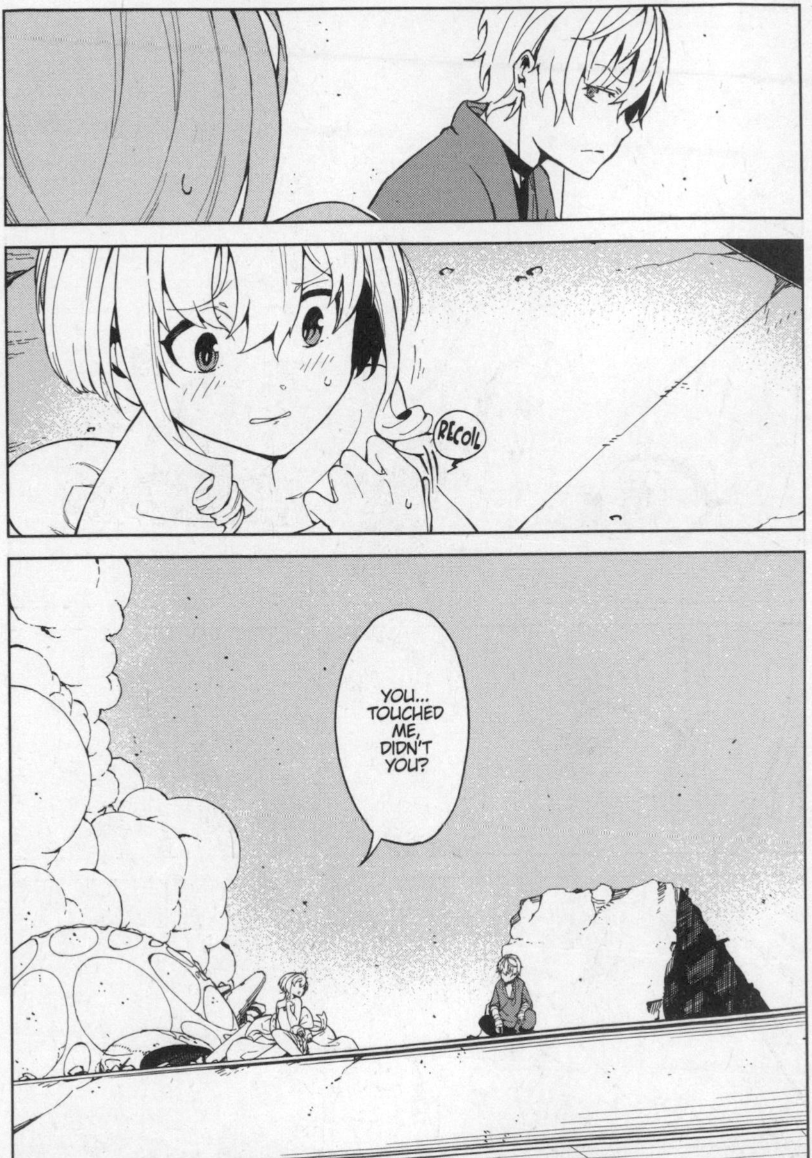
RECOIL
YOU... TOUCHED ME, DIDN'T YOU?

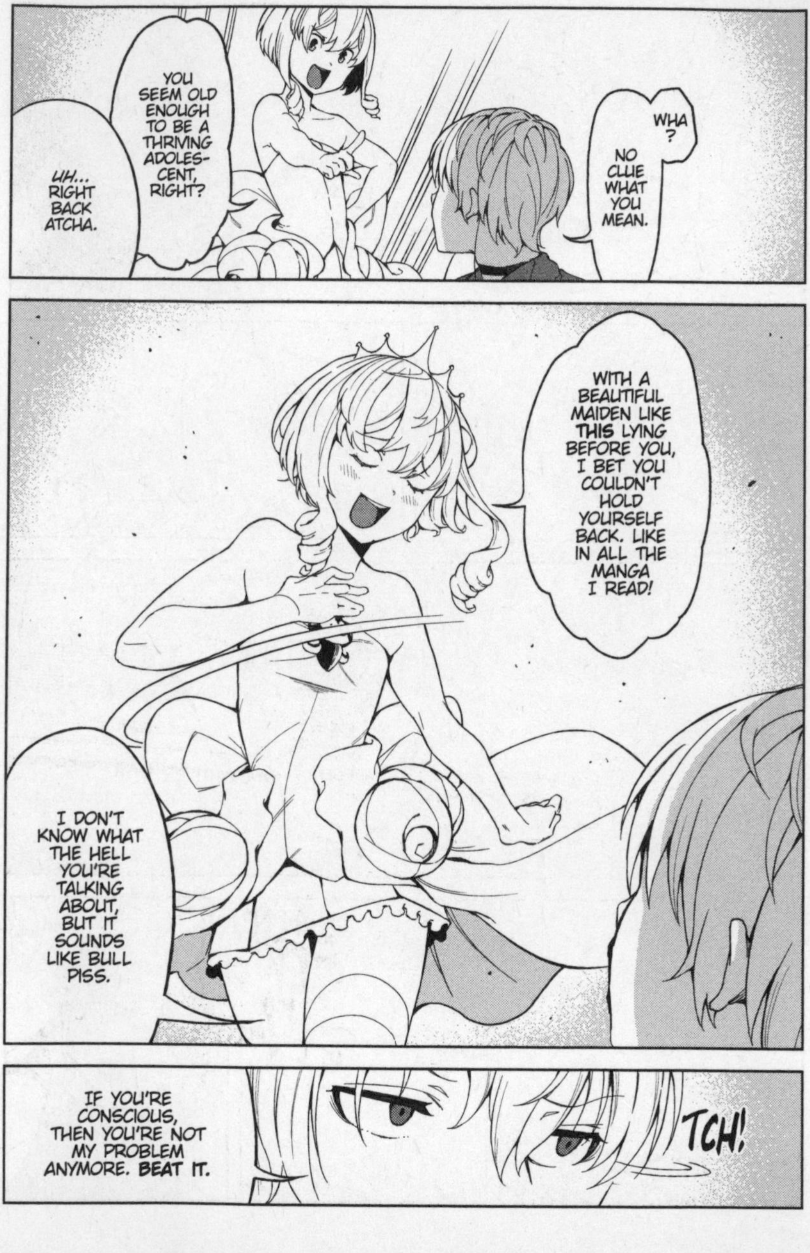
WHA? NO CLUE WHAT YOU MEAN.
YOU SEEM OLD ENOUGH TO BE A THRIVING ADOLESCENT, RIGHT?
UH... RIGHT BACK ATCHA.
WITH A BEAUTIFUL MAIDEN LIKE **THIS** LYING BEFORE YOU, I BET YOU COULDN'T HOLD YOURSELF BACK. LIKE IN ALL THE MANGA I READ!
I DON'T KNOW WHAT THE HELL YOU'RE TALKING ABOUT, BUT IT SOUNDS LIKE BULL PISS.
TCH!
IF YOU'RE CONSCIOUS, THEN YOU'RE NOT MY PROBLEM ANYMORE. **BEAT IT.**

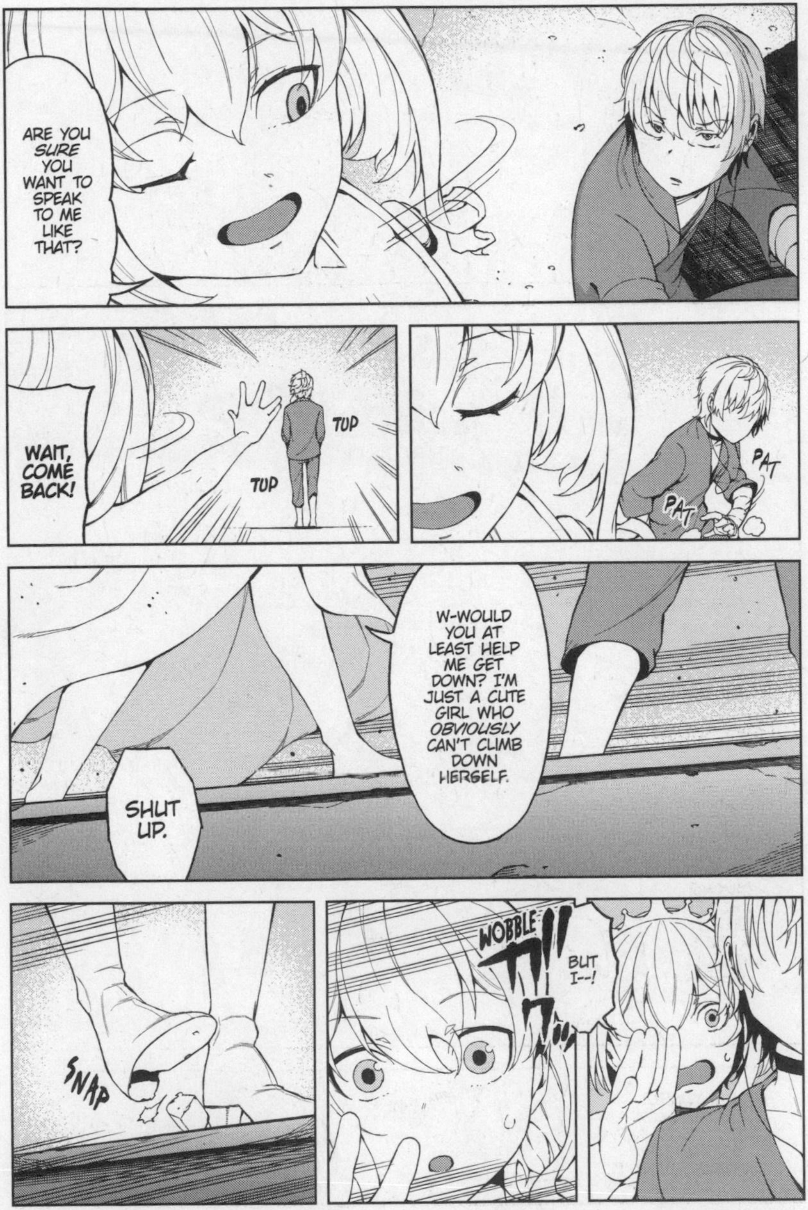
ARE YOU SURE YOU WANT TO SPEAK TO ME LIKE THAT?
PAT
PAT
TUP
WAIT, COME BACK!
TUP
W-WOULD YOU AT LEAST HELP ME GET DOWN? I'M JUST A CUTE GIRL WHO OBVIOUSLY CAN'T CLIMB DOWN HERSELF.
SHUT UP.
WOBBLE
BUT I--!
SNAP

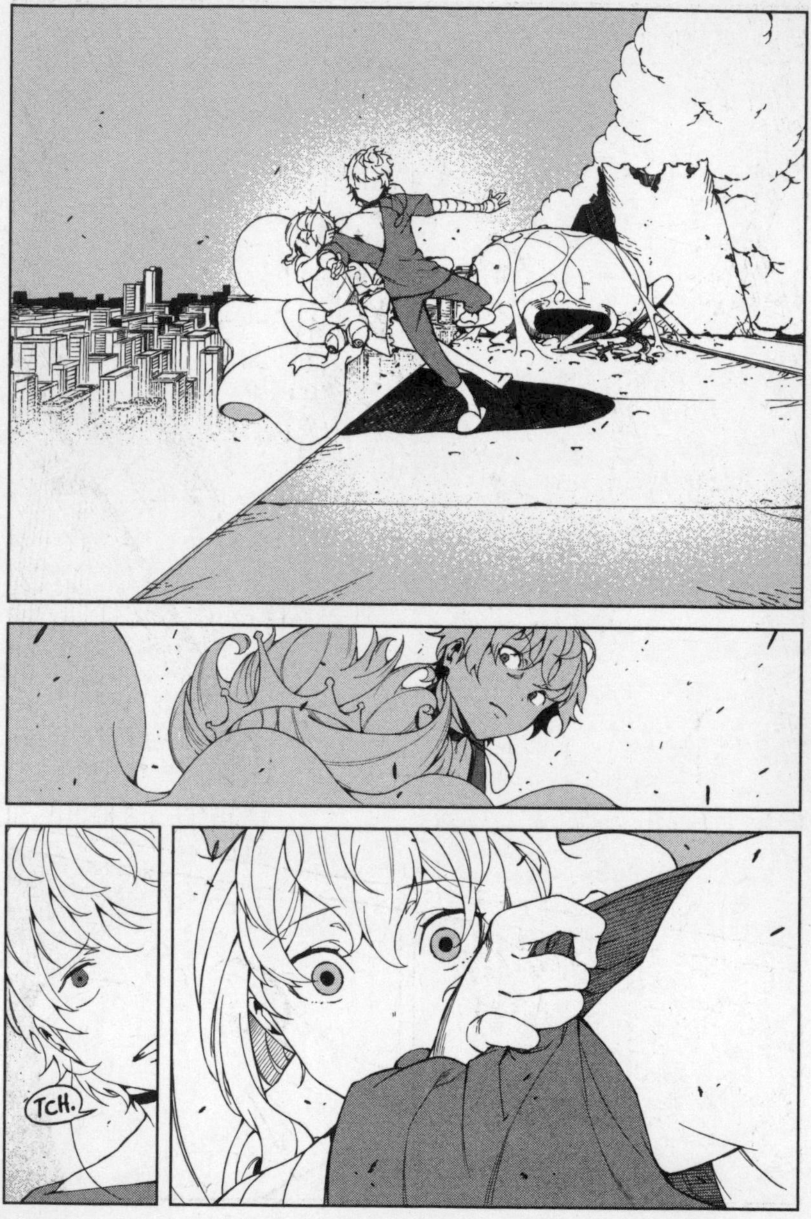
TCH.

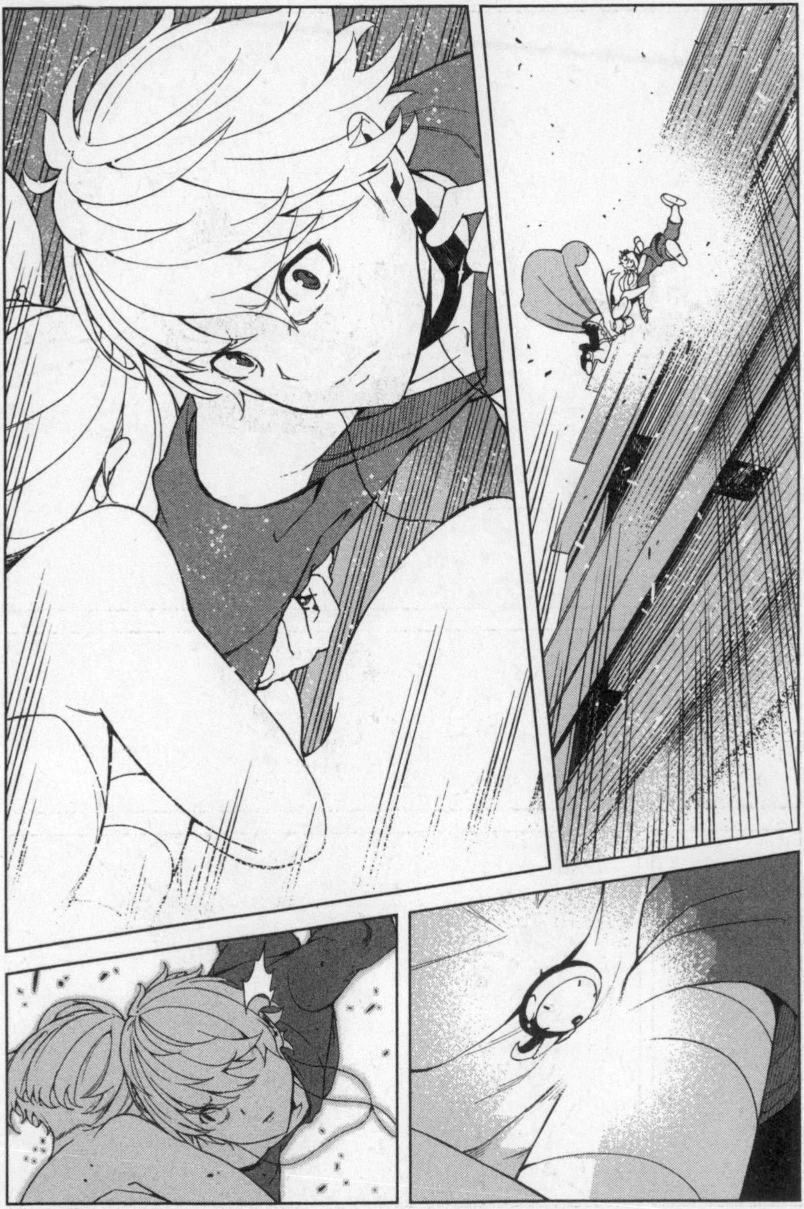

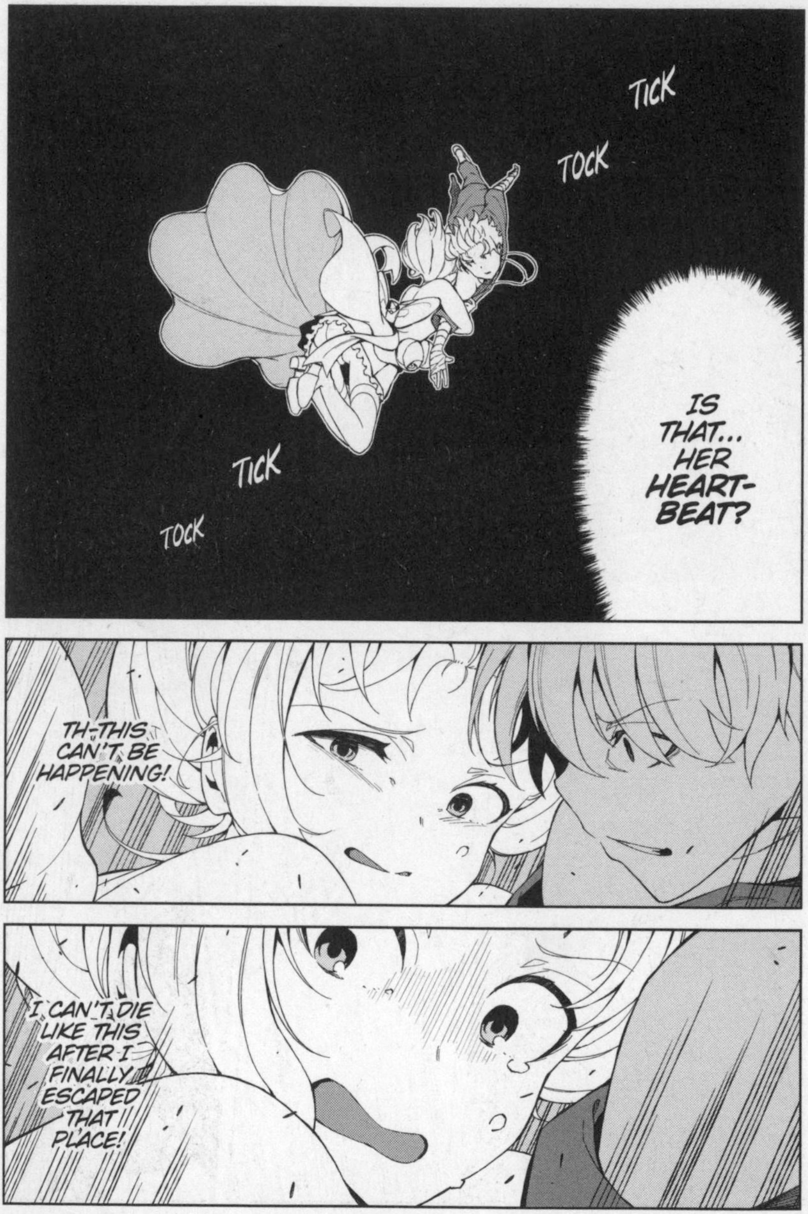
TICK
TOCK
IS THAT... HER HEART-BEAT?
TICK
TOCK
TH-THIS CAN'T BE HAPPENING!
I CAN'T DIE LIKE THIS AFTER I FINALLY ESCAPED THAT PLACE!

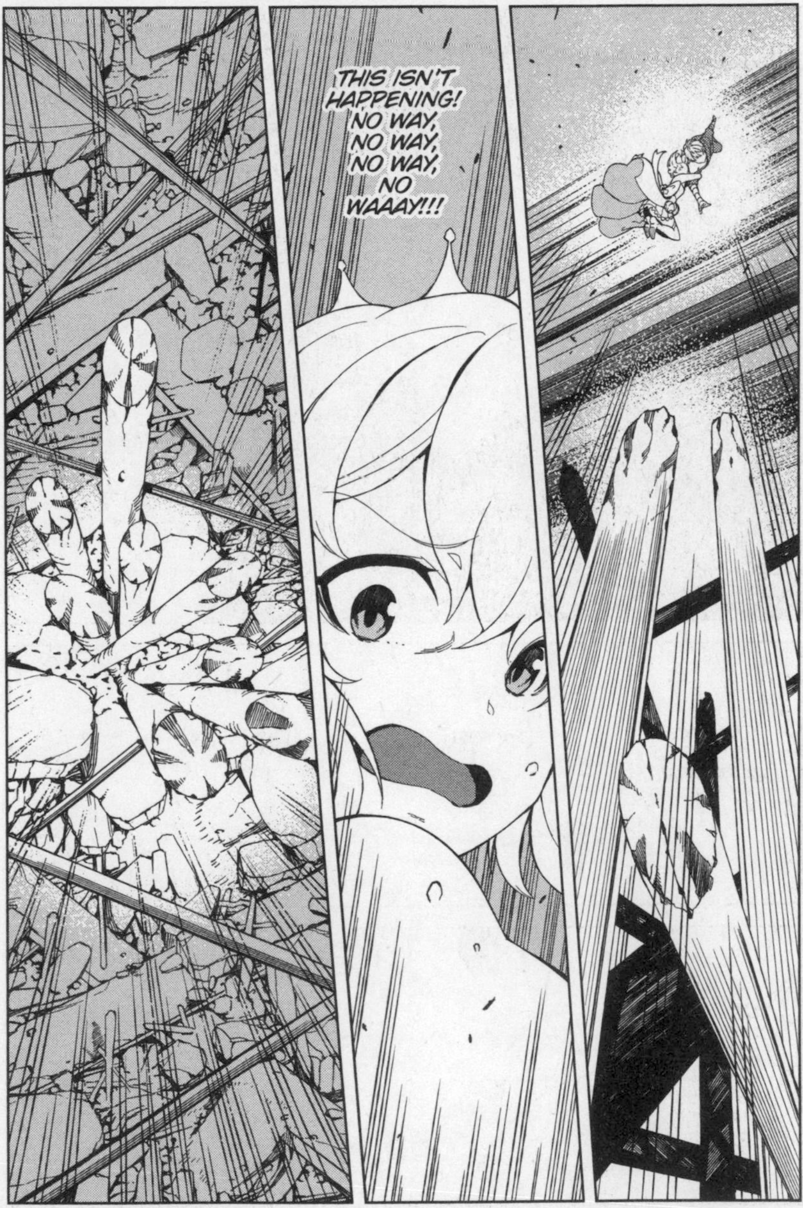
THIS ISN'T HAPPENING! NO WAY, NO WAY, NO WAY, NO WAAAY!!!

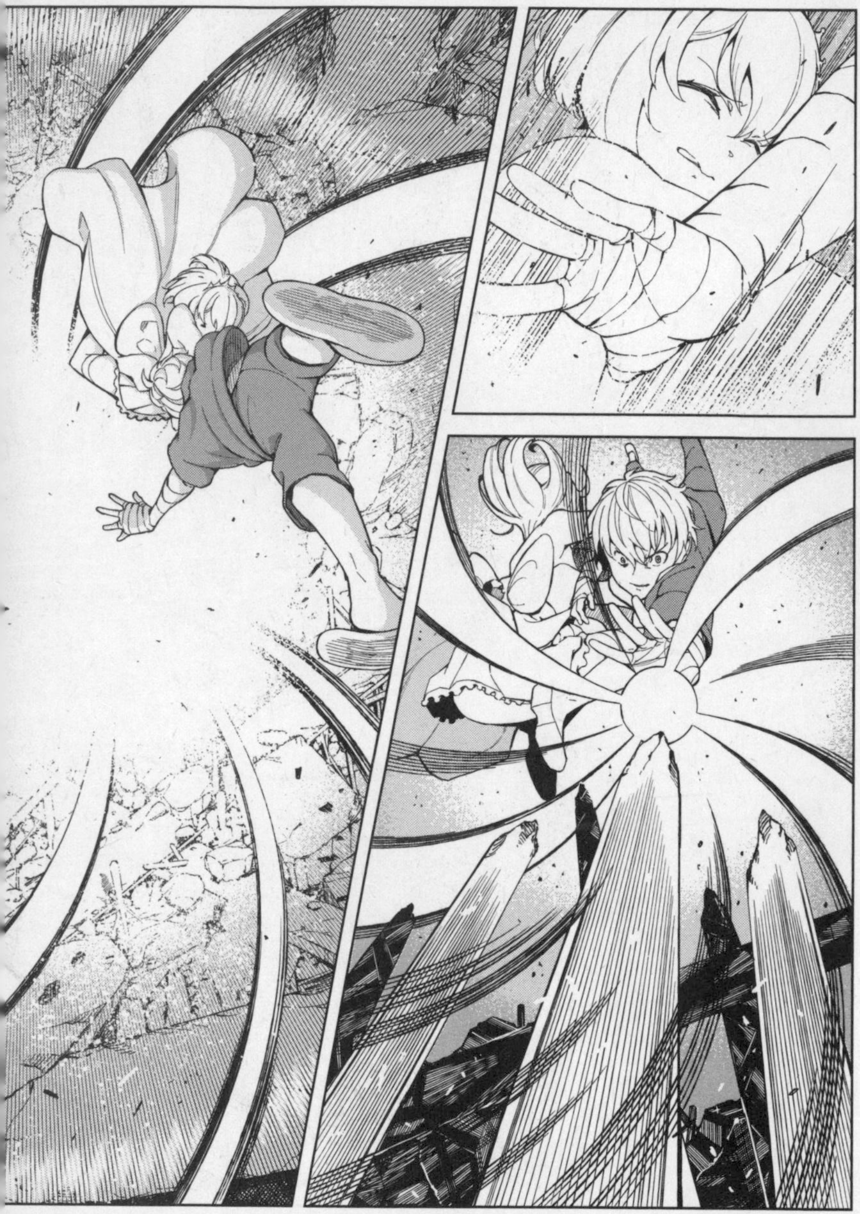

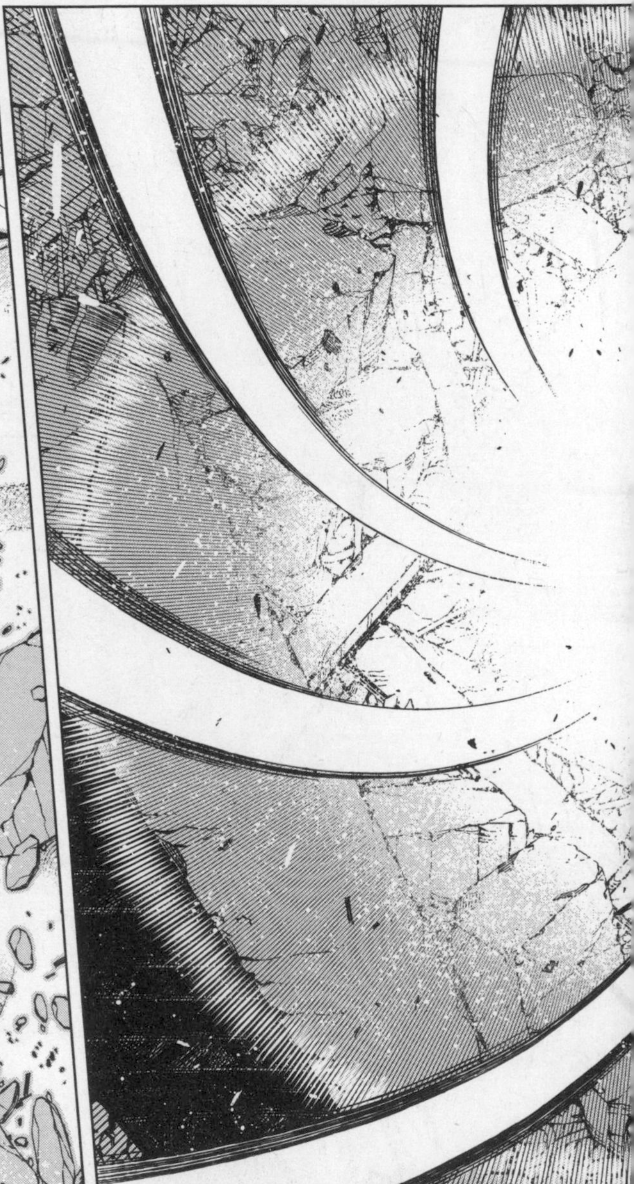
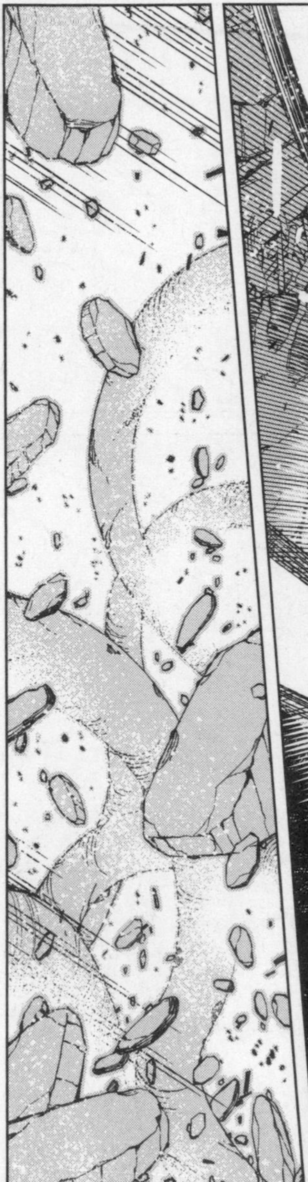

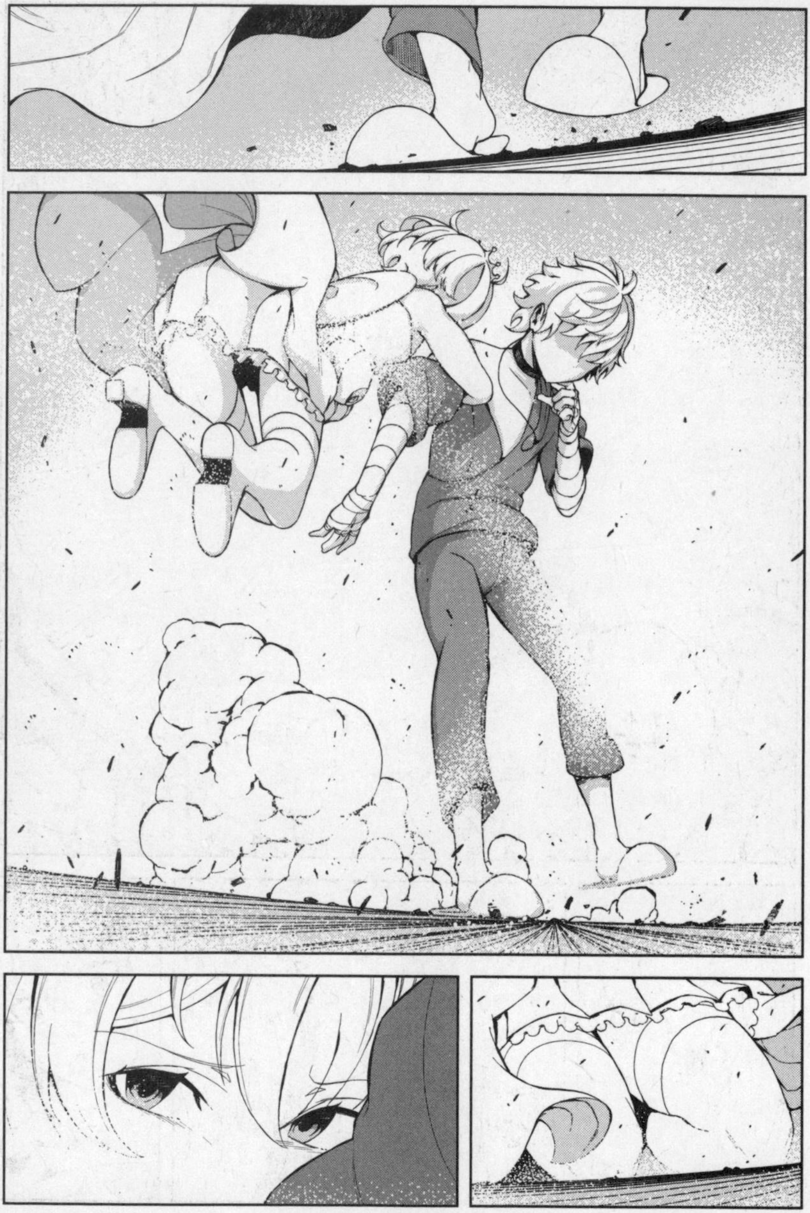

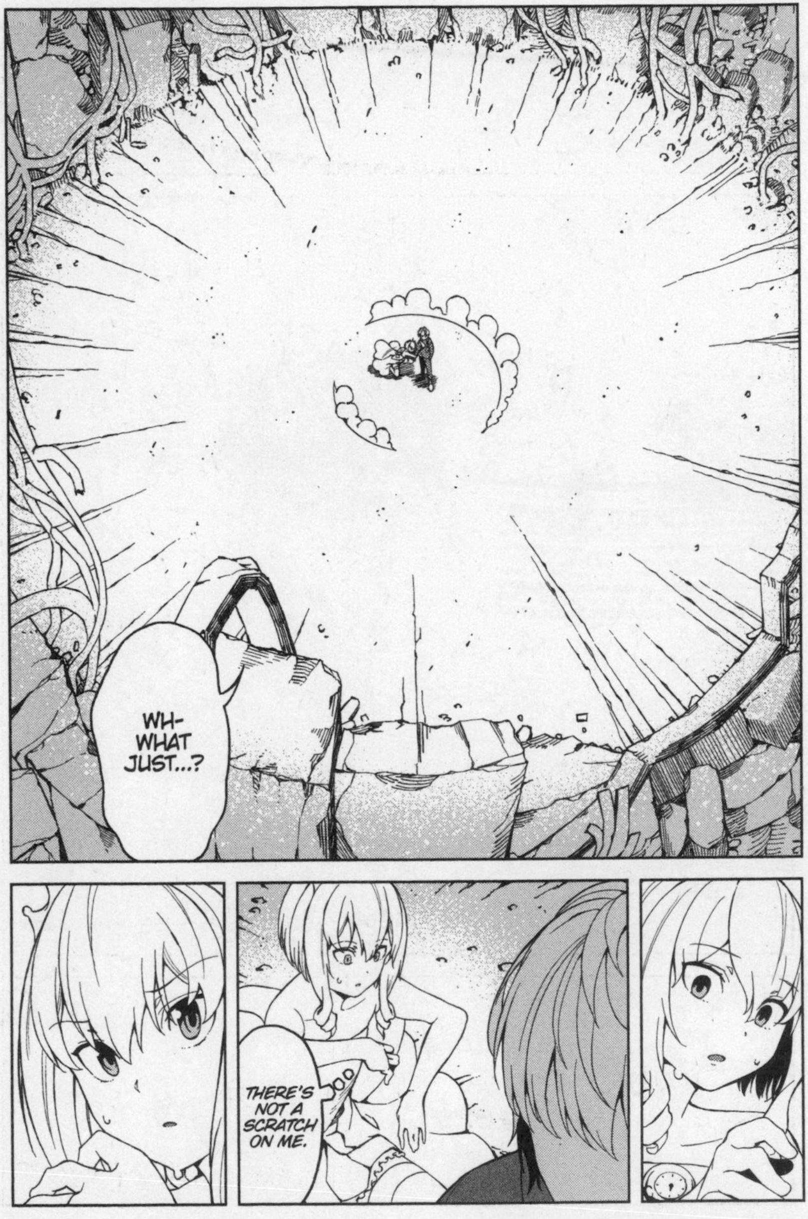
WH- WHAT JUST...?
THERE'S NOT A SCRATCH ON ME.

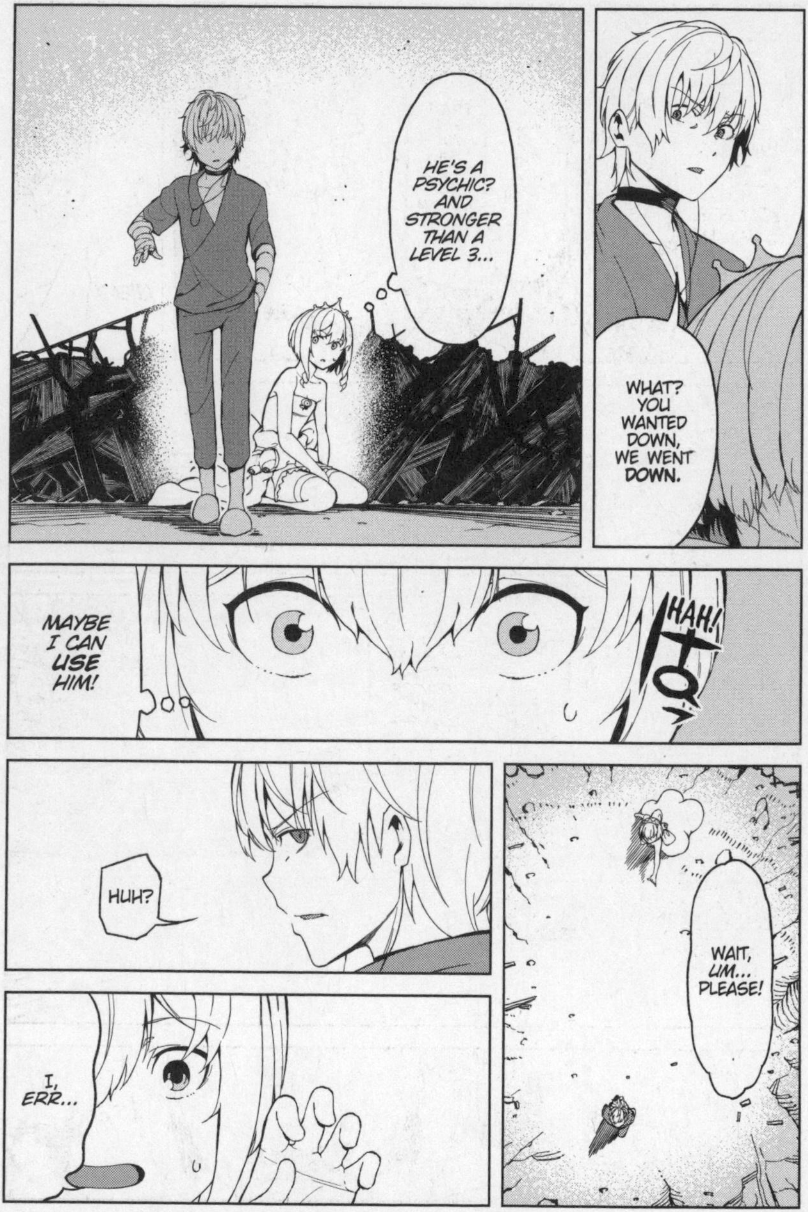
WHAT? YOU WANTED DOWN, WE WENT DOWN.
HE'S A PSYCHIC? AND STRONGER THAN A LEVEL 3...
HAH!
MAYBE I CAN USE HIM!
WAIT, UM... PLEASE!
HUH?
I, ERR...

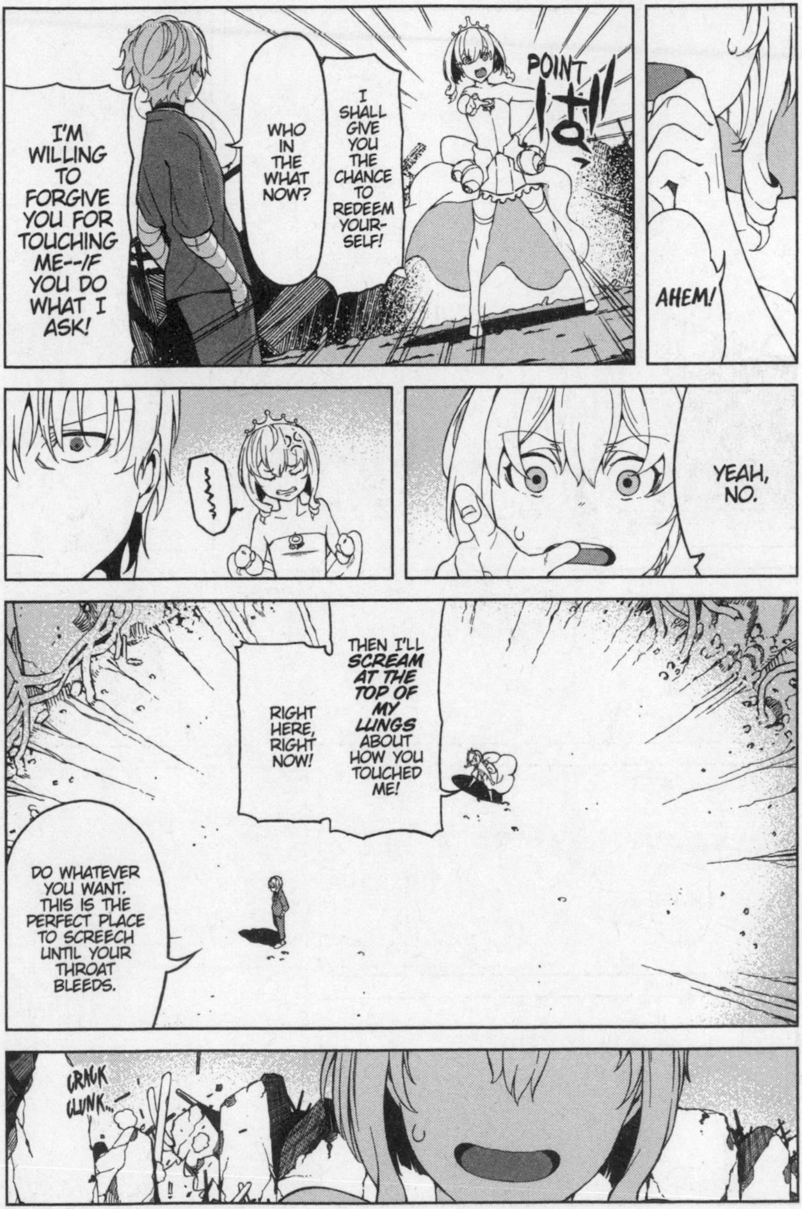
AHEM!
POINT
I SHALL GIVE YOU THE CHANCE TO REDEEM YOURSELF!
WHO IN THE WHAT NOW?
I'M WILLING TO FORGIVE YOU FOR TOUCHING ME--IF YOU DO WHAT I ASK!
YEAH, NO.
THEN I'LL SCREAM AT THE TOP OF MY LUNGS ABOUT HOW YOU TOUCHED ME!
RIGHT HERE, RIGHT NOW!
DO WHATEVER YOU WANT. THIS IS THE PERFECT PLACE TO SCREECH UNTIL YOUR THROAT BLEEDS.
CRACK
CLUNK...

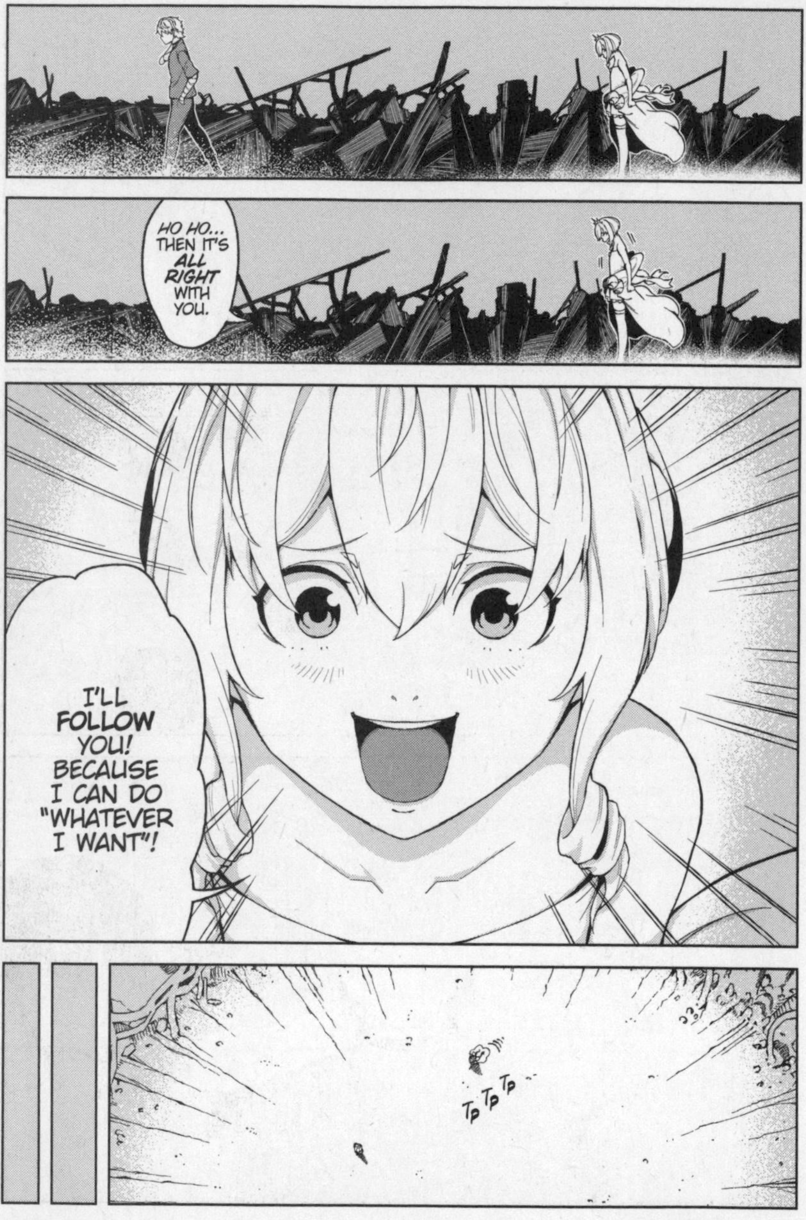
HO HO... THEN IT'S ALL RIGHT WITH YOU.
I'LL FOLLOW YOU! BECAUSE I CAN DO "WHATEVER I WANT"!
Tp Tp Tp

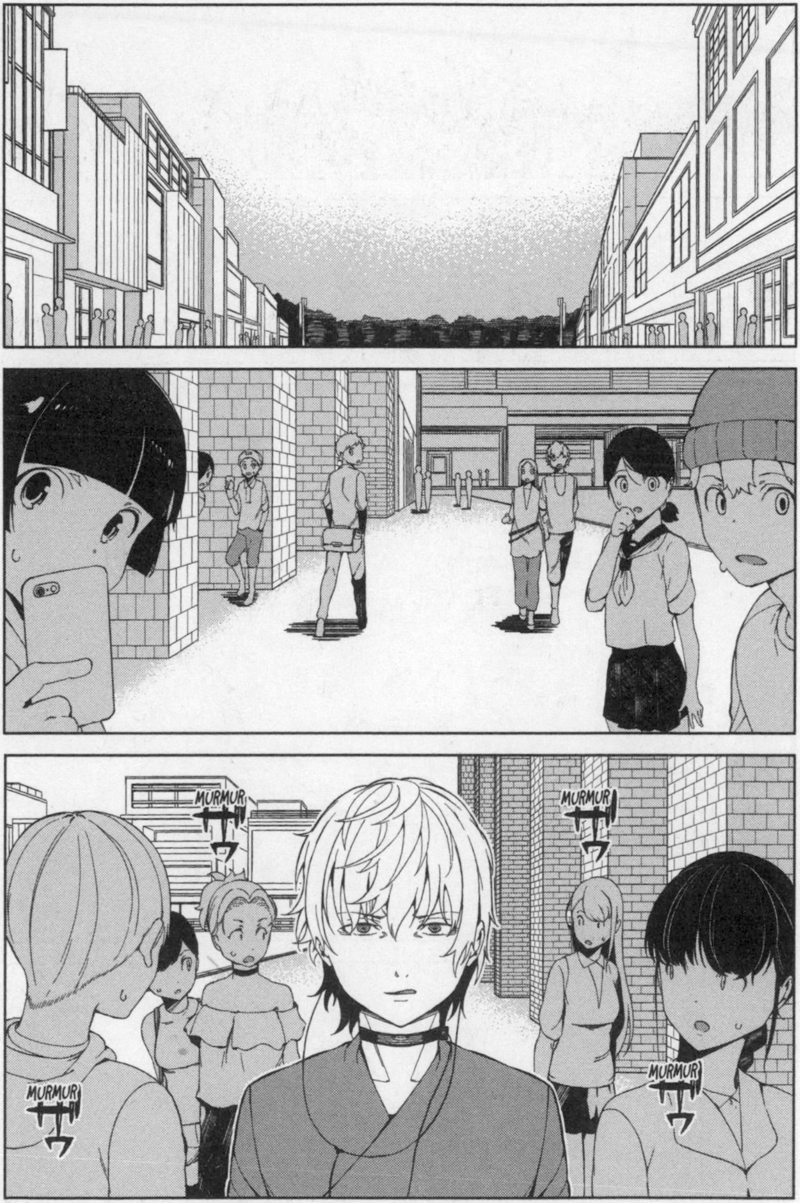
MURMUR
MURMUR
MURMUR
MURMUR

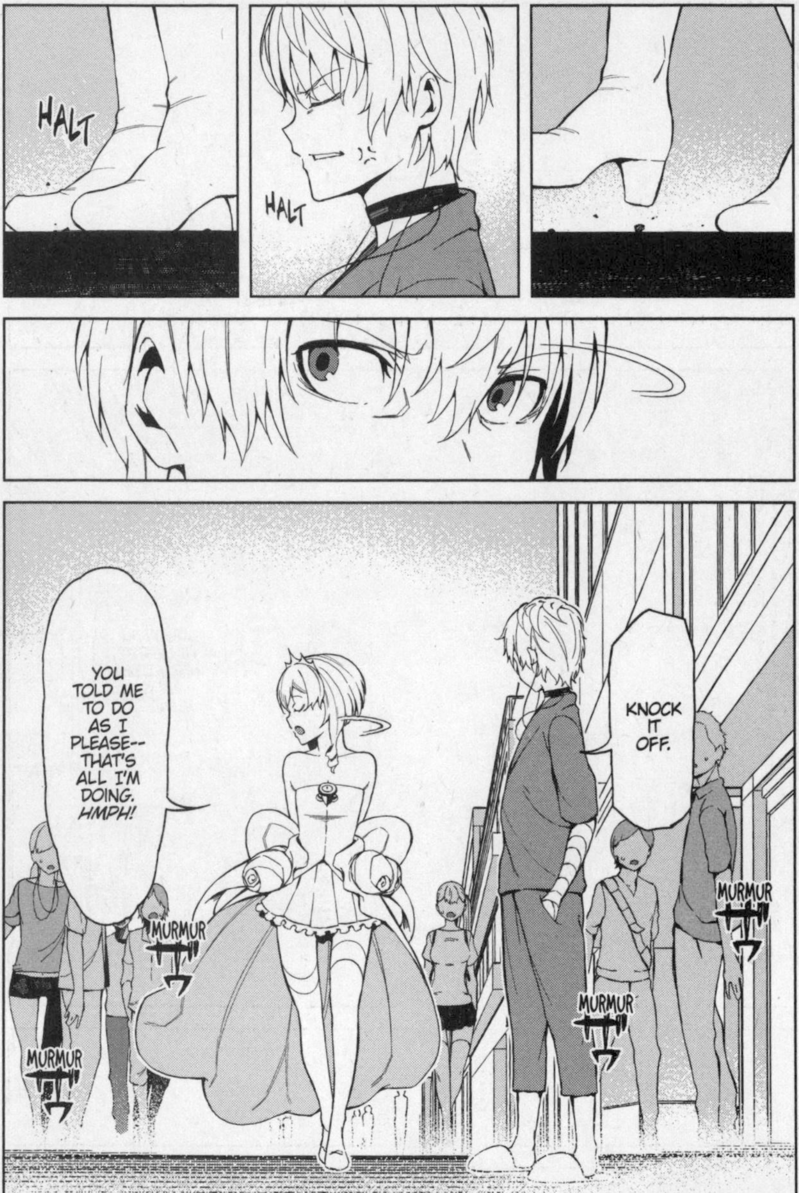
HALT
HALT
KNOCK IT OFF.
YOU TOLD ME TO DO AS I PLEASE-- THAT'S ALL I'M DOING. HMPH!
MURMUR
MURMUR
MURMUR
MURMUR

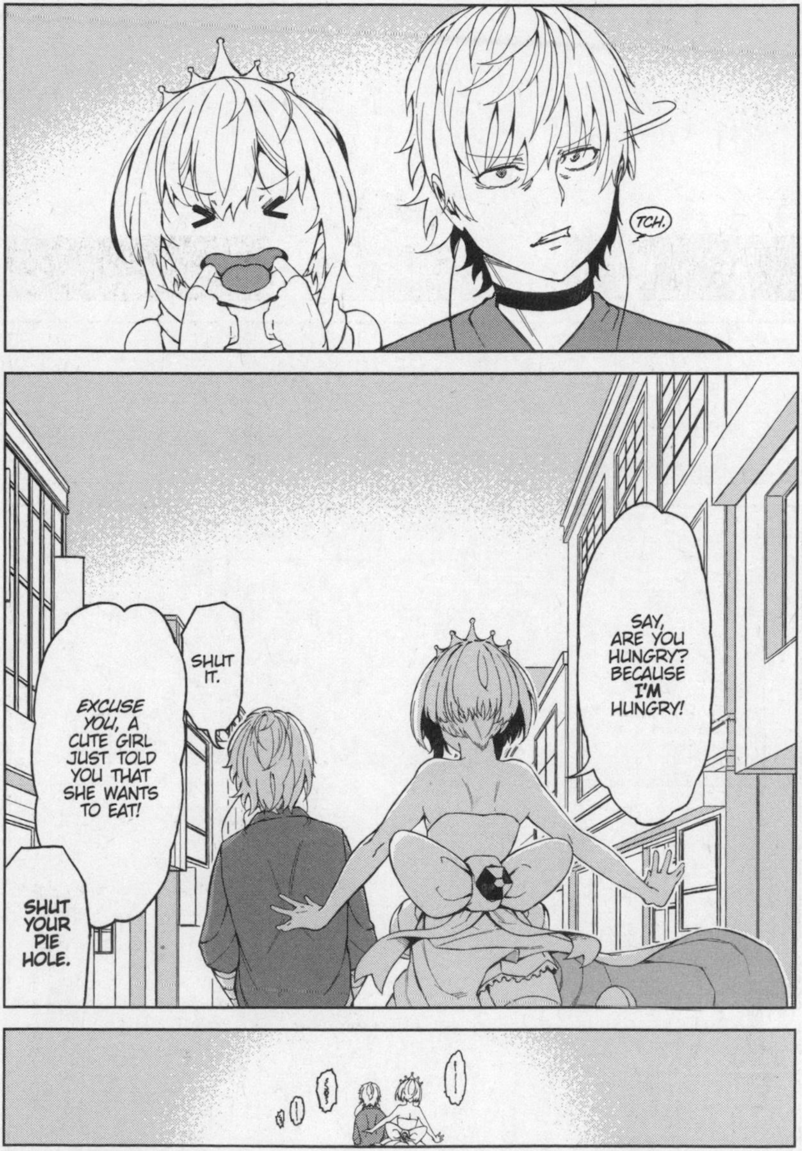
TCH.
SAY, ARE YOU HUNGRY? BECAUSE I'M HUNGRY!
SHUT IT.
EXCUSE YOU, A CUTE GIRL JUST TOLD YOU THAT SHE WANTS TO EAT!
SHUT YOUR PIE HOLE.

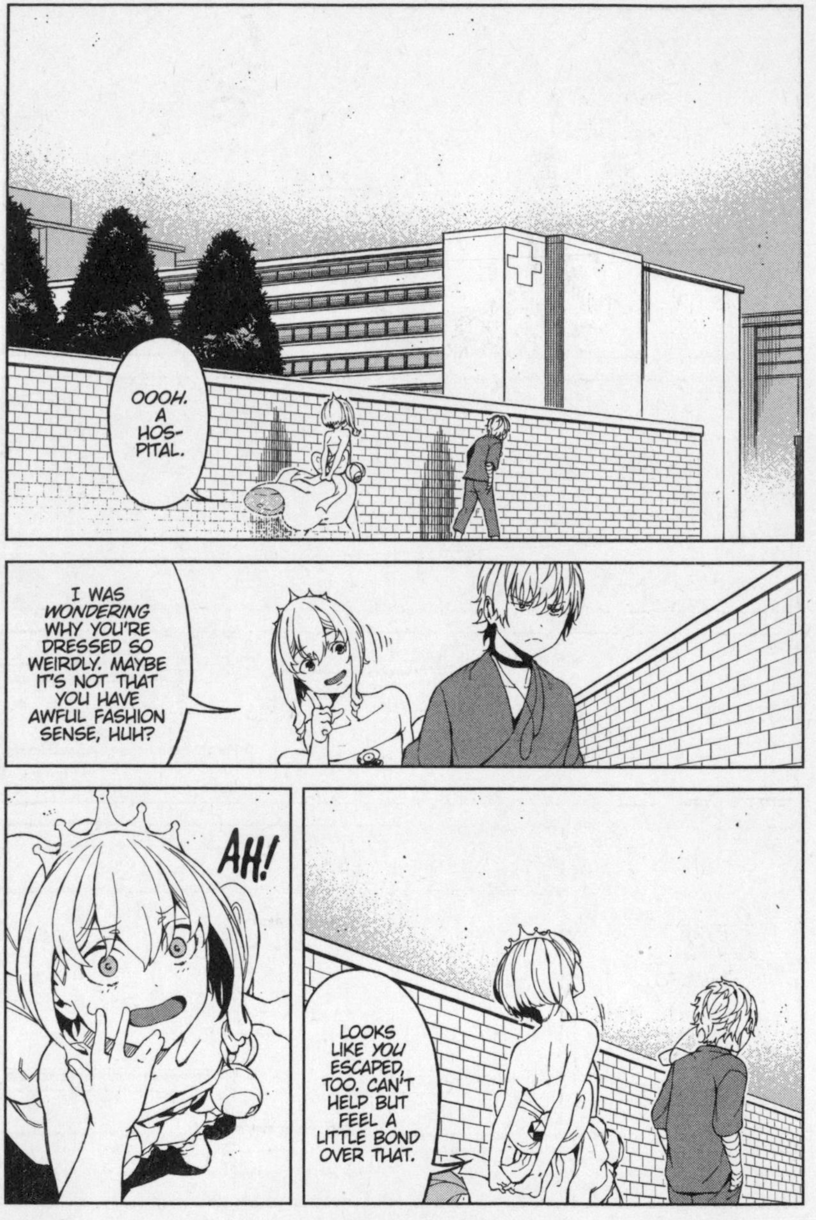
OOOH. A HOS-PITAL.
I WAS *WONDERING* WHY YOU'RE DRESSED SO WEIRDLY. MAYBE IT'S NOT THAT YOU HAVE AWFUL FASHION SENSE, HUH?
LOOKS LIKE *YOU* ESCAPED, TOO. CAN'T HELP BUT FEEL A LITTLE BOND OVER THAT.
AH!

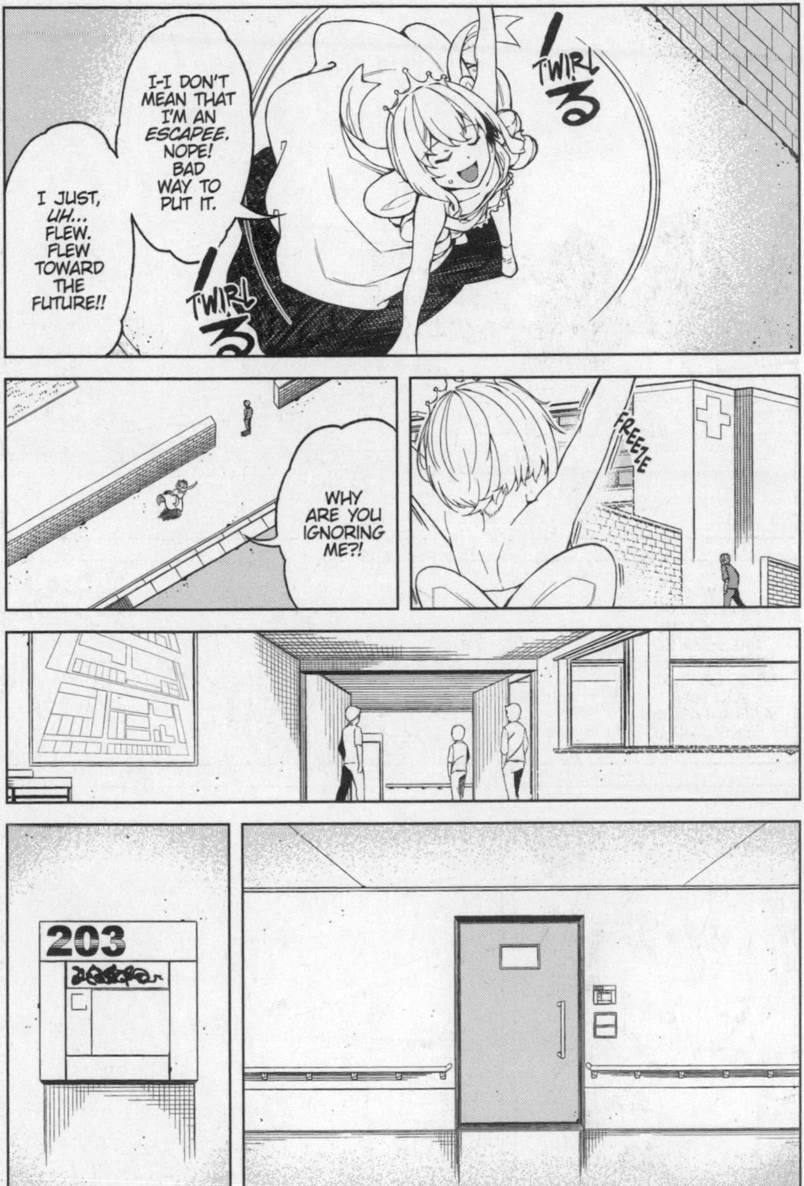
TWIRL る
I-I DON'T MEAN THAT I'M AN *ESCAPEE.* NOPE! BAD WAY TO PUT IT.
I JUST, *UH...* FLEW. FLEW TOWARD THE FUTURE!!
TWIRL る
FREEZE
WHY ARE YOU IGNORING ME?!
203

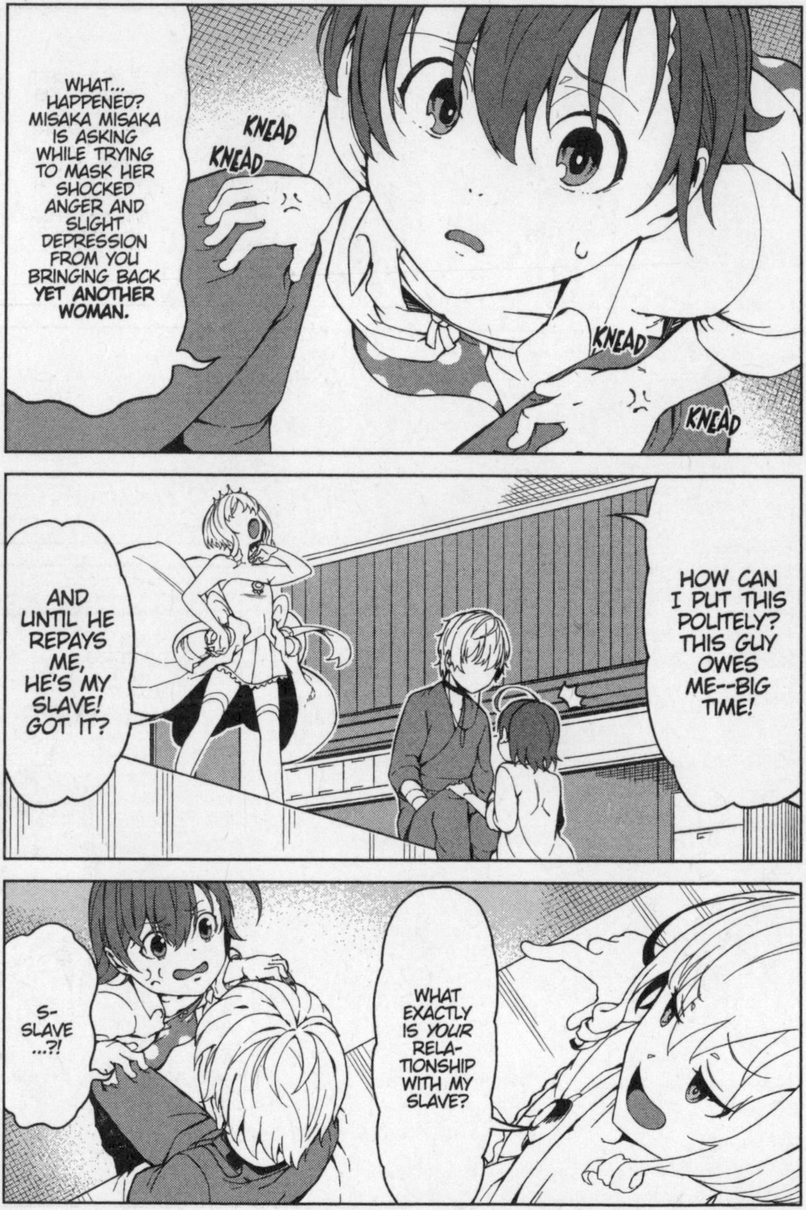
WHAT... HAPPENED? MISAKA MISAKA IS ASKING WHILE TRYING TO MASK HER SHOCKED ANGER AND SLIGHT DEPRESSION FROM YOU BRINGING BACK *YET ANOTHER WOMAN.*
KNEAD
KNEAD
KNEAD
KNEAD
HOW CAN I PUT THIS POLITELY? THIS GUY OWES ME--BIG TIME!
AND UNTIL HE REPAYS ME, HE'S MY SLAVE! GOT IT?
WHAT EXACTLY IS *YOUR* RELATIONSHIP WITH MY SLAVE?
S-SLAVE ...?!

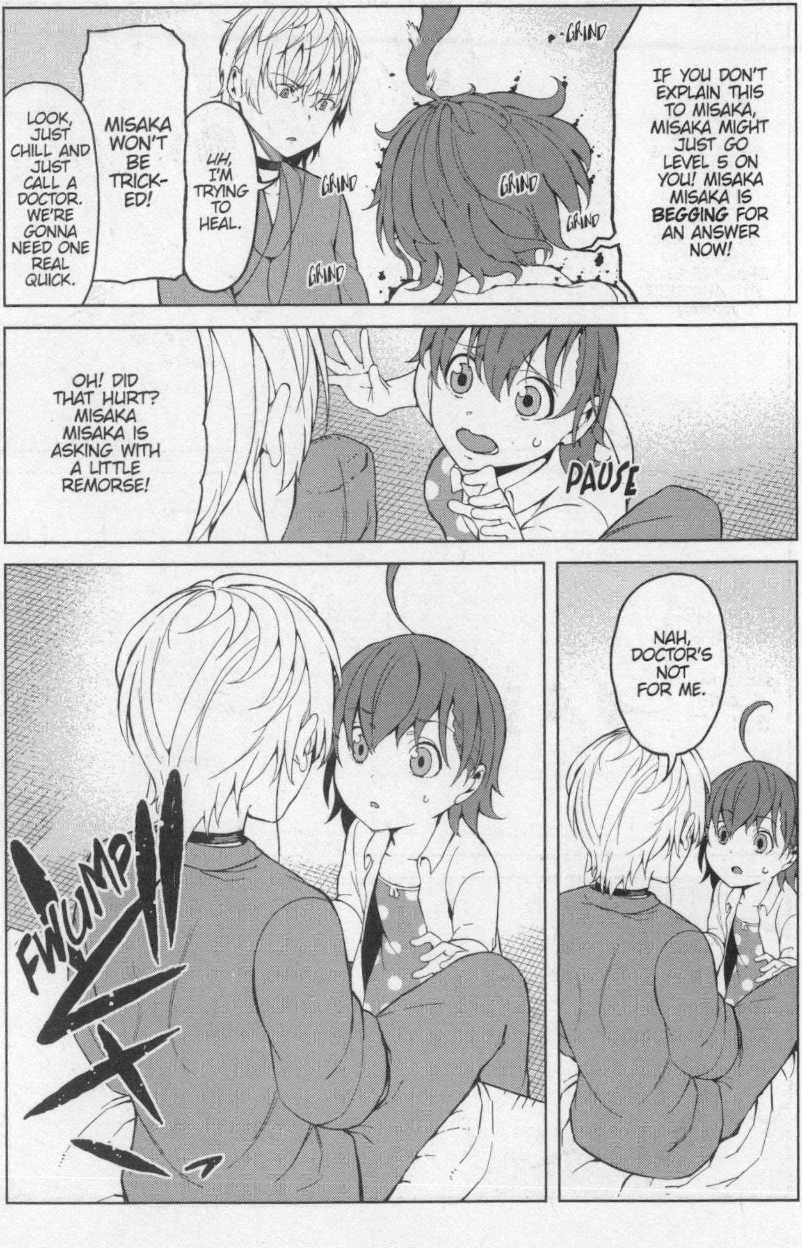
GRIND
IF YOU DON'T EXPLAIN THIS TO MISAKA, MISAKA MIGHT JUST GO LEVEL 5 ON YOU! MISAKA MISAKA IS **BEGGING** FOR AN ANSWER NOW!
GRIND
GRIND
GRIND
GRIND
UH, I'M TRYING TO HEAL.
MISAKA WON'T BE TRICK-ED!
LOOK, JUST CHILL AND JUST CALL A DOCTOR. WE'RE GONNA NEED ONE REAL QUICK.
PAUSE
OH! DID THAT HURT? MISAKA MISAKA IS ASKING WITH A LITTLE REMORSE!
NAH, DOCTOR'S NOT FOR ME.
FWUMP!!

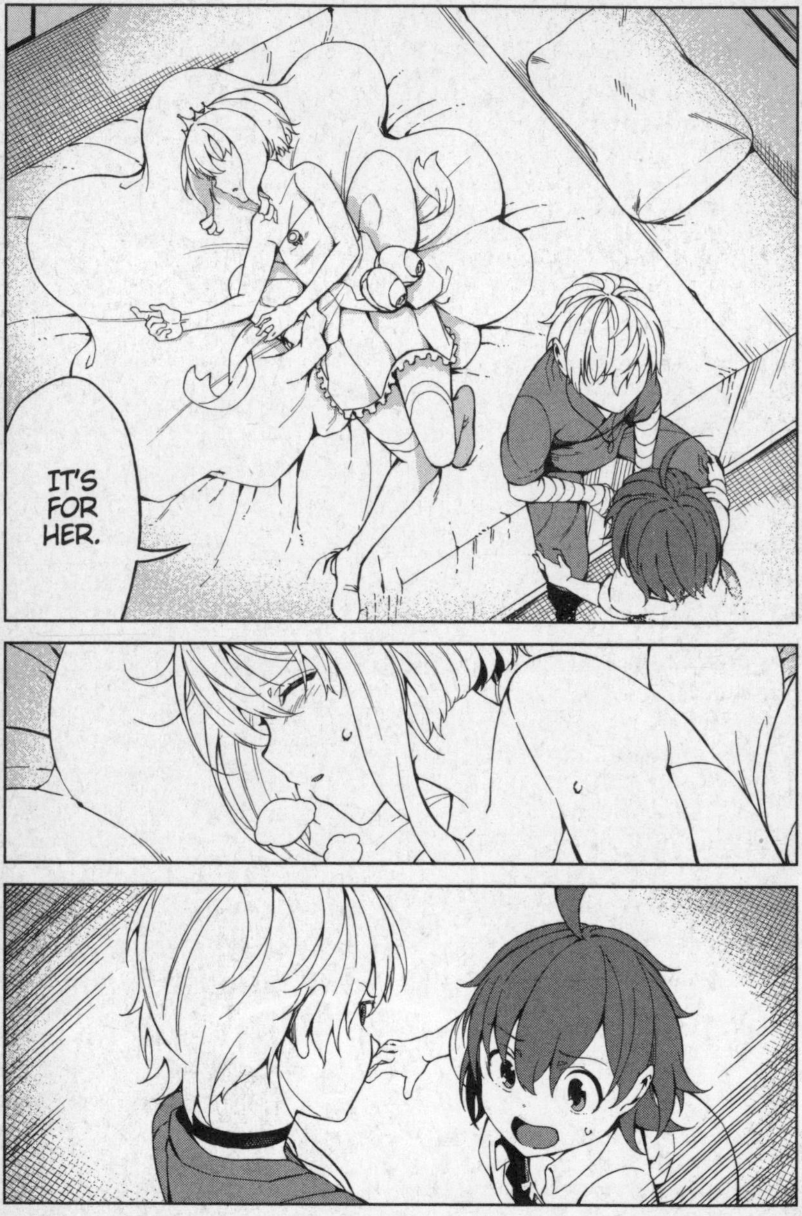
IT'S FOR HER.

a certain
SCIENTIFIC
ACCELERATOR

とある科学の一方通行

アクセラレータ

とある魔術の禁書目録外伝

CHAPTER 39

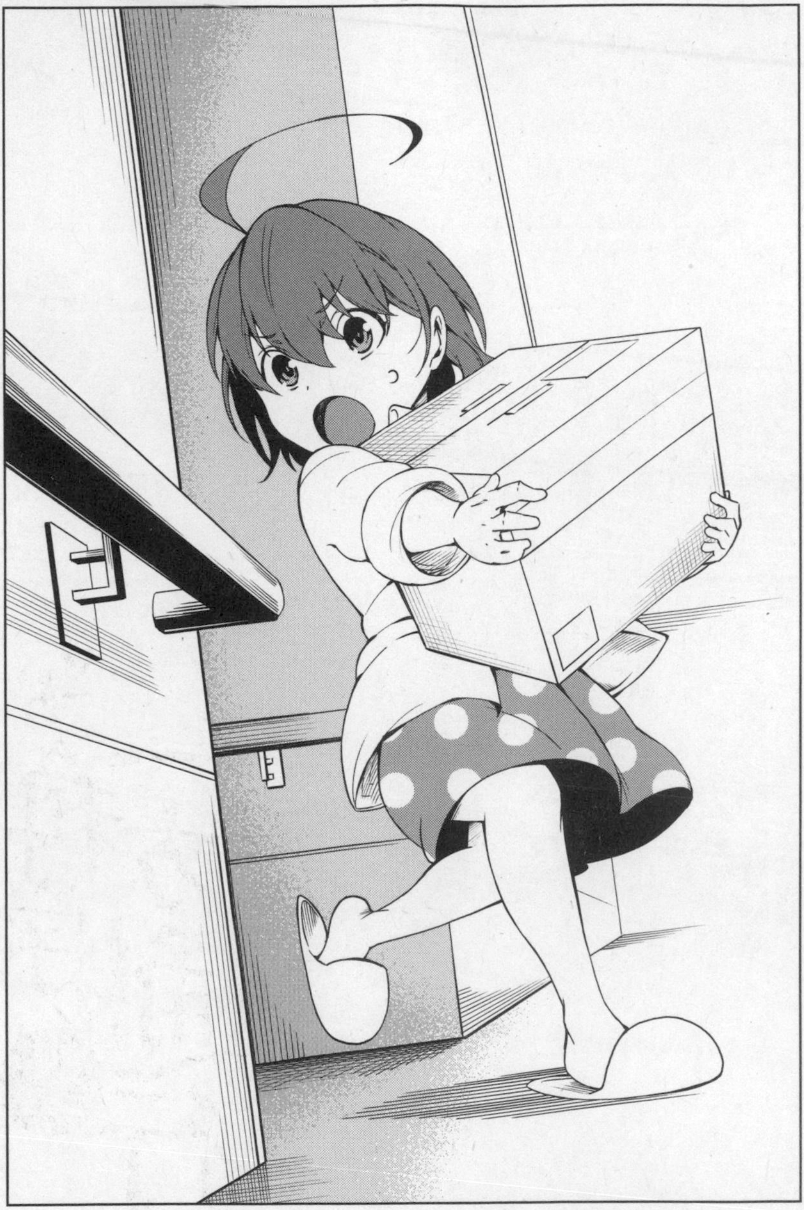

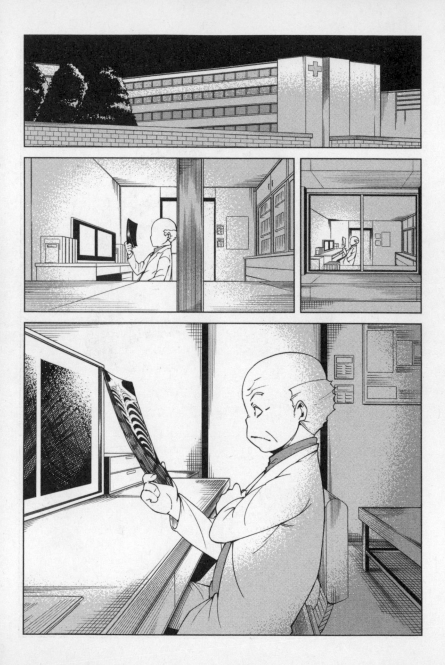

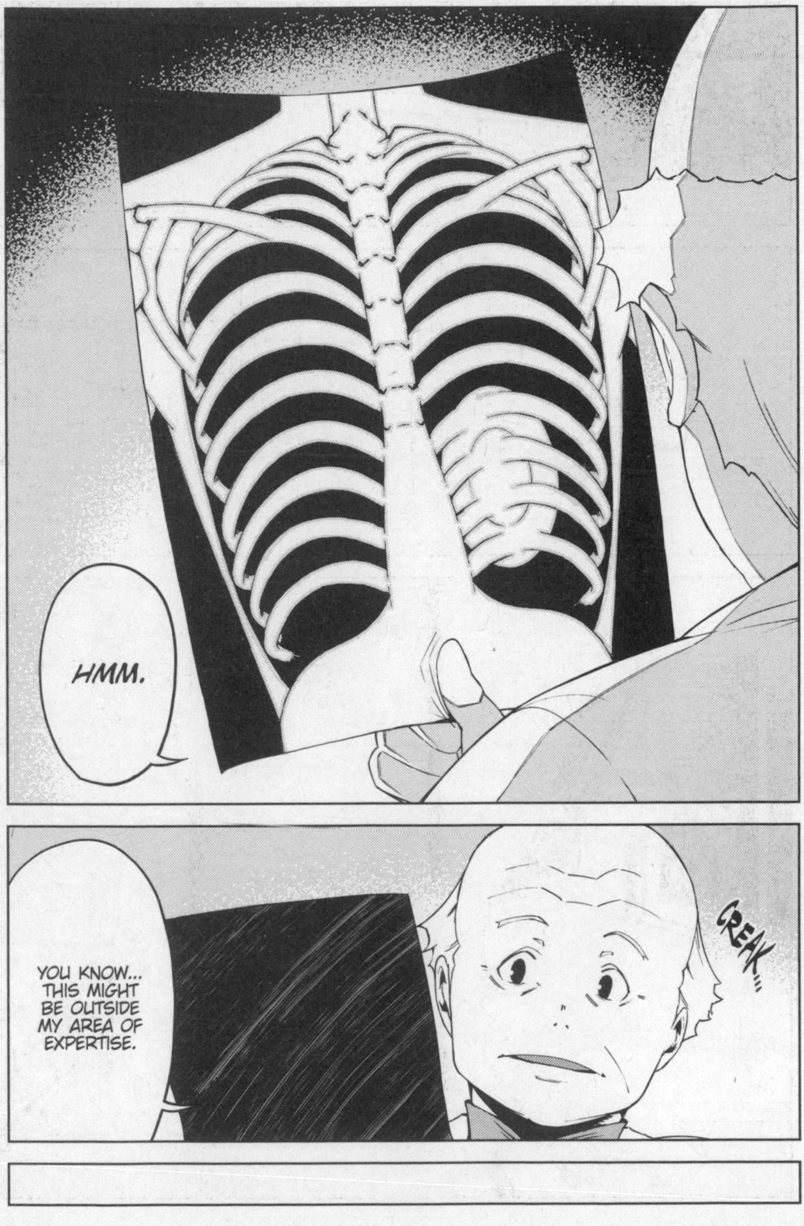
HMM.
CREAK...
YOU KNOW... THIS MIGHT BE OUTSIDE MY AREA OF EXPERTISE.

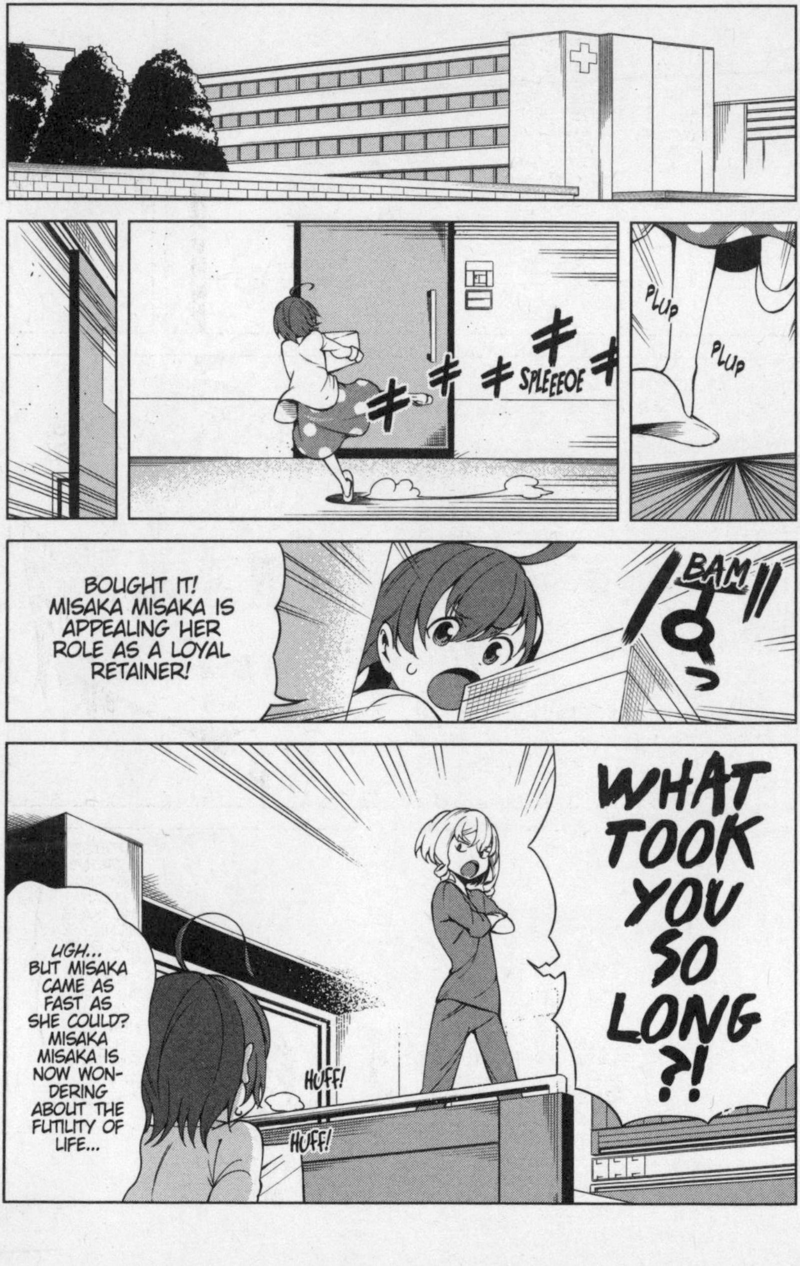
PLUP
PLUP
SPLEEEOE
BAM
BOUGHT IT! MISAKA MISAKA IS APPEALING HER ROLE AS A LOYAL RETAINER!
WHAT TOOK YOU SO LONG?!
HUFF!
HUFF!
UGH... BUT MISAKA CAME AS FAST AS SHE COULD? MISAKA MISAKA IS NOW WON-DERING ABOUT THE FUTILITY OF LIFE...

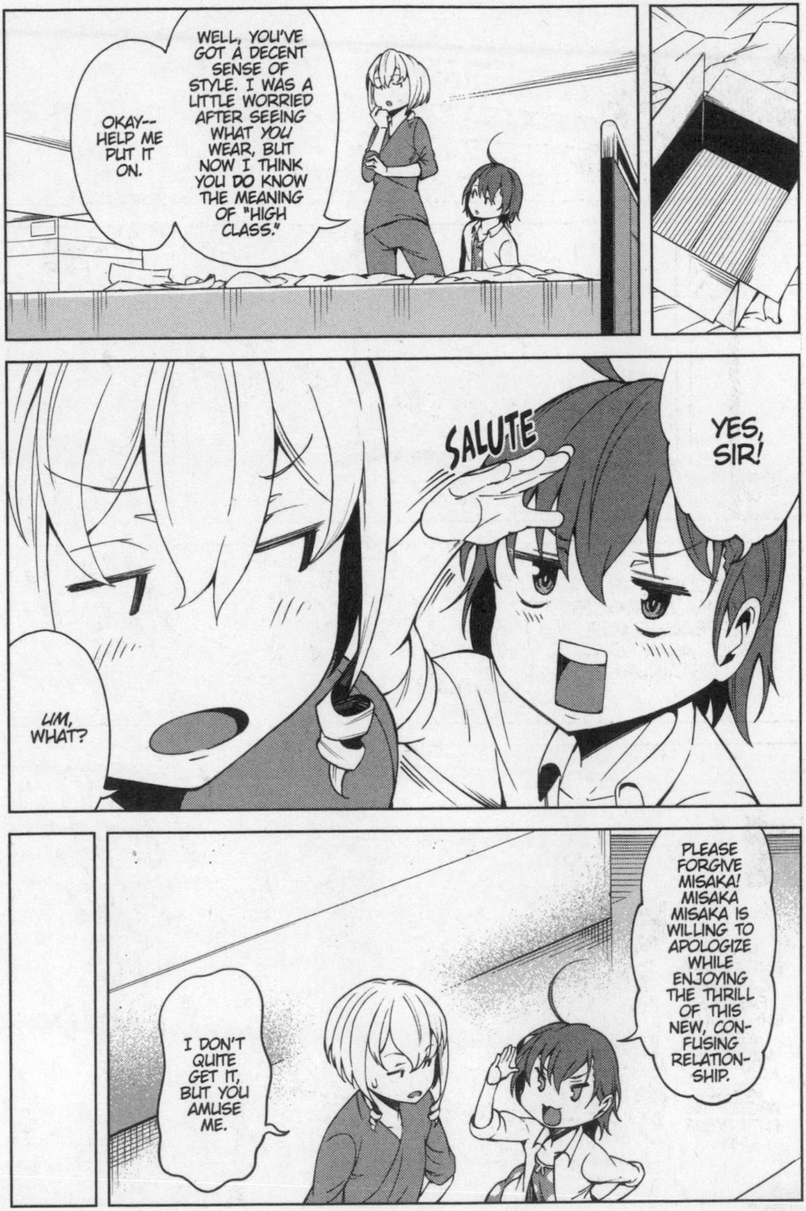
WELL, YOU'VE GOT A DECENT SENSE OF STYLE. I WAS A LITTLE WORRIED AFTER SEEING WHAT YOU WEAR, BUT NOW I THINK YOU DO KNOW THE MEANING OF "HIGH CLASS."
OKAY-- HELP ME PUT IT ON.
YES, SIR!
SALUTE
UM, WHAT?
PLEASE FORGIVE MISAKA! MISAKA MISAKA IS WILLING TO APOLOGIZE WHILE ENJOYING THE THRILL OF THIS NEW, CONFUSING RELATIONSHIP.
I DON'T QUITE GET IT, BUT YOU AMUSE ME.

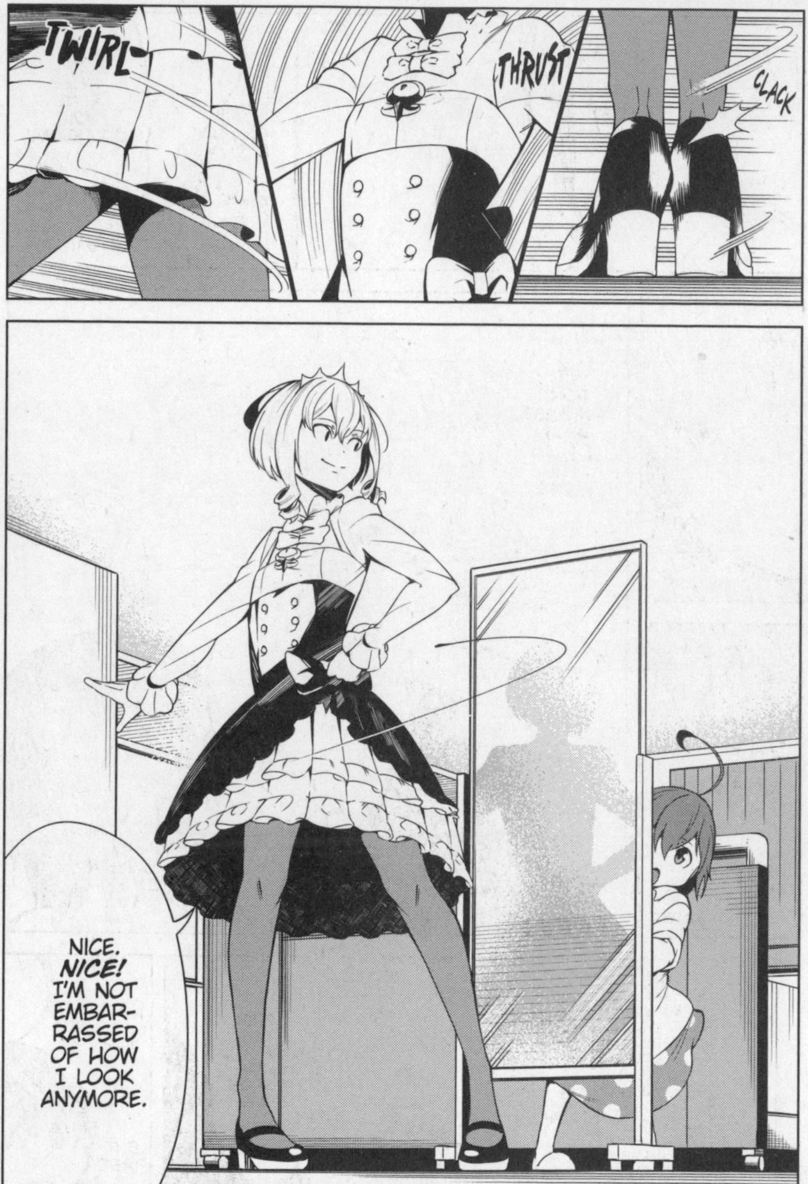
CLACK
THRUST
TWIRL
NICE. NICE! I'M NOT EMBARRASSED OF HOW I LOOK ANYMORE.

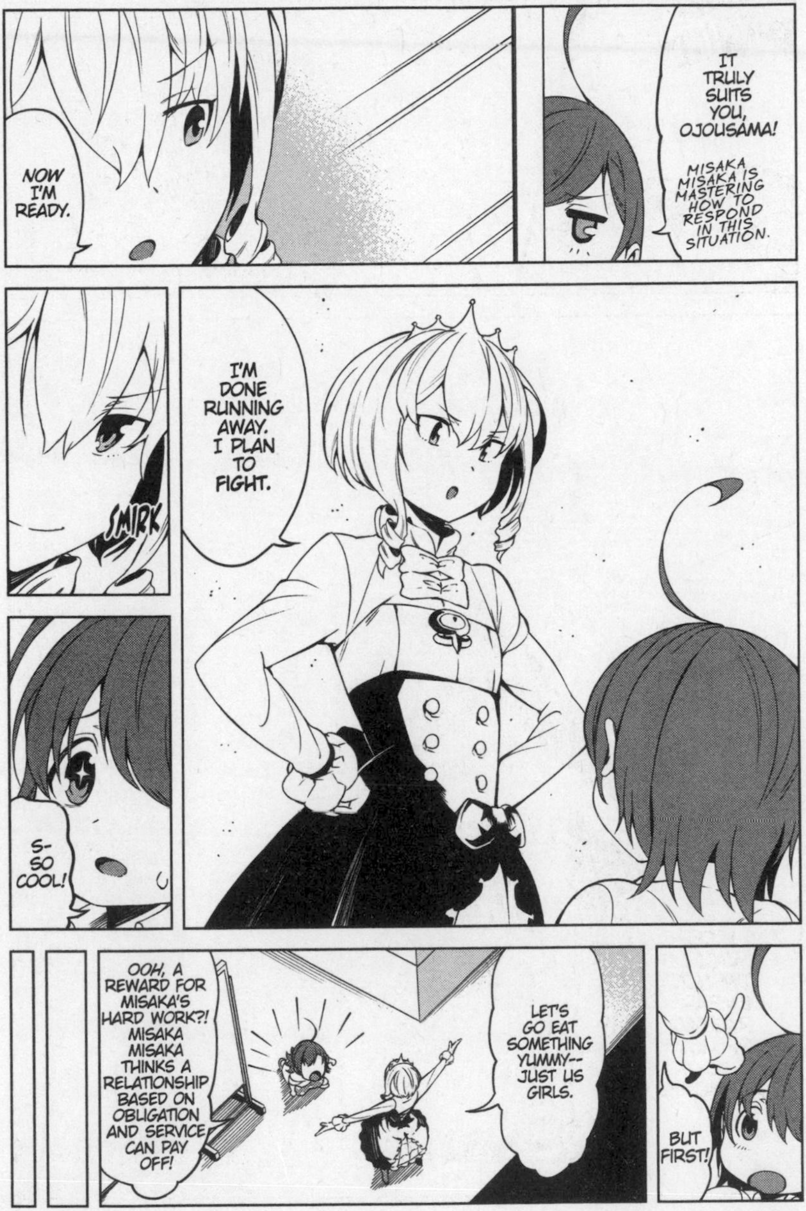
IT TRULY SUITS YOU, OJOUSAMA!
MISAKA MISAKA IS MASTERING HOW TO RESPOND IN THIS SITUATION.
NOW I'M READY.
I'M DONE RUNNING AWAY. I PLAN TO FIGHT.
SMIRK
S-SO COOL!
BUT FIRST!
LET'S GO EAT SOMETHING YUMMY--JUST US GIRLS.
OOH, A REWARD FOR MISAKA'S HARD WORK?! MISAKA MISAKA THINKS A RELATIONSHIP BASED ON OBLIGATION AND SERVICE CAN PAY OFF!

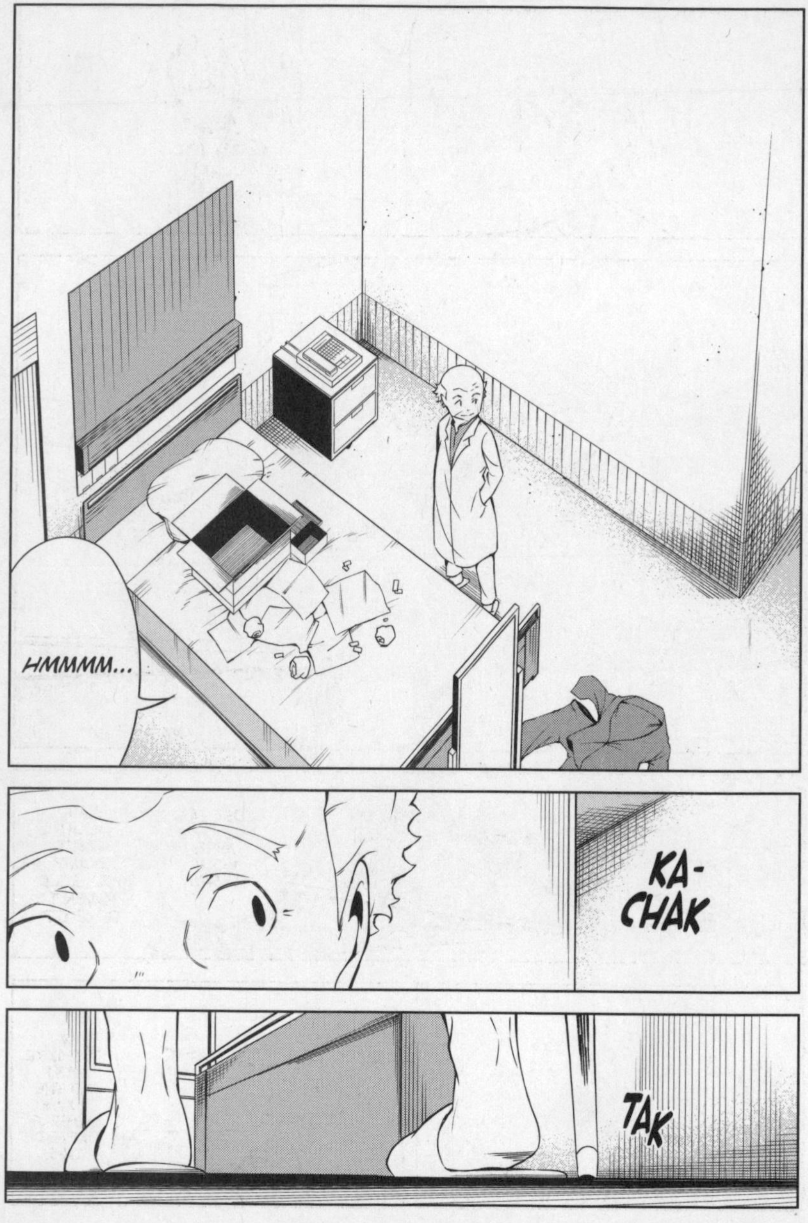
HMMMM...
KA-
CHAK
TAK

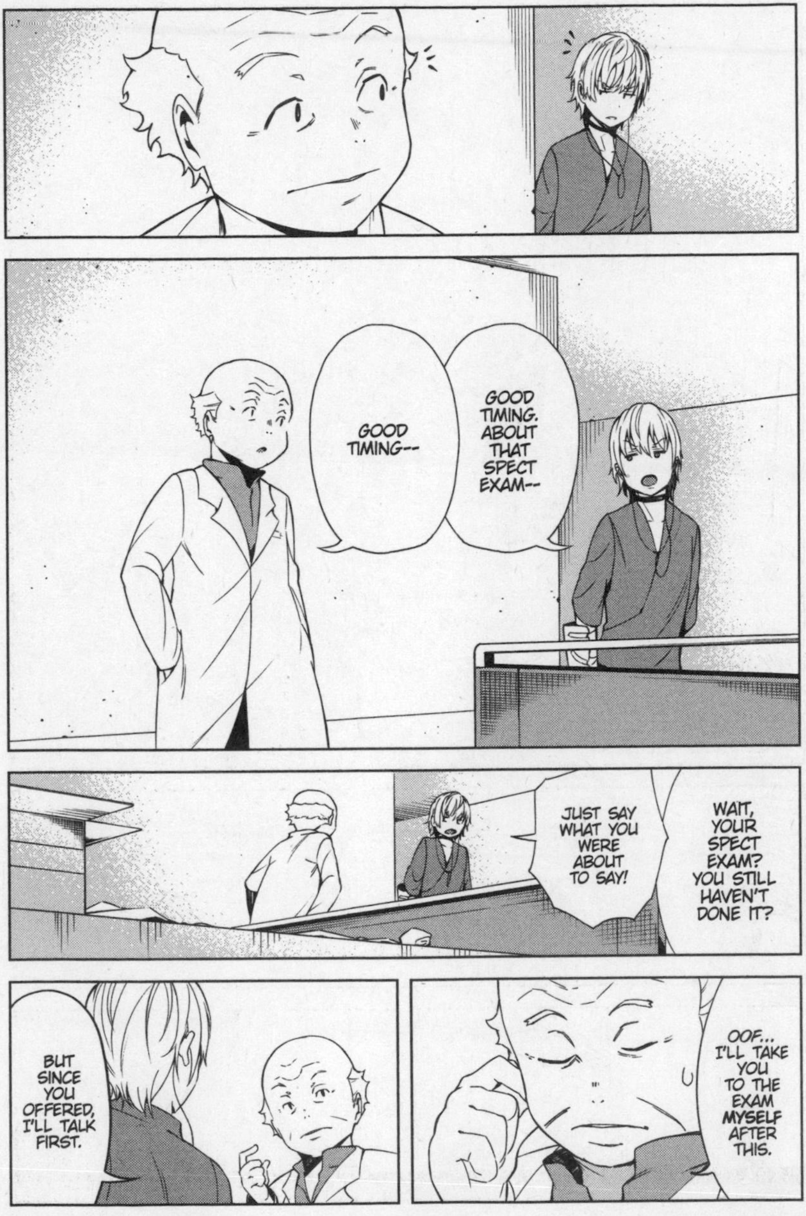
GOOD TIMING. ABOUT THAT SPECT EXAM--
GOOD TIMING--
WAIT, YOUR SPECT EXAM? YOU STILL HAVEN'T DONE IT?
JUST SAY WHAT YOU WERE ABOUT TO SAY!
OOF... I'LL TAKE YOU TO THE EXAM MYSELF AFTER THIS.
BUT SINCE YOU OFFERED, I'LL TALK FIRST.

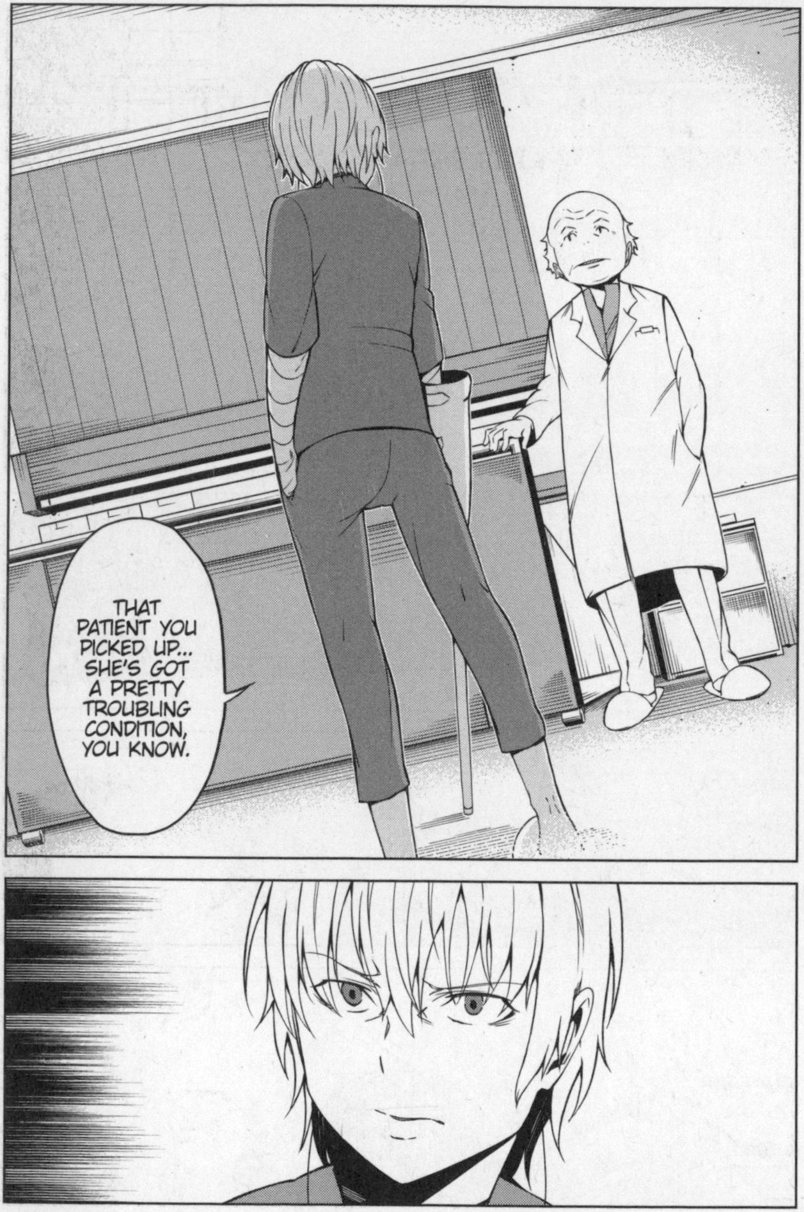
THAT PATIENT YOU PICKED UP... SHE'S GOT A PRETTY TROUBLING CONDITION, YOU KNOW.

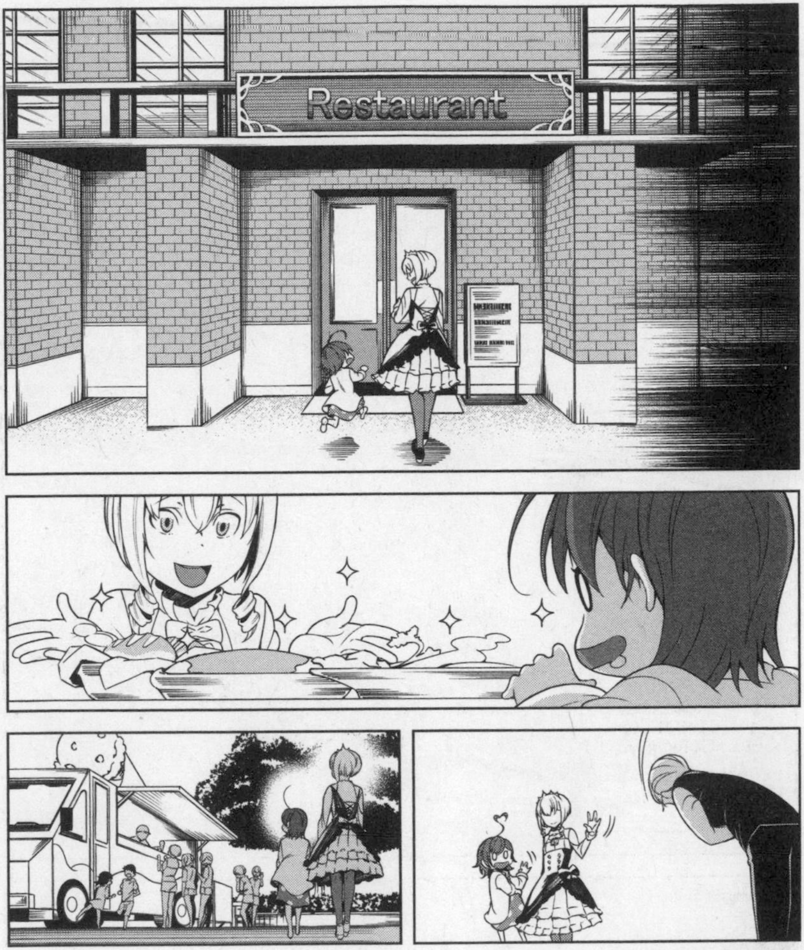
Restaurant

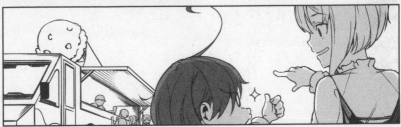

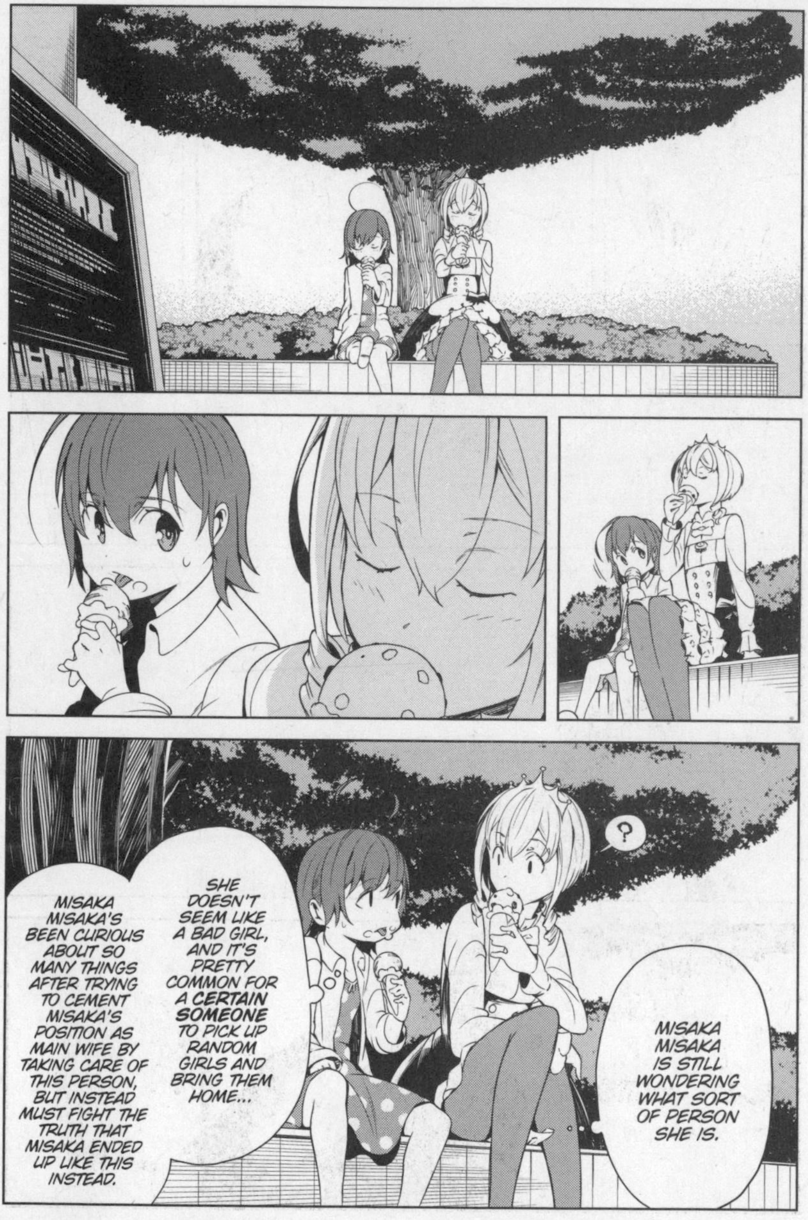
?
MISAKA MISAKA IS STILL WONDERING WHAT SORT OF PERSON SHE IS.
SHE DOESN'T SEEM LIKE A BAD GIRL, AND IT'S PRETTY COMMON FOR A **CERTAIN SOMEONE** TO PICK UP RANDOM GIRLS AND BRING THEM HOME...
MISAKA MISAKA'S BEEN CURIOUS ABOUT SO MANY THINGS AFTER TRYING TO CEMENT MISAKA'S POSITION AS MAIN WIFE BY TAKING CARE OF THIS PERSON, BUT INSTEAD MUST FIGHT THE TRUTH THAT MISAKA ENDED UP LIKE THIS INSTEAD.

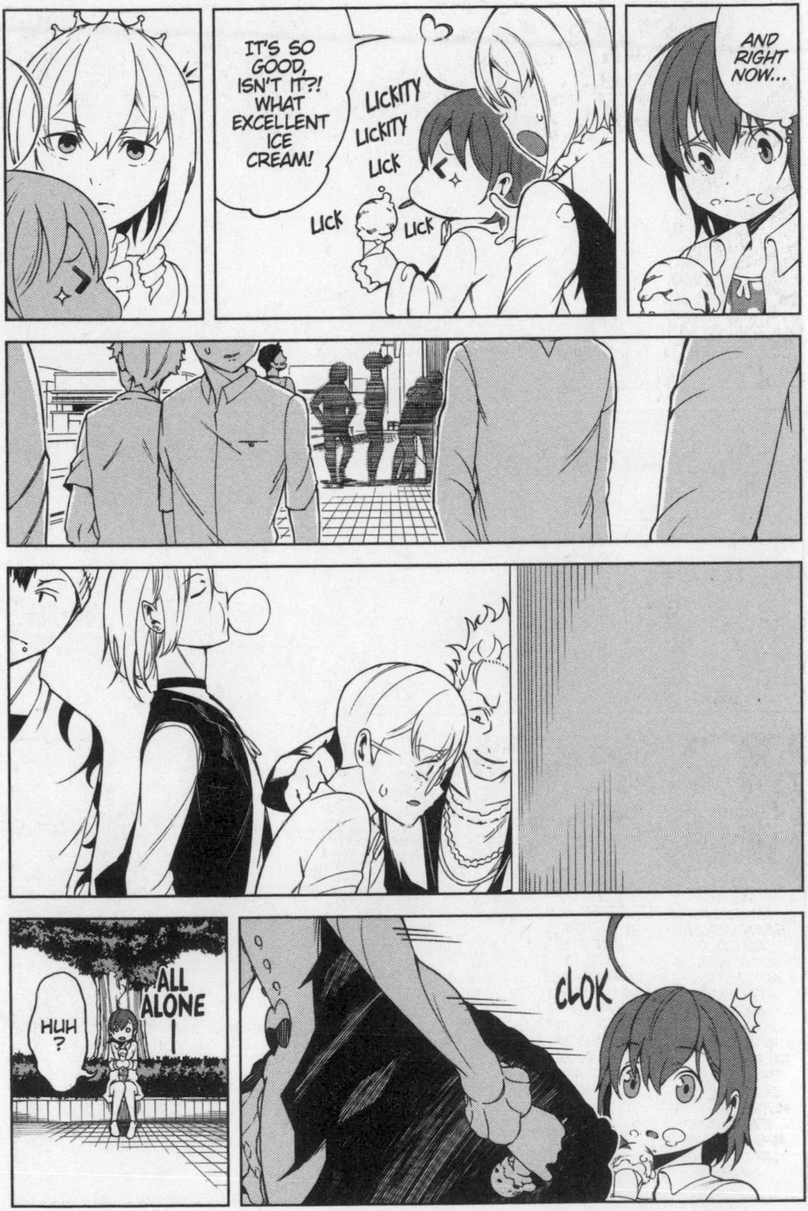
AND RIGHT NOW...
IT'S SO GOOD, ISN'T IT?! WHAT EXCELLENT ICE CREAM!
LICKITY
LICKITY
LICK
LICK
LICK
CLOK
ALL ALONE
HUH?

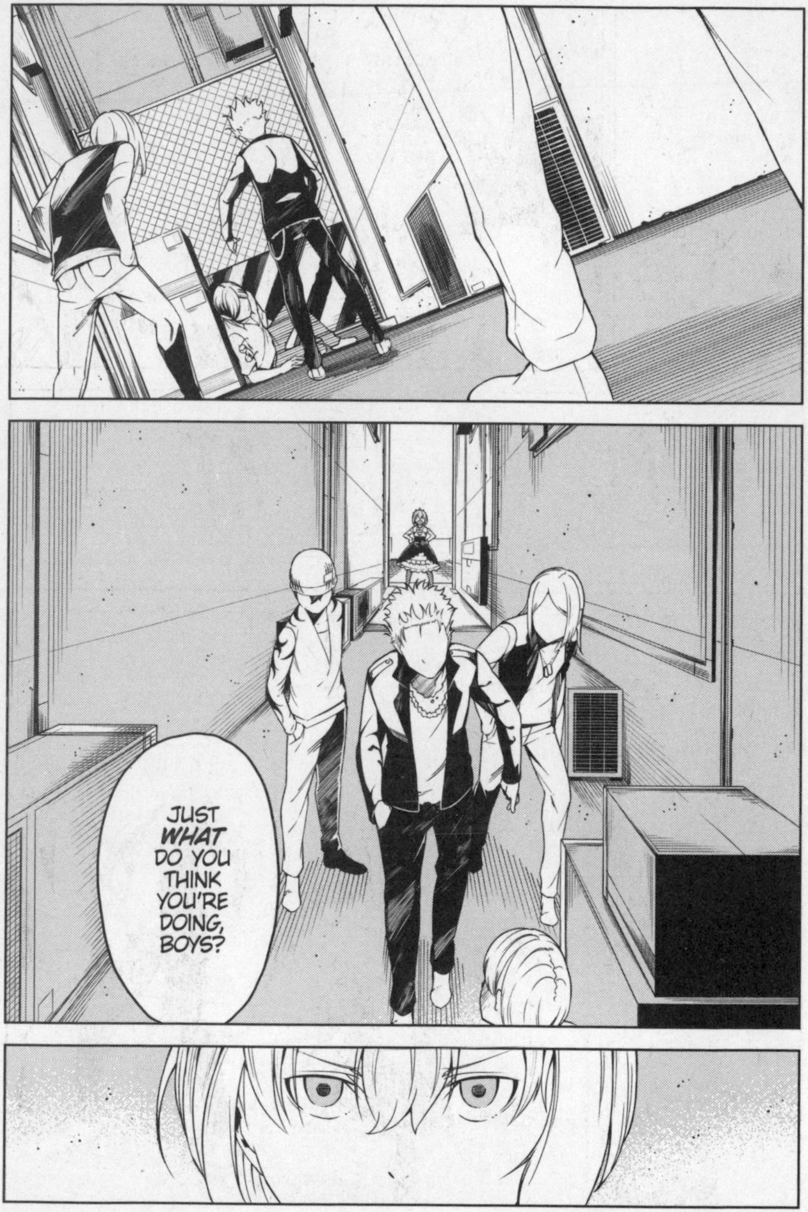
JUST ***WHAT*** DO YOU THINK YOU'RE DOING, BOYS?

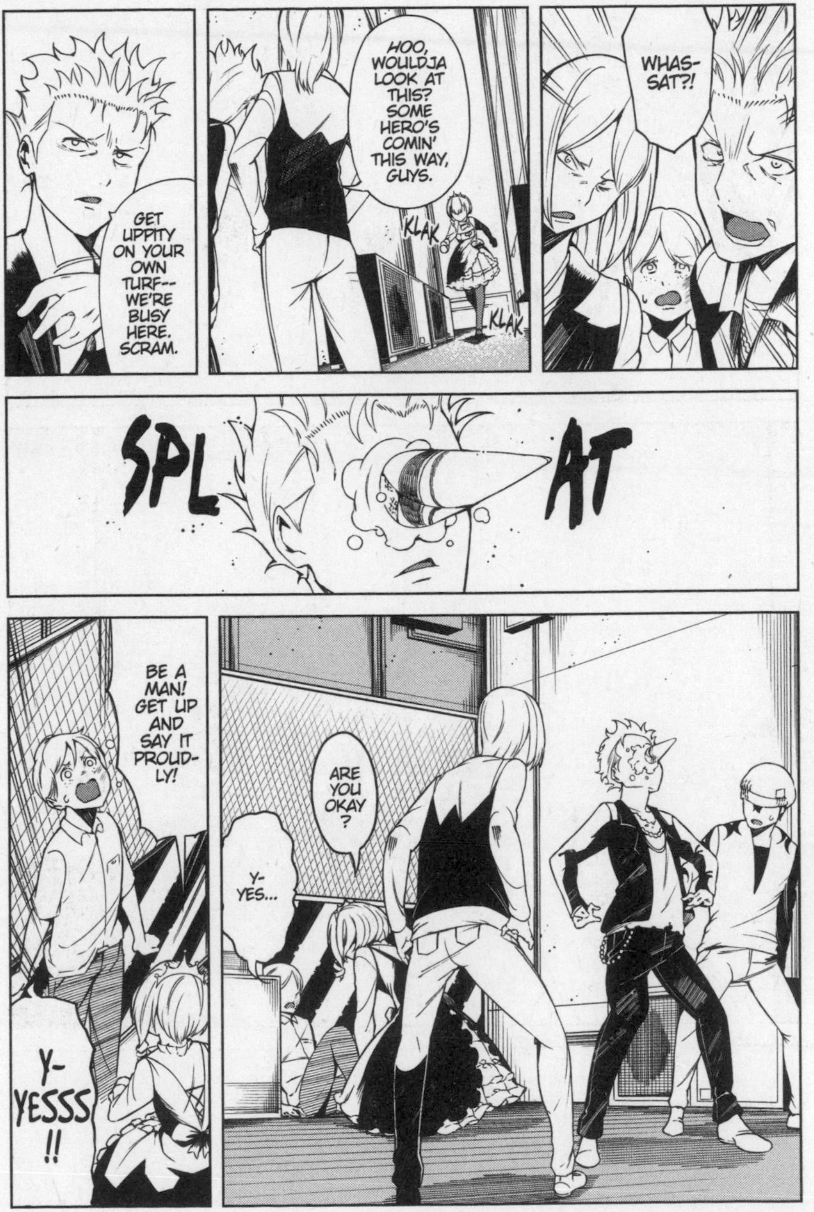
WHAS-SAT?!
HOO, WOULDJA LOOK AT THIS? SOME HERO'S COMIN' THIS WAY, GUYS.
KLAK
KLAK
GET UPPITY ON YOUR OWN TURF--WE'RE BUSY HERE. SCRAM.
SPLAT
ARE YOU OKAY?
Y-YES...
BE A MAN! GET UP AND SAY IT PROUDLY!
Y-YESSS!!

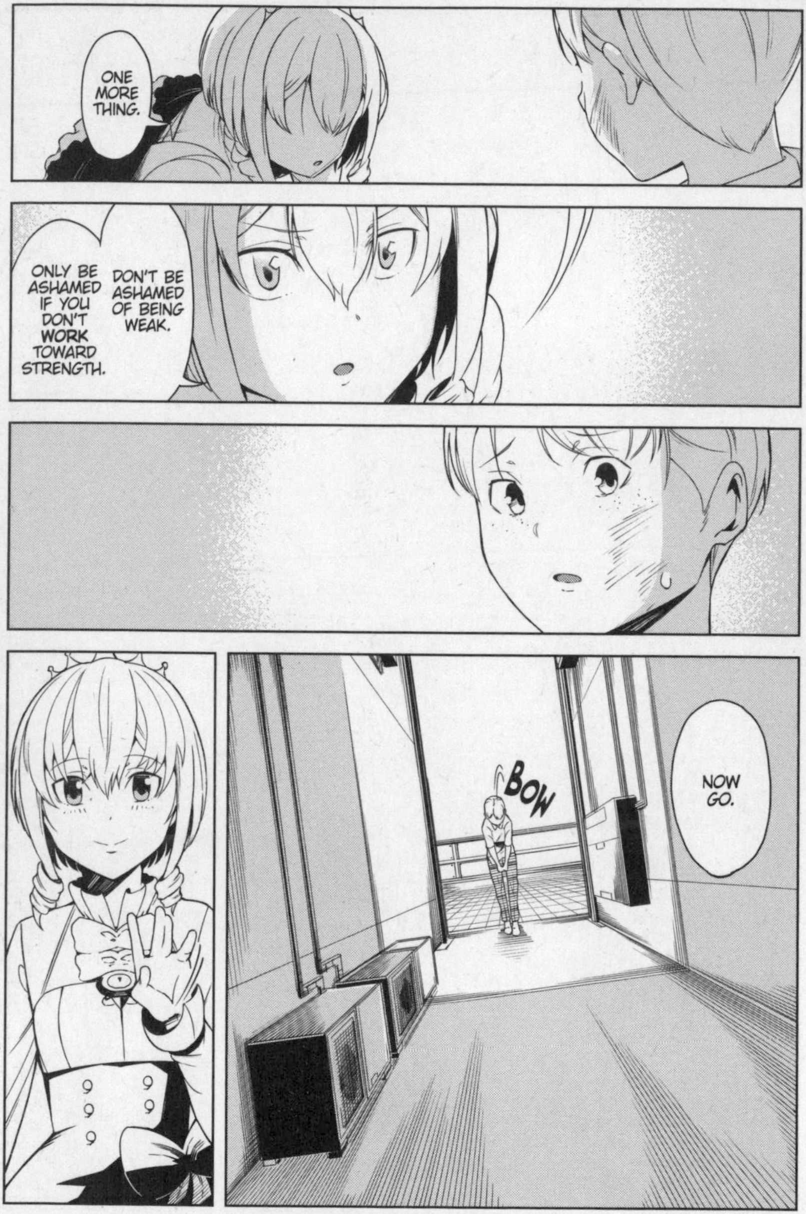
ONE MORE THING.
DON'T BE ASHAMED OF BEING WEAK.
ONLY BE ASHAMED IF YOU DON'T WORK TOWARD STRENGTH.
NOW GO.
BOW

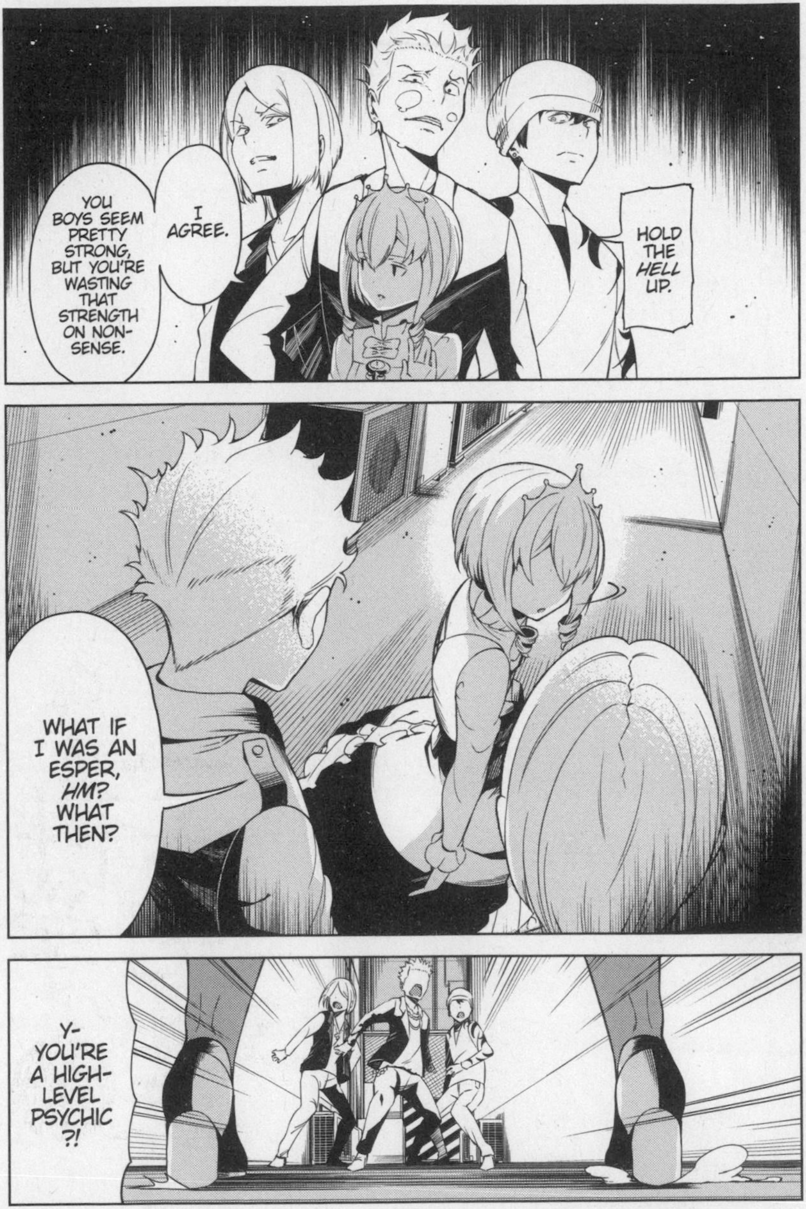
HOLD THE HELL UP.
I AGREE.
YOU BOYS SEEM PRETTY STRONG, BUT YOU'RE WASTING THAT STRENGTH ON NON-SENSE.
WHAT IF I WAS AN ESPER, HM? WHAT THEN?
Y-YOU'RE A HIGH-LEVEL PSYCHIC?!

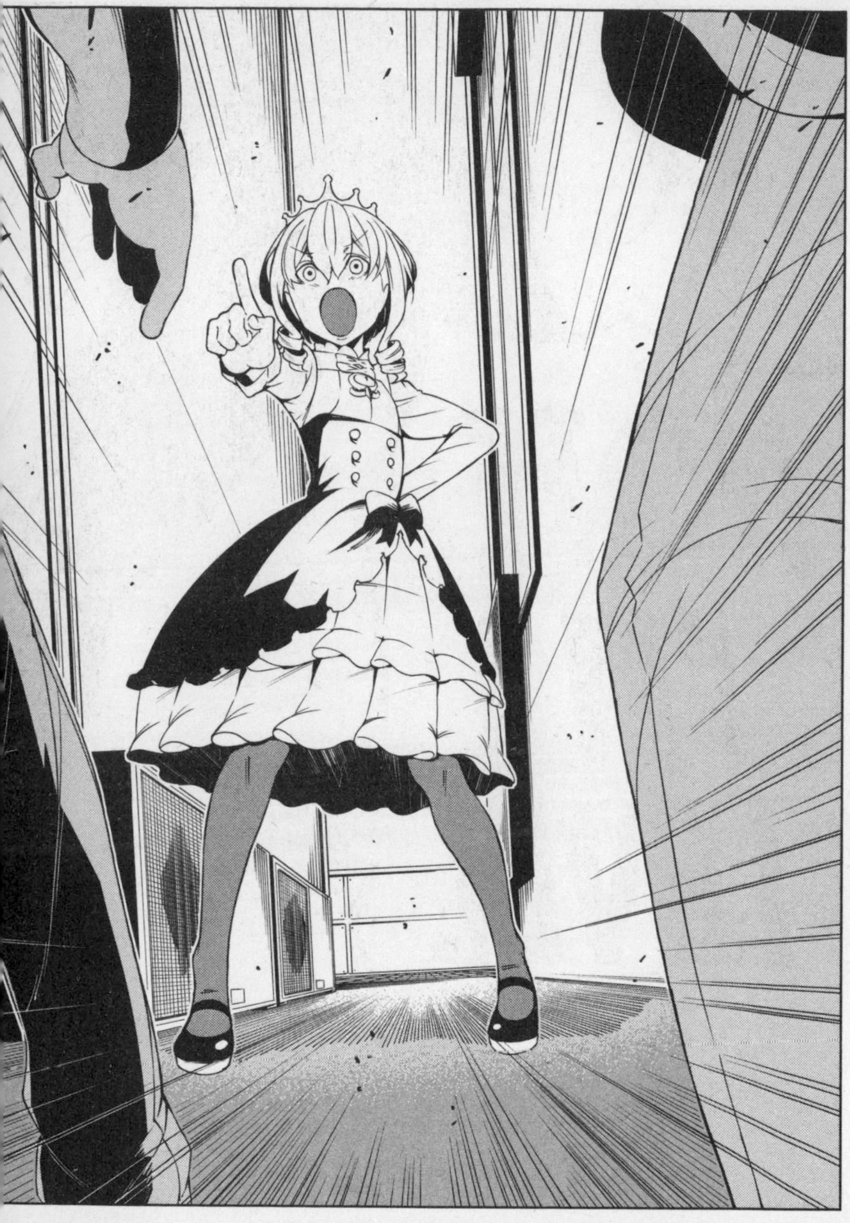

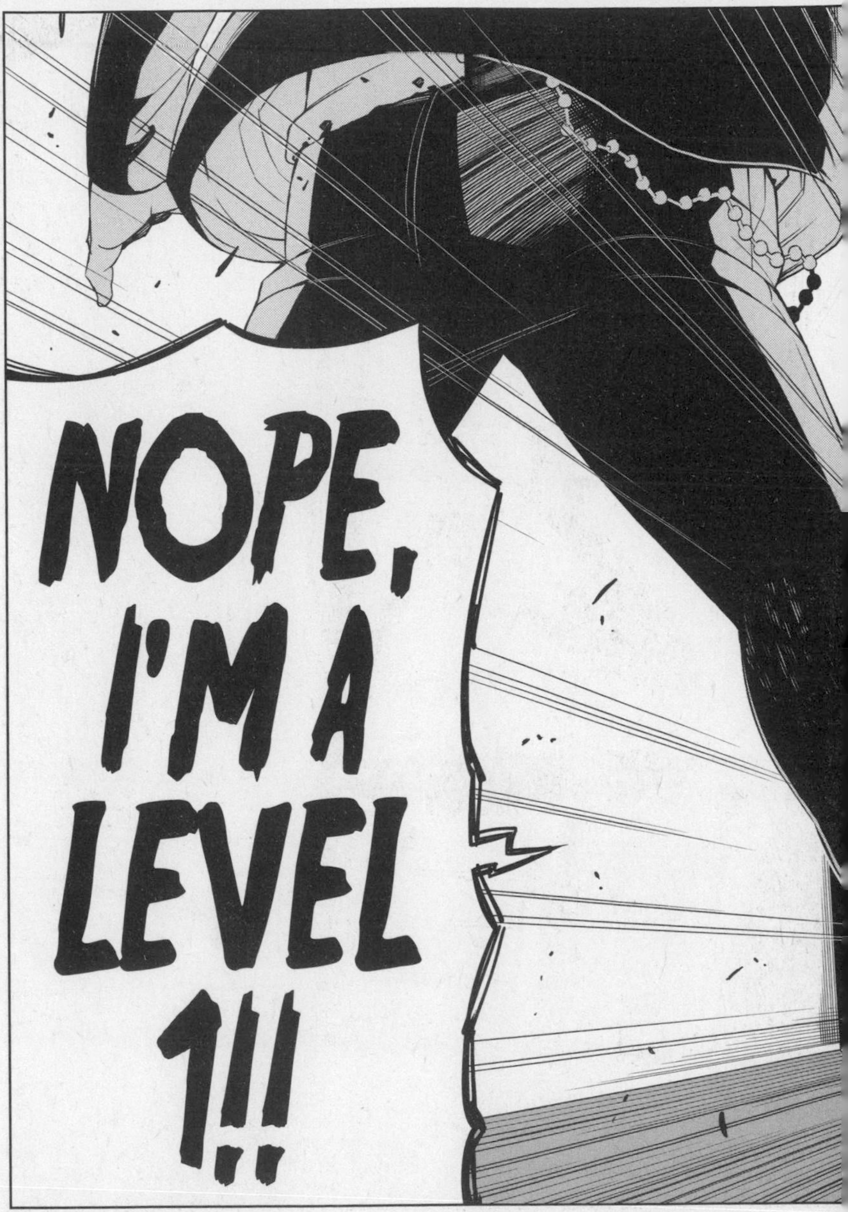
NOPE, I'M A LEVEL 1!!

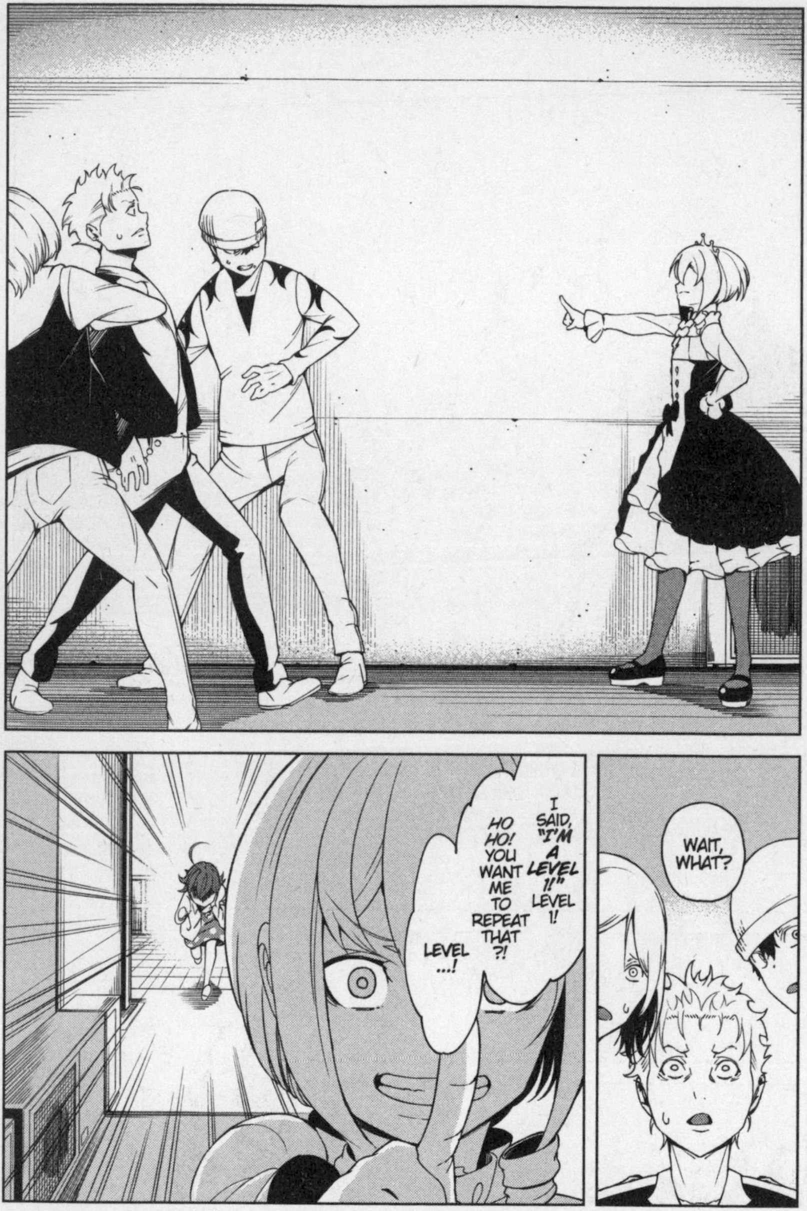
WAIT, WHAT?
I SAID, "I'M A LEVEL 1!" LEVEL 1!
HO HO! YOU WANT ME TO REPEAT THAT?!
LEVEL ...!

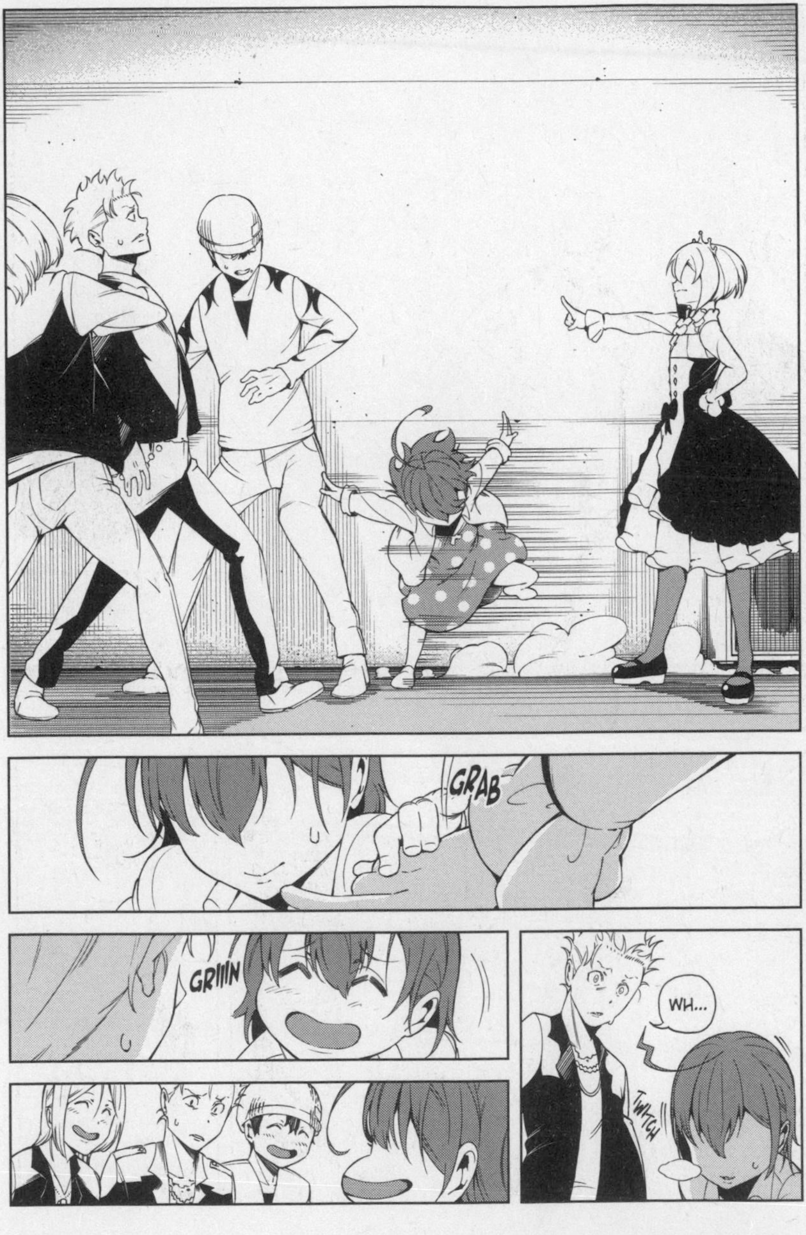
GRAB
WH...
TWITCH
GRIIIN

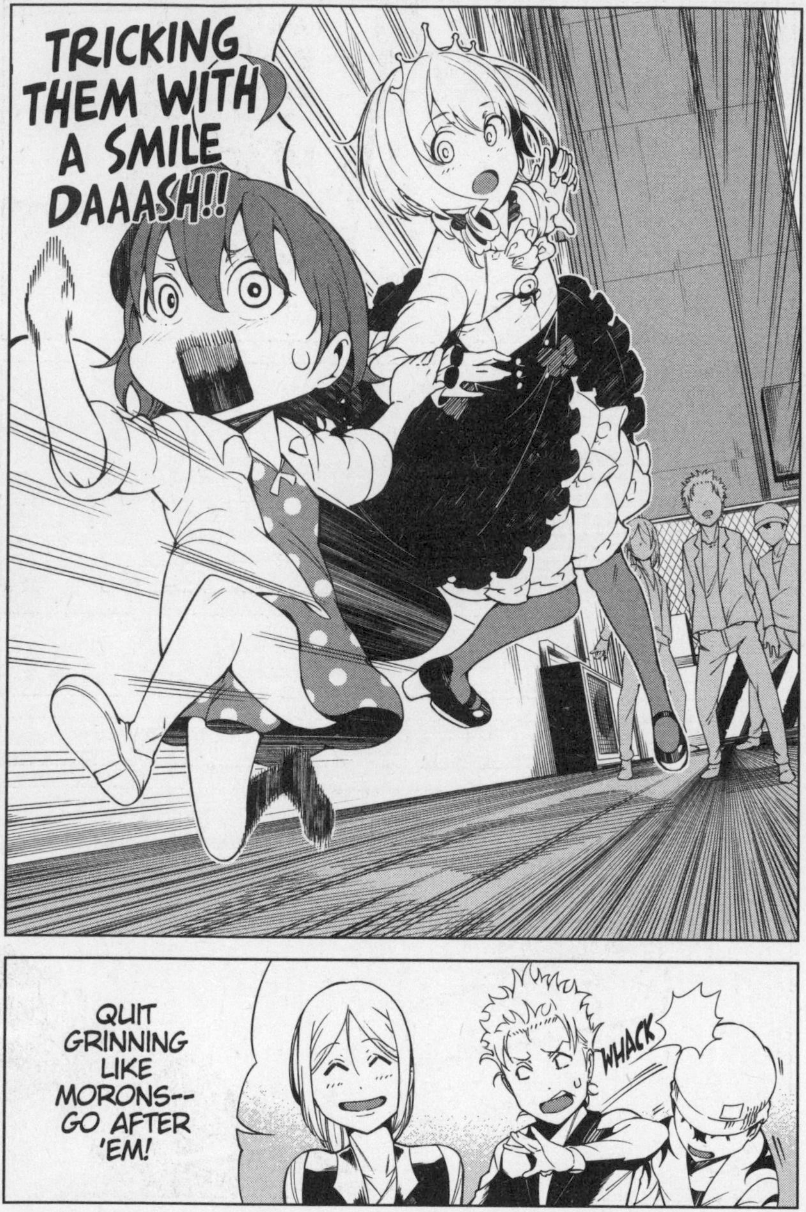
TRICKING THEM WITH A SMILE DAAASH!!
QUIT GRINNING LIKE MORONS-- GO AFTER 'EM!
WHACK

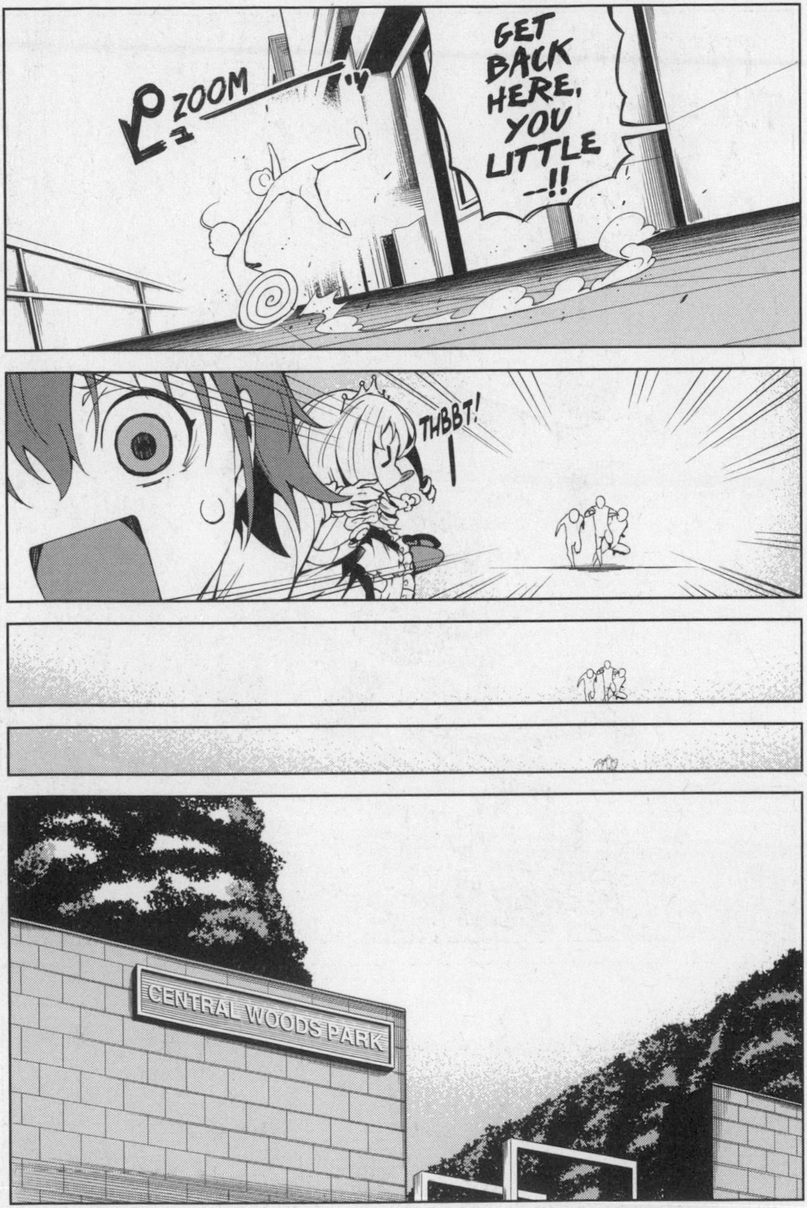
GET BACK HERE, YOU LITTLE --!!
ZOOM
THBBT!
CENTRAL WOODS PARK

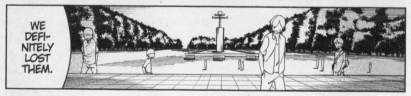

WE DEFI-
NITELY
LOST
THEM.

PHEW!

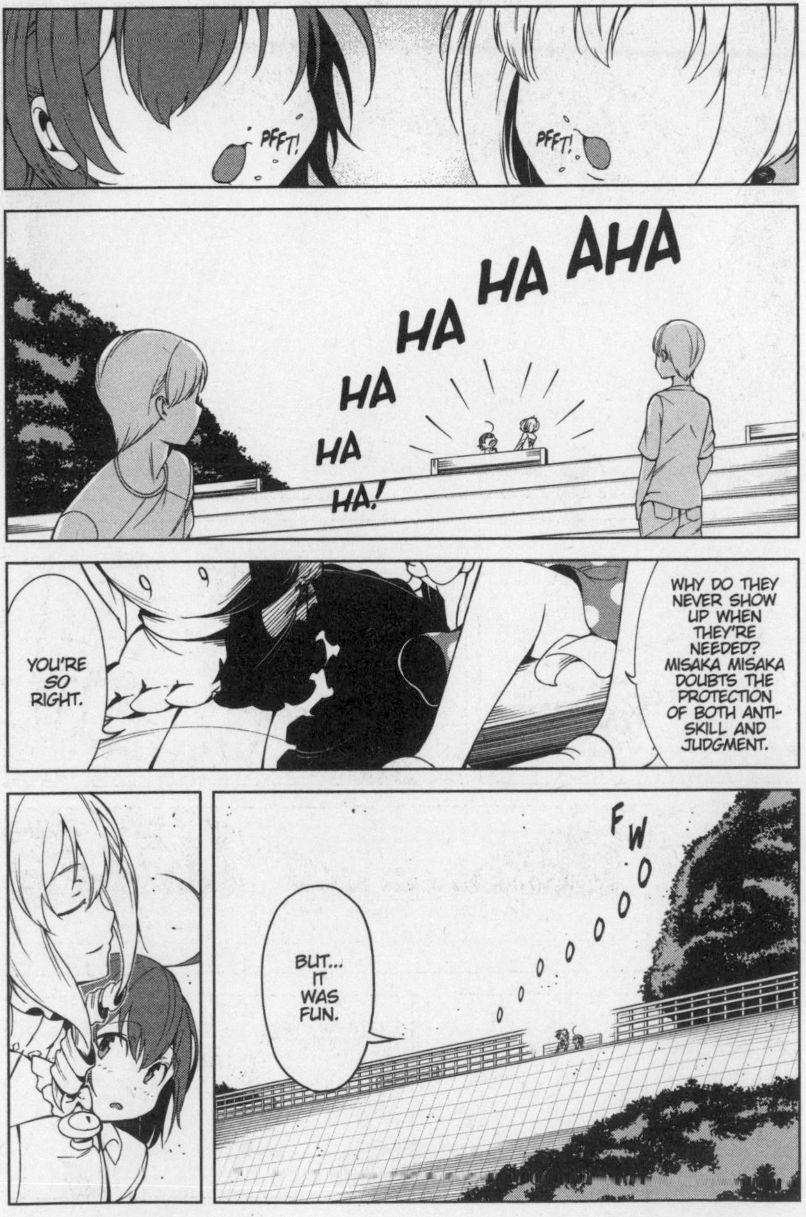
PFFT!
PFFT!
AHA
HA
HA
HA
HA
HA!
WHY DO THEY NEVER SHOW UP WHEN THEY'RE NEEDED? MISAKA MISAKA DOUBTS THE PROTECTION OF BOTH ANTI-SKILL AND JUDGMENT.
YOU'RE SO RIGHT.
FWOOOOOOOO
BUT... IT WAS FUN.

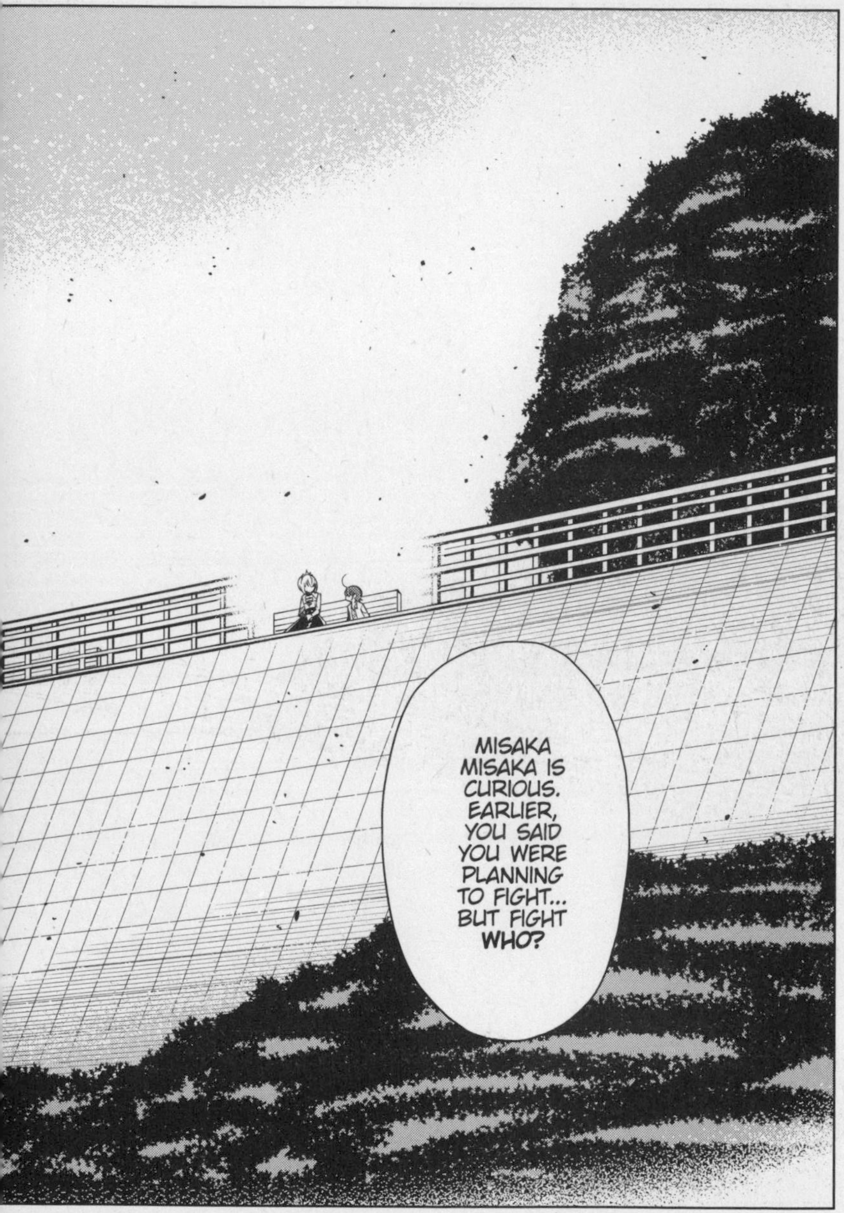
MISAKA MISAKA IS CURIOUS. EARLIER, YOU SAID YOU WERE PLANNING TO FIGHT... BUT FIGHT WHO?

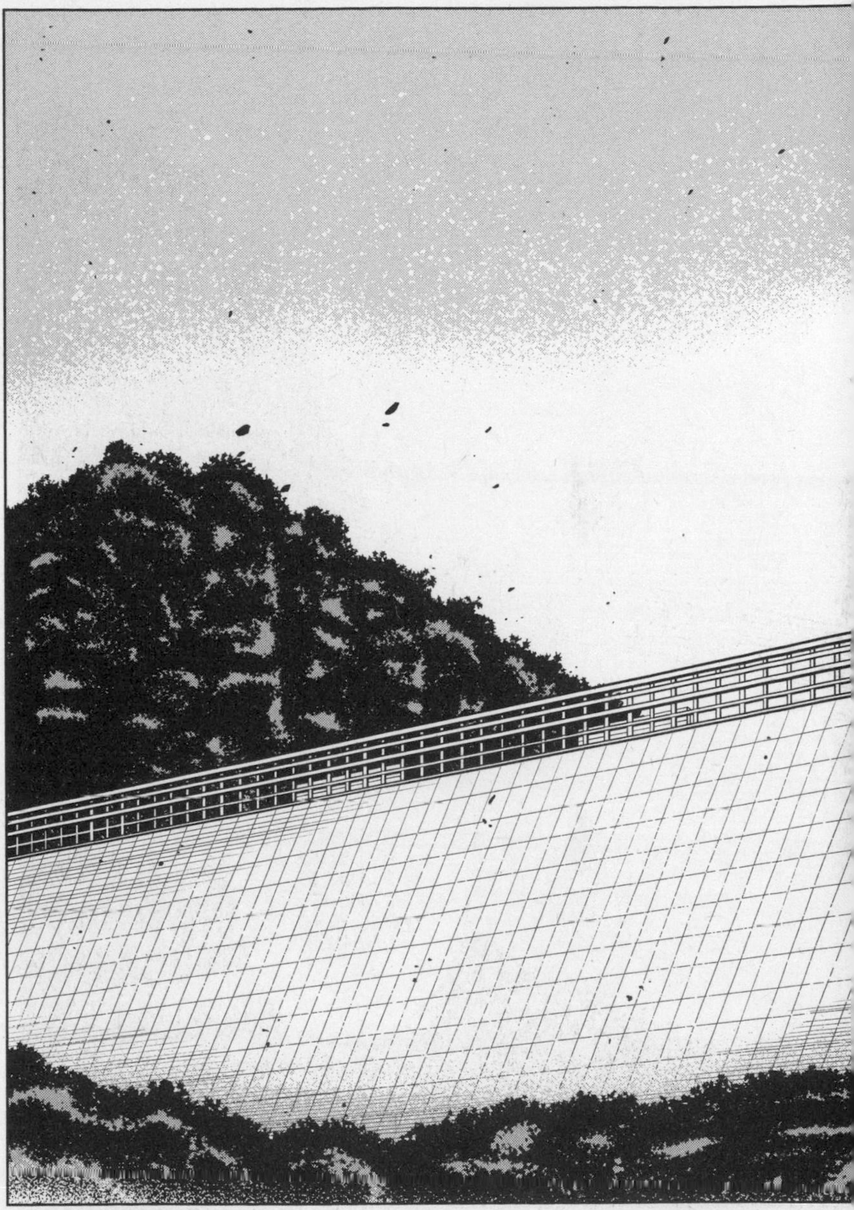

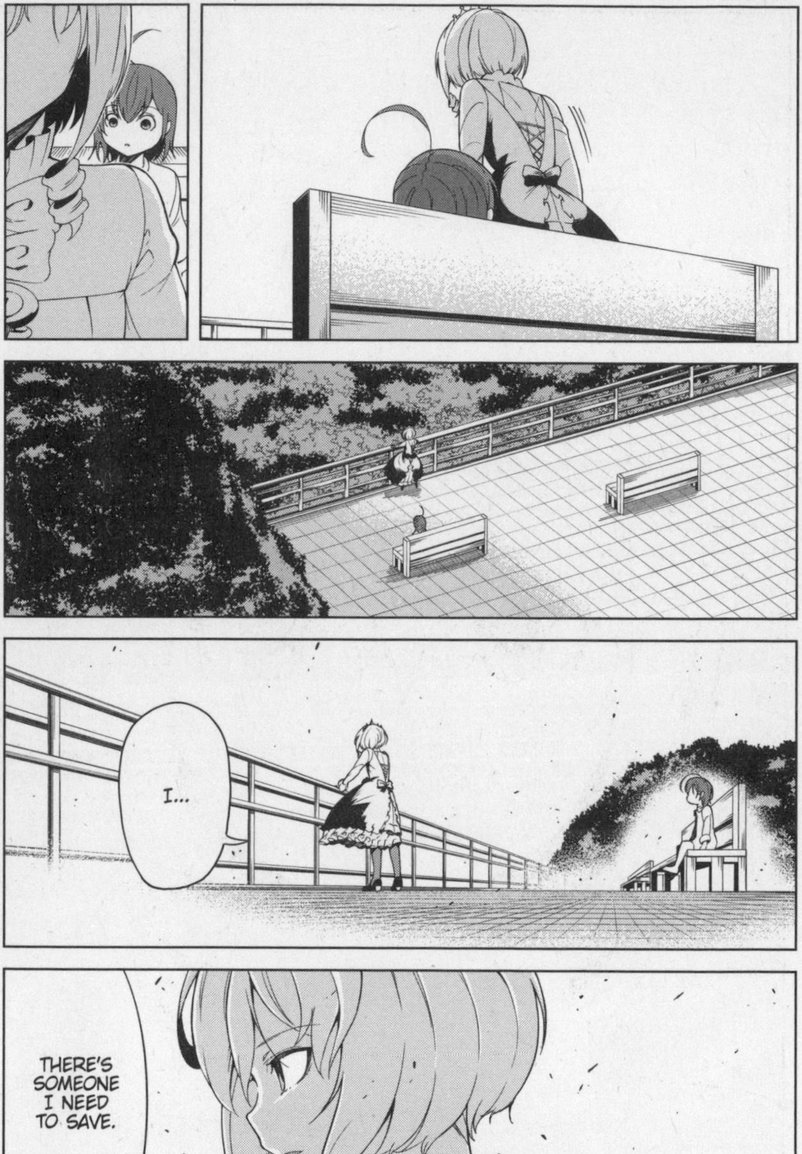
I...
THERE'S SOMEONE I NEED TO SAVE.

CHAPTER 40

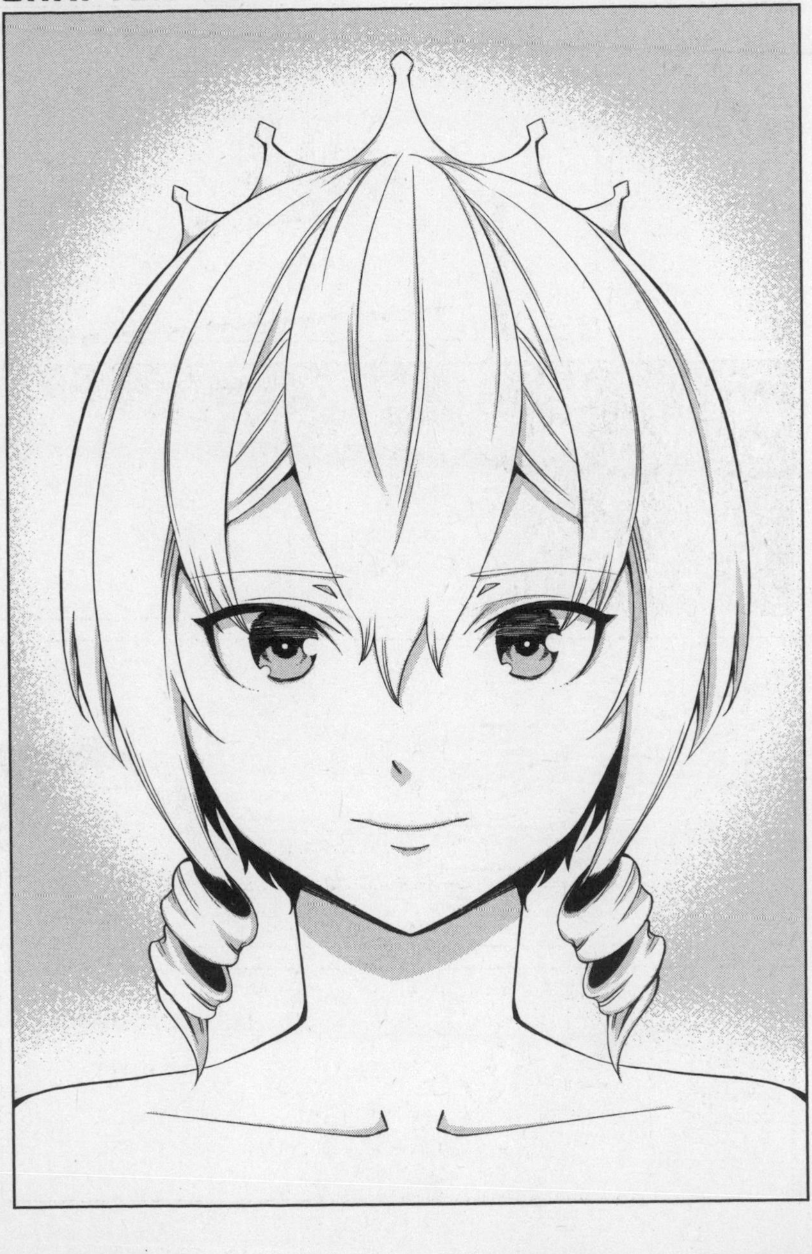

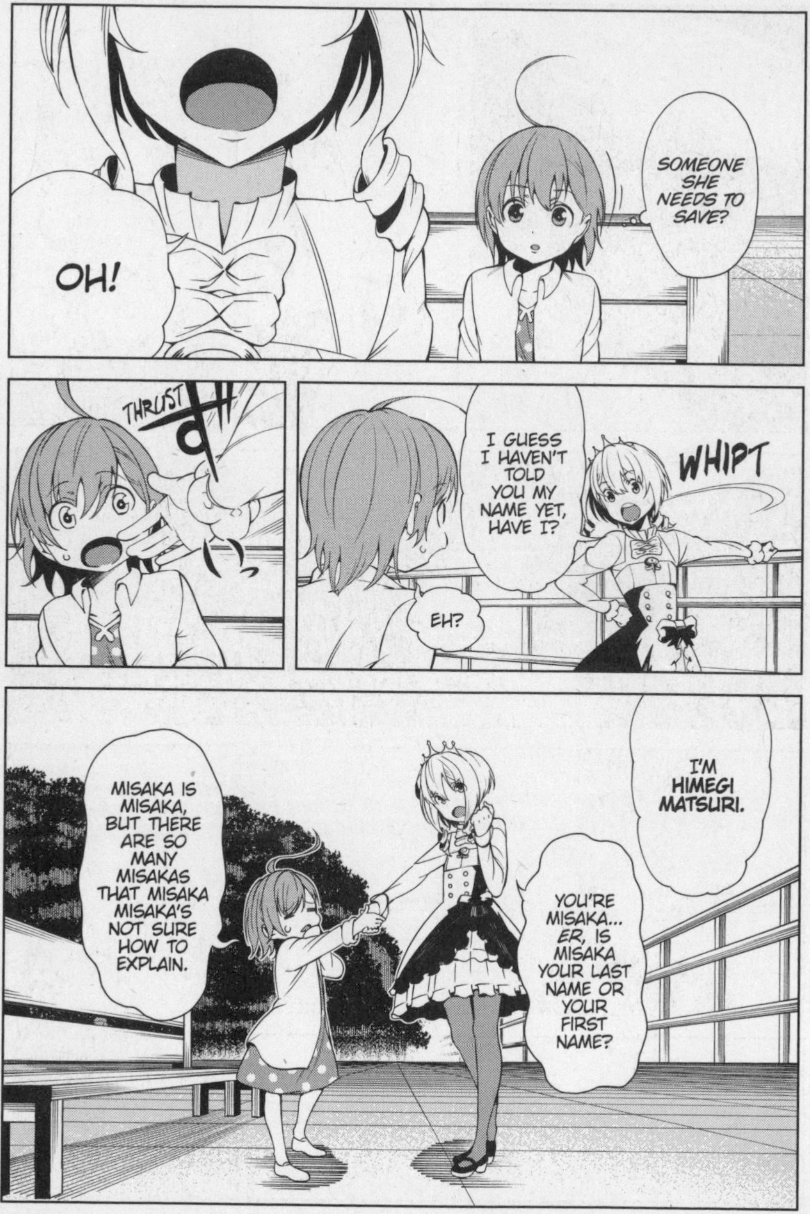
SOMEONE SHE NEEDS TO SAVE?
OH!
I GUESS I HAVEN'T TOLD YOU MY NAME YET, HAVE I?
WHIPT
EH?
THRUST
I'M HIMEGI MATSURI.
YOU'RE MISAKA... ER, IS MISAKA YOUR LAST NAME OR YOUR FIRST NAME?
MISAKA IS MISAKA, BUT THERE ARE SO MANY MISAKAS THAT MISAKA MISAKA'S NOT SURE HOW TO EXPLAIN.

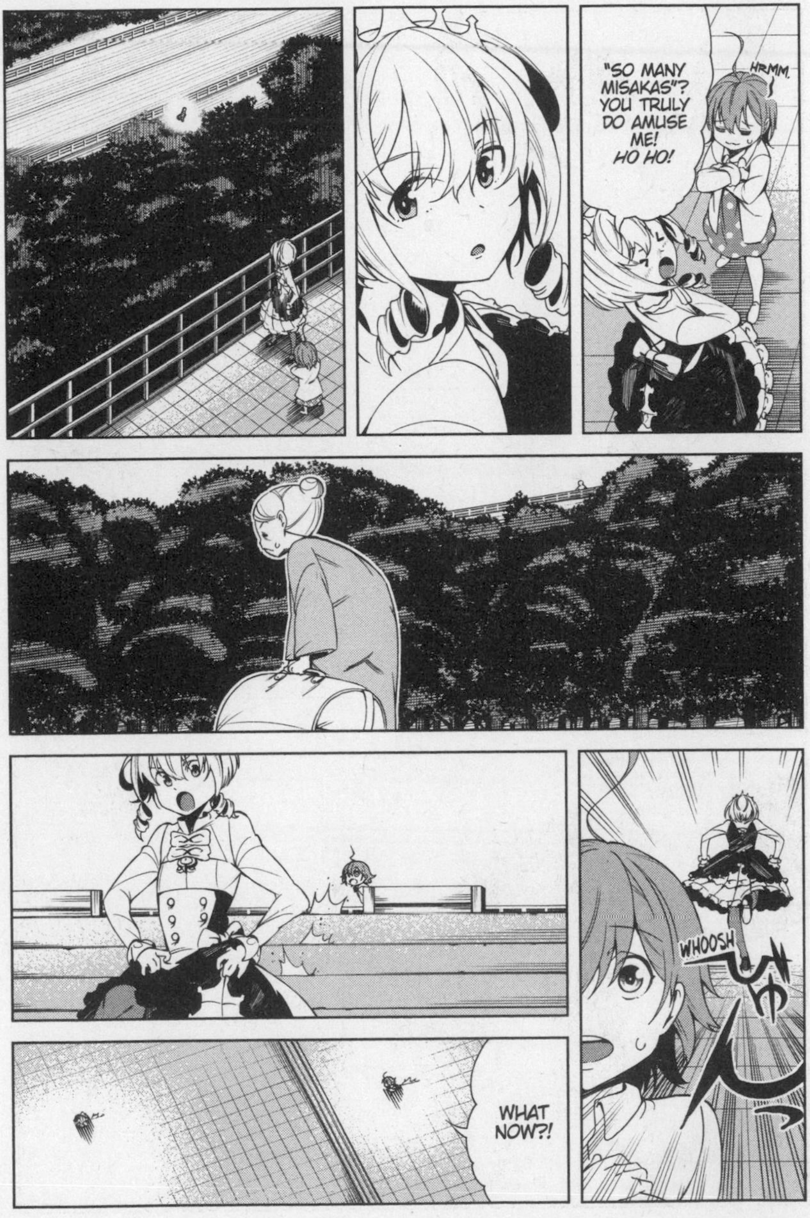
"SO MANY MISAKAS"? YOU TRULY DO AMUSE ME! HO HO!
HRMM.
WHOOSH
WHAT NOW?!

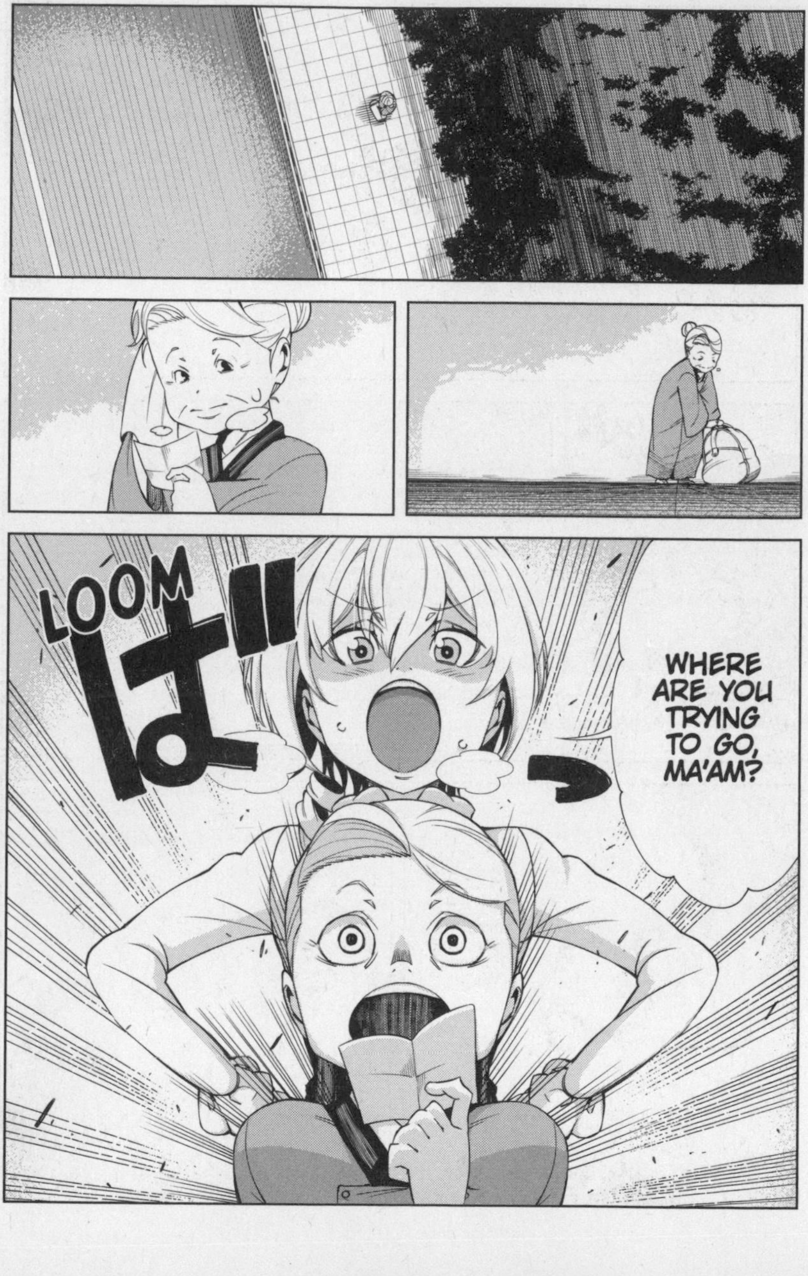
LOOM
WHERE ARE YOU TRYING TO GO, MA'AM?

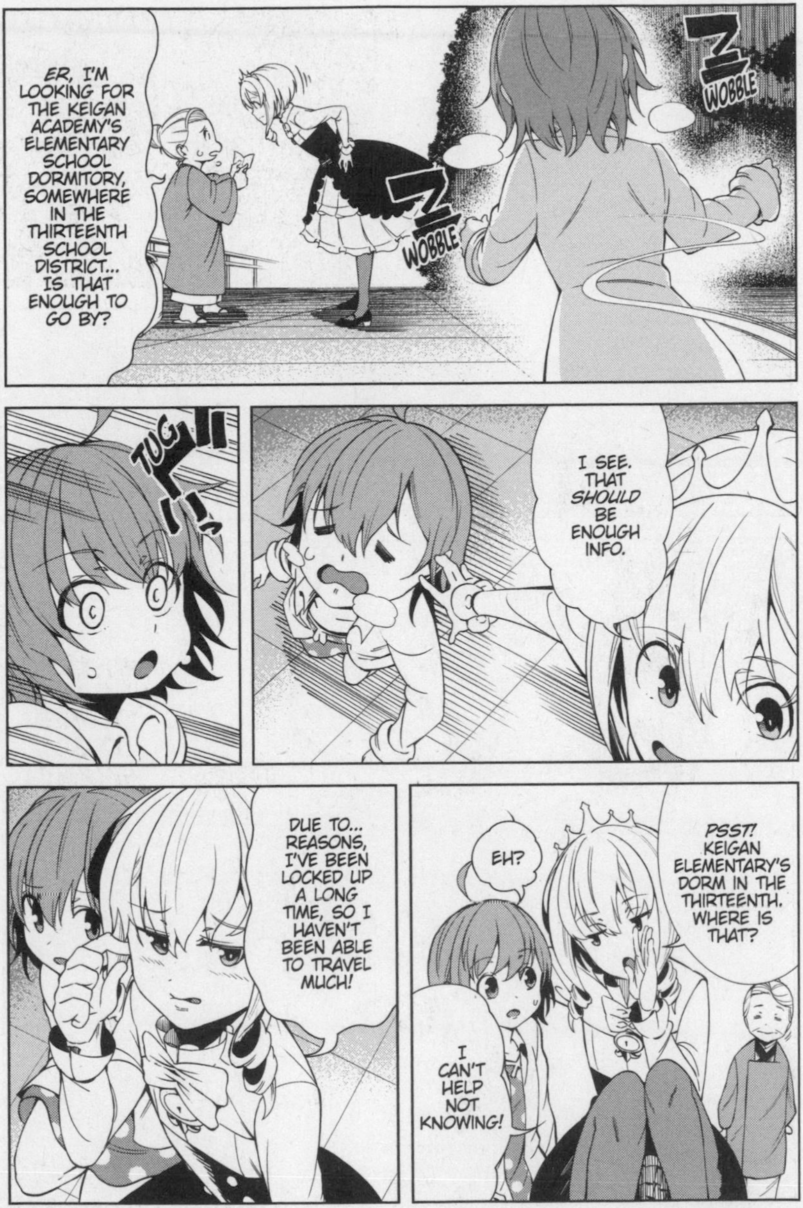
WOBBLE
WOBBLE
ER, I'M LOOKING FOR THE KEIGAN ACADEMY'S ELEMENTARY SCHOOL DORMITORY, SOMEWHERE IN THE THIRTEENTH SCHOOL DISTRICT... IS THAT ENOUGH TO GO BY?
I SEE. THAT SHOULD BE ENOUGH INFO.
TUG
PSST! KEIGAN ELEMENTARY'S DORM IN THE THIRTEENTH. WHERE IS THAT?
EH?
I CAN'T HELP NOT KNOWING!
DUE TO... REASONS, I'VE BEEN LOCKED UP A LONG TIME, SO I HAVEN'T BEEN ABLE TO TRAVEL MUCH!

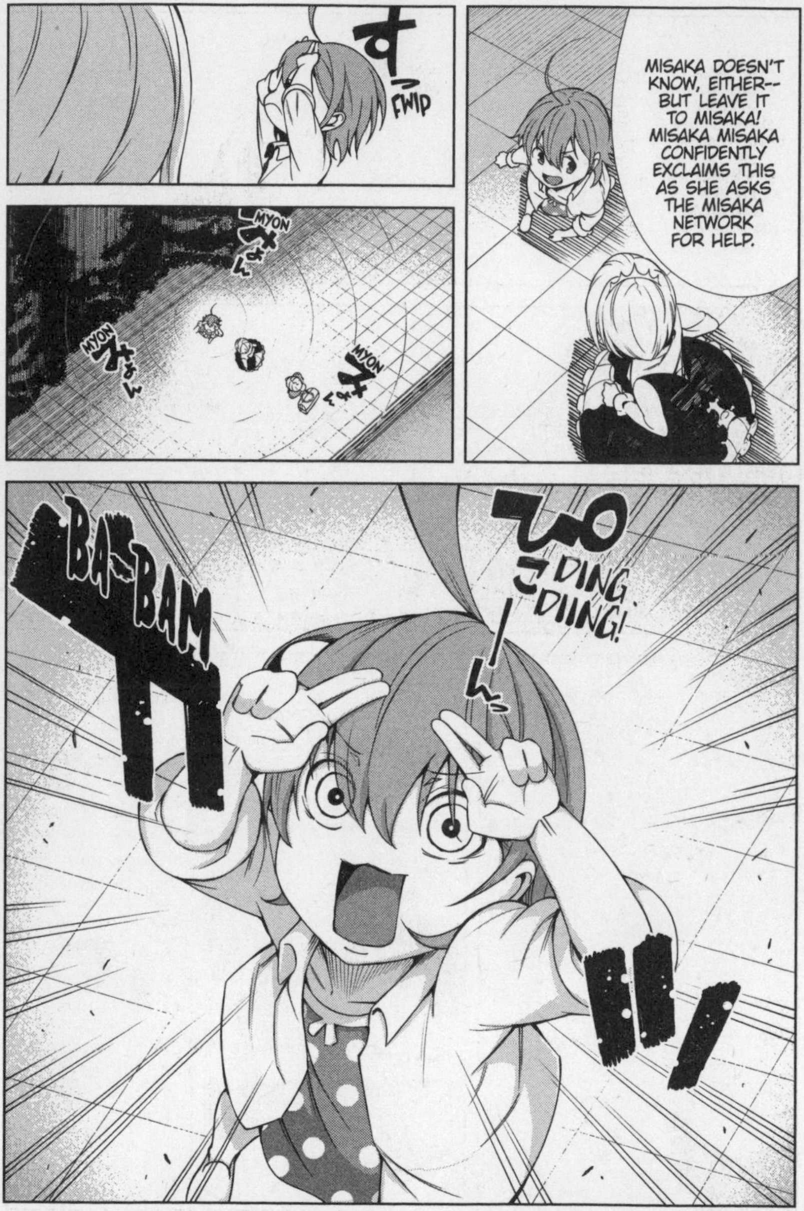
MISAKA DOESN'T KNOW, EITHER-- BUT LEAVE IT TO MISAKA! MISAKA MISAKA CONFIDENTLY EXCLAIMS THIS AS SHE ASKS THE MISAKA NETWORK FOR HELP.
FWIP
MYON
MYON
MYON
DING DIING!
BA-BAM

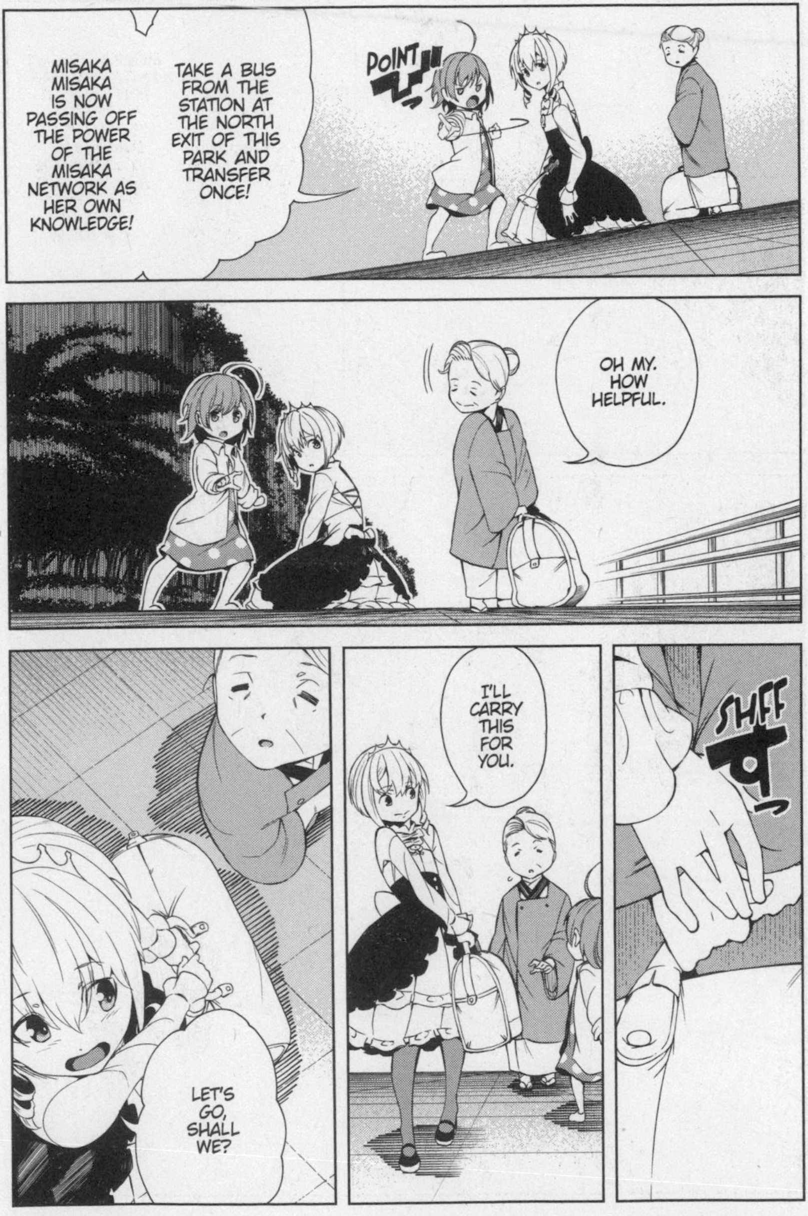
POINT
TAKE A BUS FROM THE STATION AT THE NORTH EXIT OF THIS PARK AND TRANSFER ONCE!
MISAKA MISAKA IS NOW PASSING OFF THE POWER OF THE MISAKA NETWORK AS HER OWN KNOWLEDGE!
OH MY. HOW HELPFUL.
SHFF
I'LL CARRY THIS FOR YOU.
LET'S GO, SHALL WE?

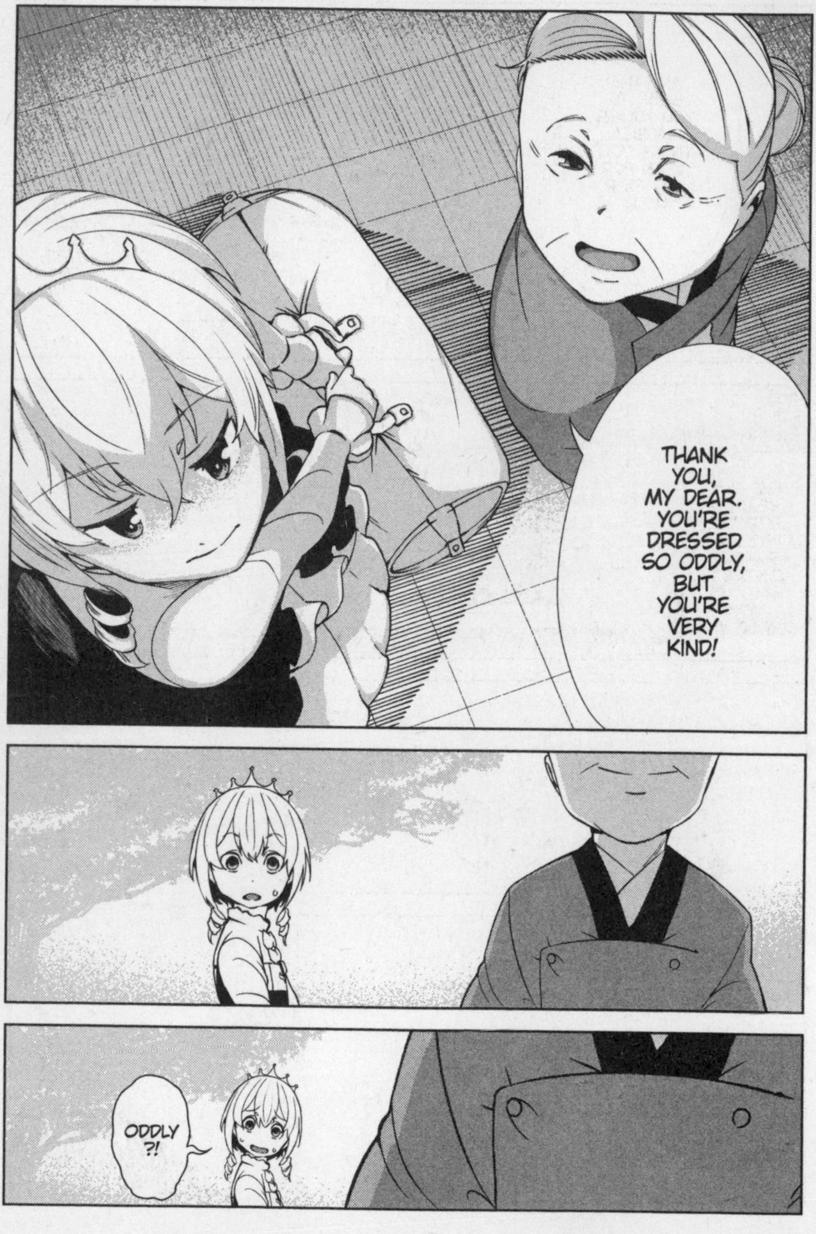
THANK YOU, MY DEAR. YOU'RE DRESSED SO ODDLY, BUT YOU'RE VERY KIND!
ODDLY?!

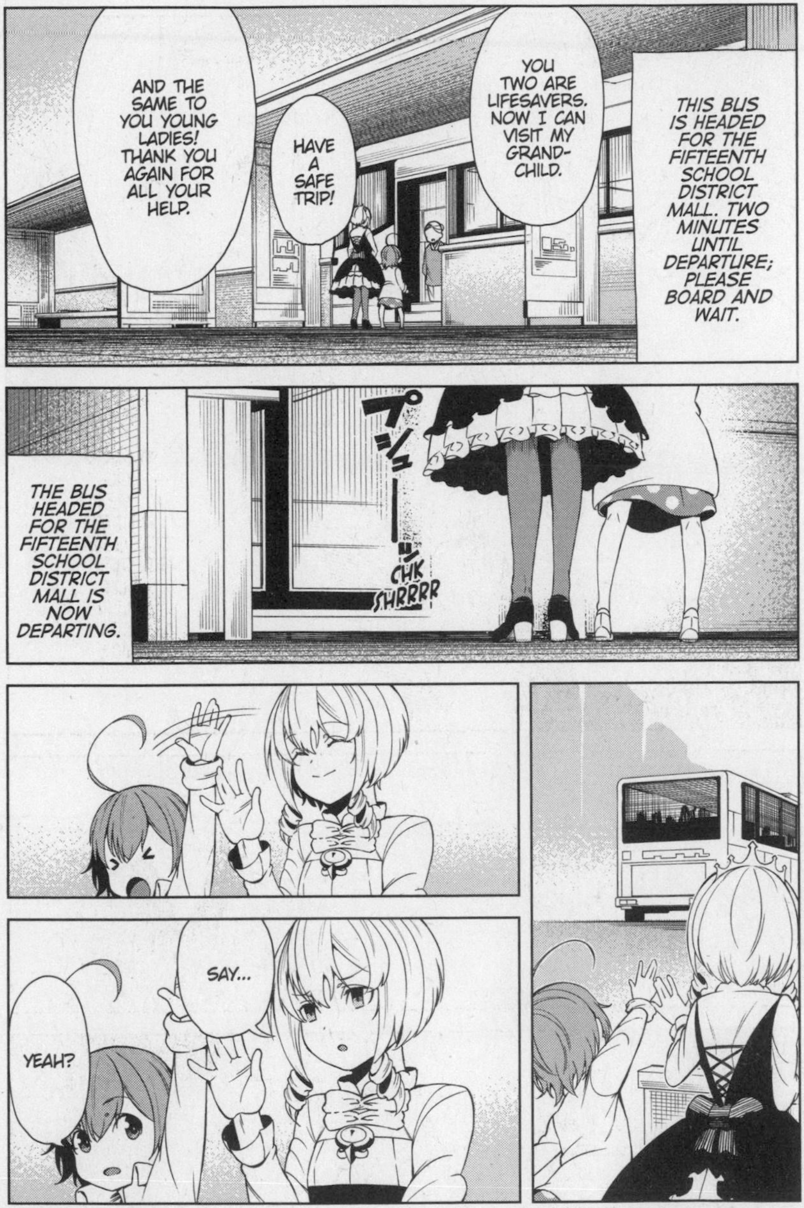
THIS BUS IS HEADED FOR THE FIFTEENTH SCHOOL DISTRICT MALL. TWO MINUTES UNTIL DEPARTURE; PLEASE BOARD AND WAIT.
YOU TWO ARE LIFESAVERS. NOW I CAN VISIT MY GRAND-CHILD.
HAVE A SAFE TRIP!
AND THE SAME TO YOU YOUNG LADIES! THANK YOU AGAIN FOR ALL YOUR HELP.
プシュー
CHK SHRRRR
THE BUS HEADED FOR THE FIFTEENTH SCHOOL DISTRICT MALL IS NOW DEPARTING.
SAY...
YEAH?

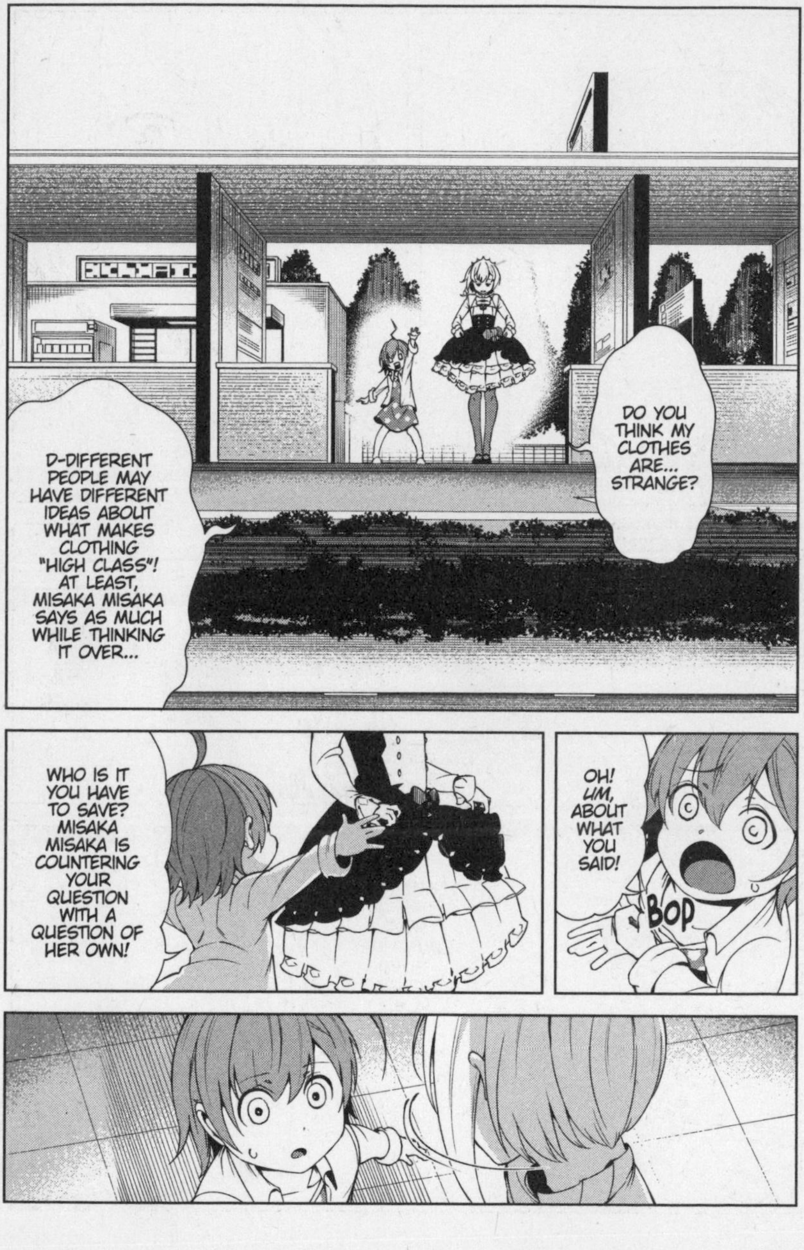
DO YOU THINK MY CLOTHES ARE... STRANGE?
D-DIFFERENT PEOPLE MAY HAVE DIFFERENT IDEAS ABOUT WHAT MAKES CLOTHING "HIGH CLASS"! AT LEAST, MISAKA MISAKA SAYS AS MUCH WHILE THINKING IT OVER...
OH! UM, ABOUT WHAT YOU SAID!
BOP
WHO IS IT YOU HAVE TO SAVE? MISAKA MISAKA IS COUNTERING YOUR QUESTION WITH A QUESTION OF HER OWN!

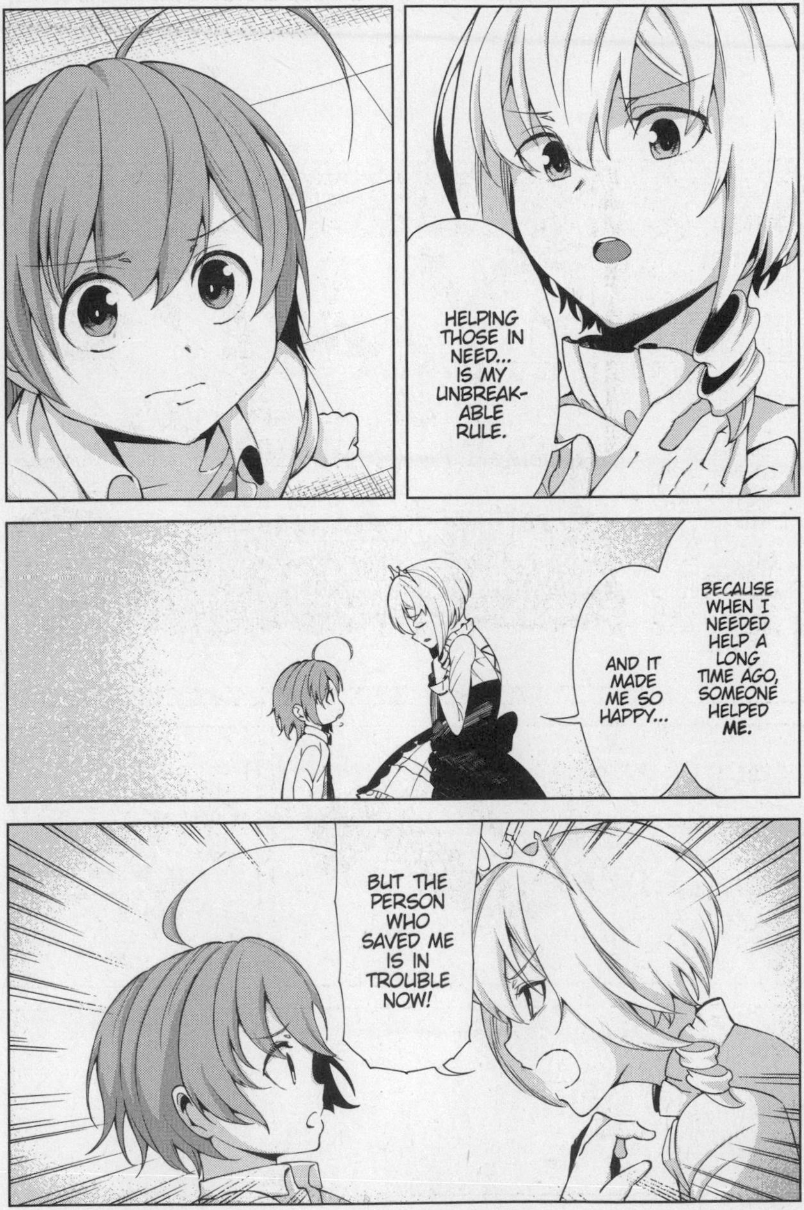
HELPING THOSE IN NEED... IS MY UNBREAKABLE RULE.
BECAUSE WHEN I NEEDED HELP A LONG TIME AGO, SOMEONE HELPED ME.
AND IT MADE ME SO HAPPY...
BUT THE PERSON WHO SAVED ME IS IN TROUBLE NOW!

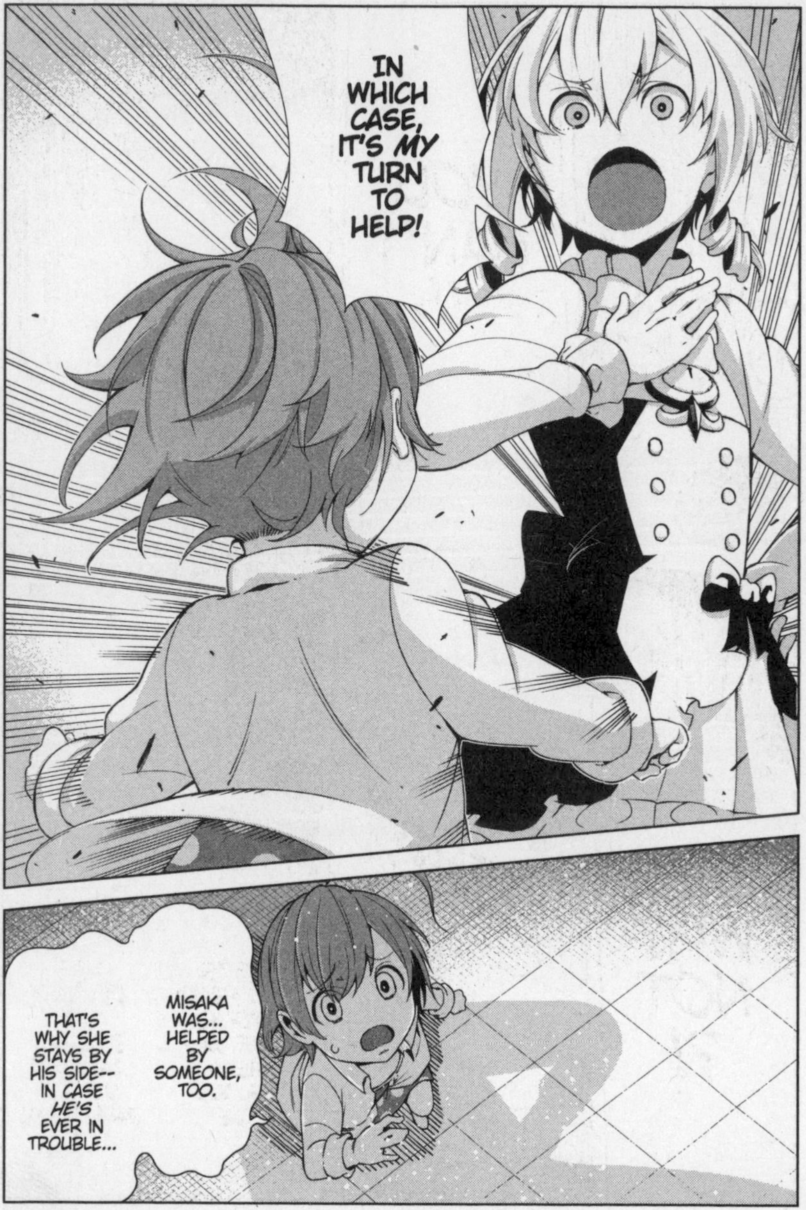
IN WHICH CASE, IT'S *MY* TURN TO HELP!
MISAKA WAS... HELPED BY SOMEONE, TOO.
THAT'S WHY SHE STAYS BY HIS SIDE-- IN CASE *HE'S* EVER IN TROUBLE...

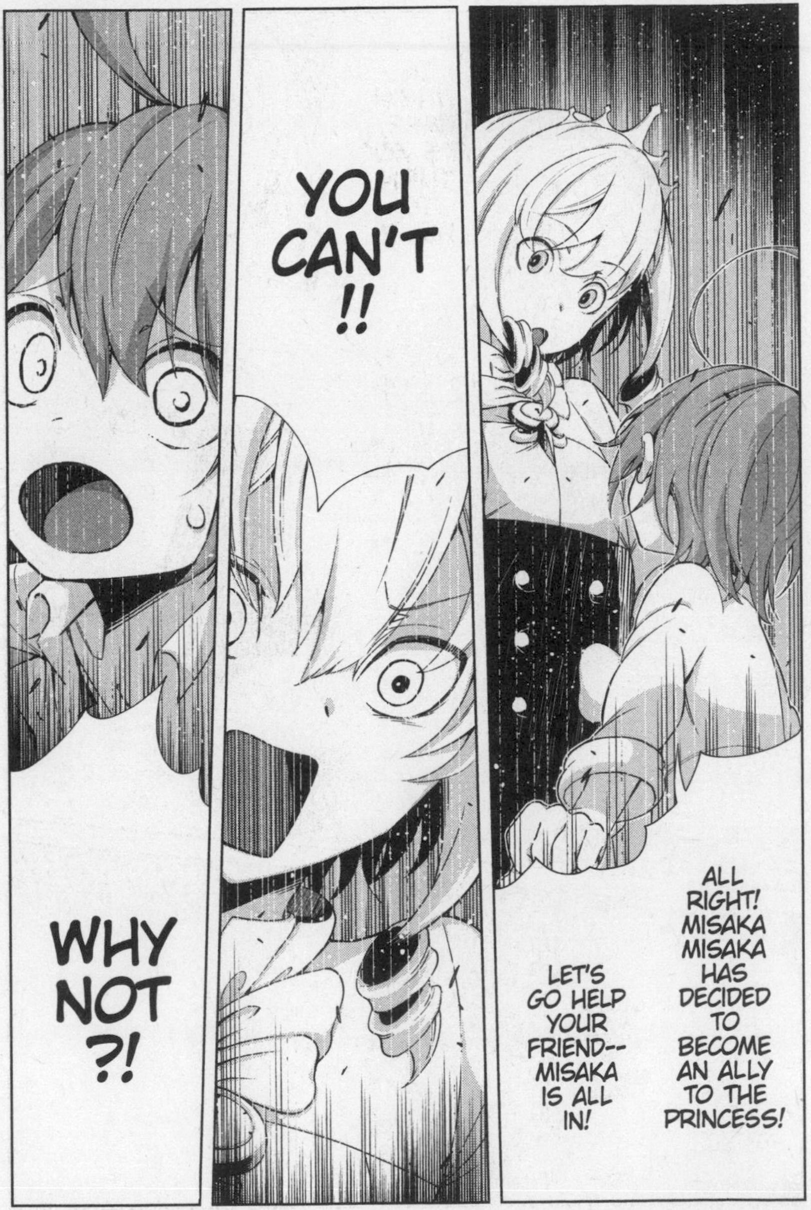
ALL RIGHT! MISAKA MISAKA HAS DECIDED TO BECOME AN ALLY TO THE PRINCESS!
LET'S GO HELP YOUR FRIEND-- MISAKA IS ALL IN!
YOU CAN'T !!
WHY NOT ?!

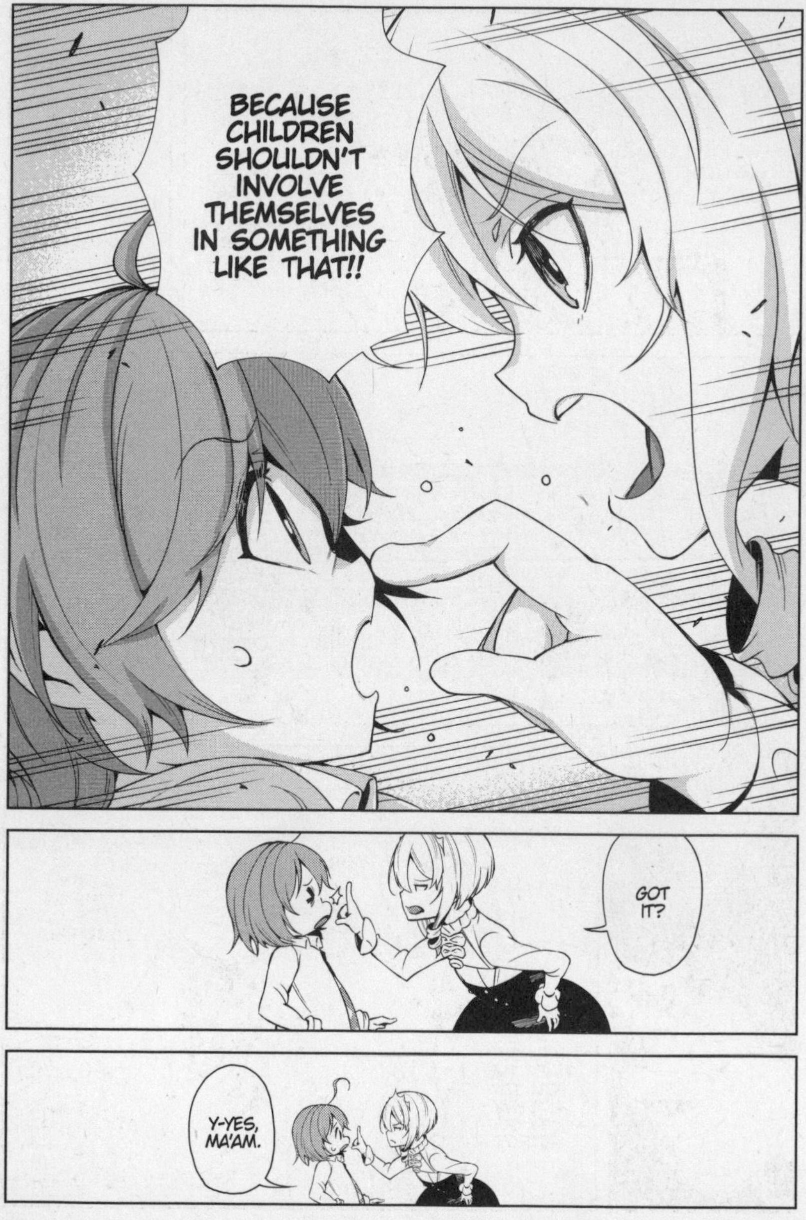
BECAUSE CHILDREN SHOULDN'T INVOLVE THEMSELVES IN SOMETHING LIKE THAT!!
GOT IT?
Y-YES, MA'AM.

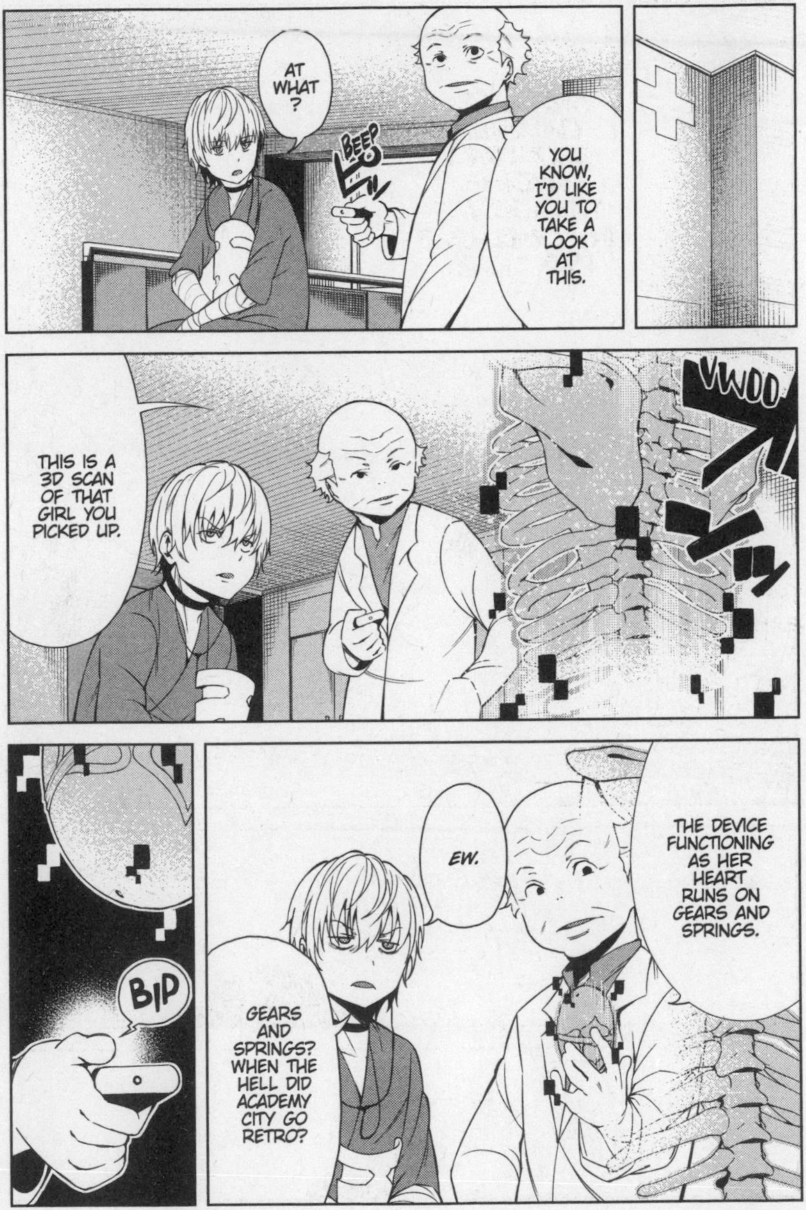
YOU KNOW, I'D LIKE YOU TO TAKE A LOOK AT THIS.
BEEP
AT WHAT?
VWOO
THIS IS A 3D SCAN OF THAT GIRL YOU PICKED UP.
THE DEVICE FUNCTIONING AS HER HEART RUNS ON GEARS AND SPRINGS.
EW.
GEARS AND SPRINGS? WHEN THE HELL DID ACADEMY CITY GO RETRO?
BIP

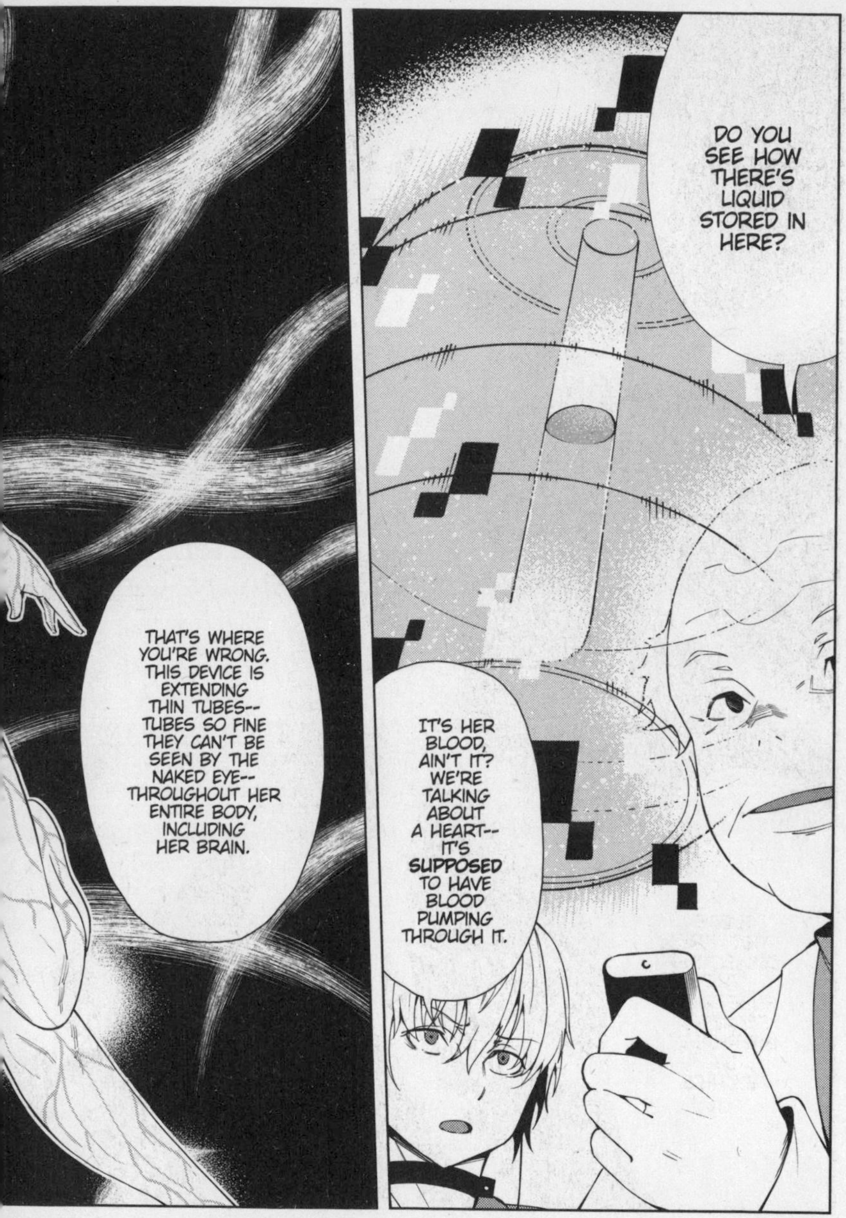
DO YOU SEE HOW THERE'S LIQUID STORED IN HERE?
IT'S HER BLOOD, AIN'T IT? WE'RE TALKING ABOUT A HEART--IT'S **SUPPOSED** TO HAVE BLOOD PUMPING THROUGH IT.
THAT'S WHERE YOU'RE WRONG. THIS DEVICE IS EXTENDING THIN TUBES--TUBES SO FINE THEY CAN'T BE SEEN BY THE NAKED EYE--THROUGHOUT HER ENTIRE BODY, INCLUDING HER BRAIN.

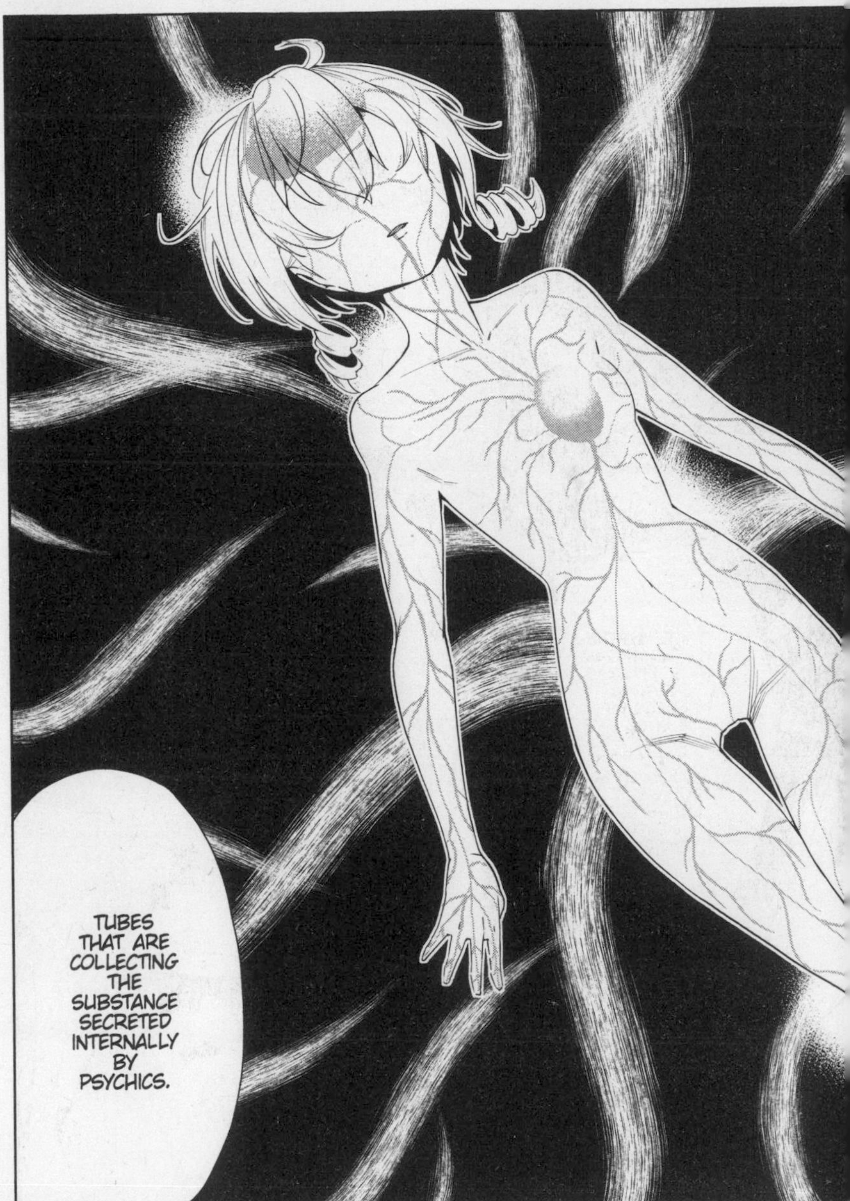
TUBES THAT ARE COLLECTING THE SUBSTANCE SECRETED INTERNALLY BY PSYCHICS.

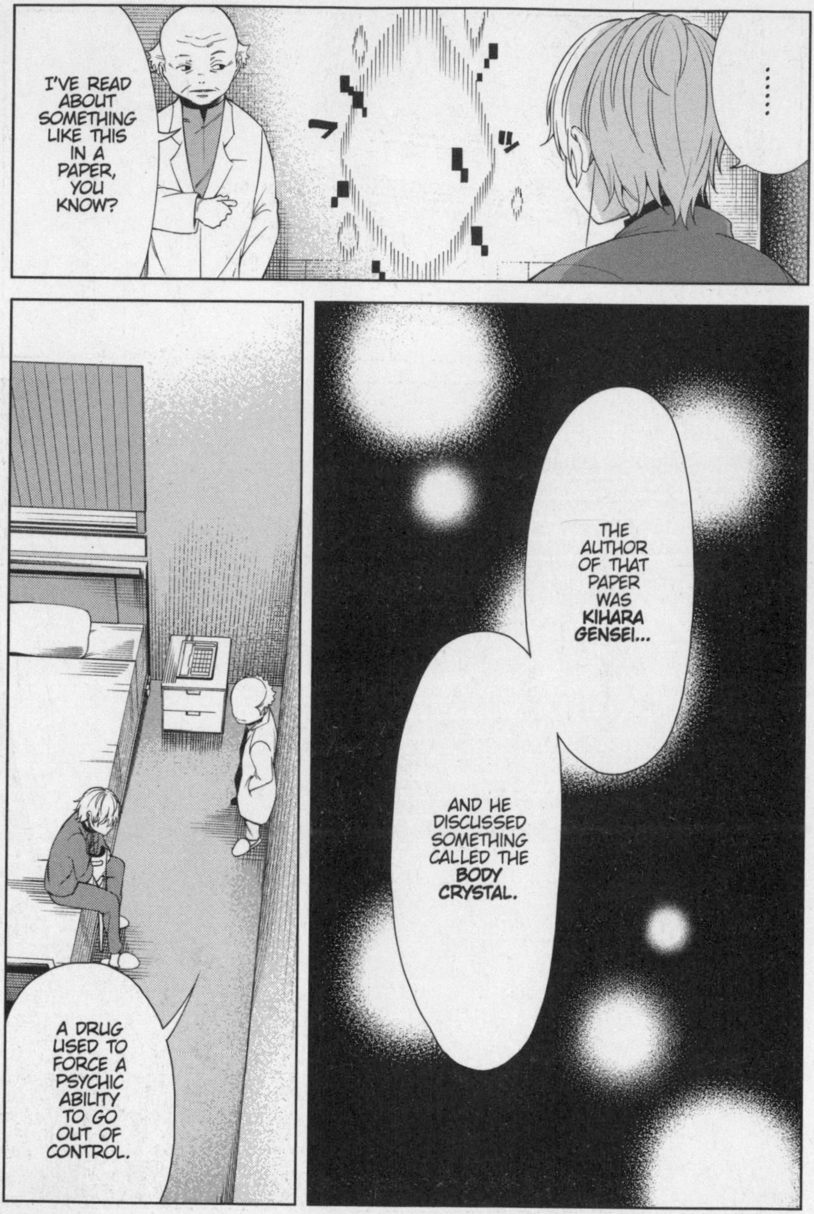
......
I'VE READ ABOUT SOMETHING LIKE THIS IN A PAPER, YOU KNOW?
THE AUTHOR OF THAT PAPER WAS KIHARA GENSEI...
AND HE DISCUSSED SOMETHING CALLED THE BODY CRYSTAL.
A DRUG USED TO FORCE A PSYCHIC ABILITY TO GO OUT OF CONTROL.

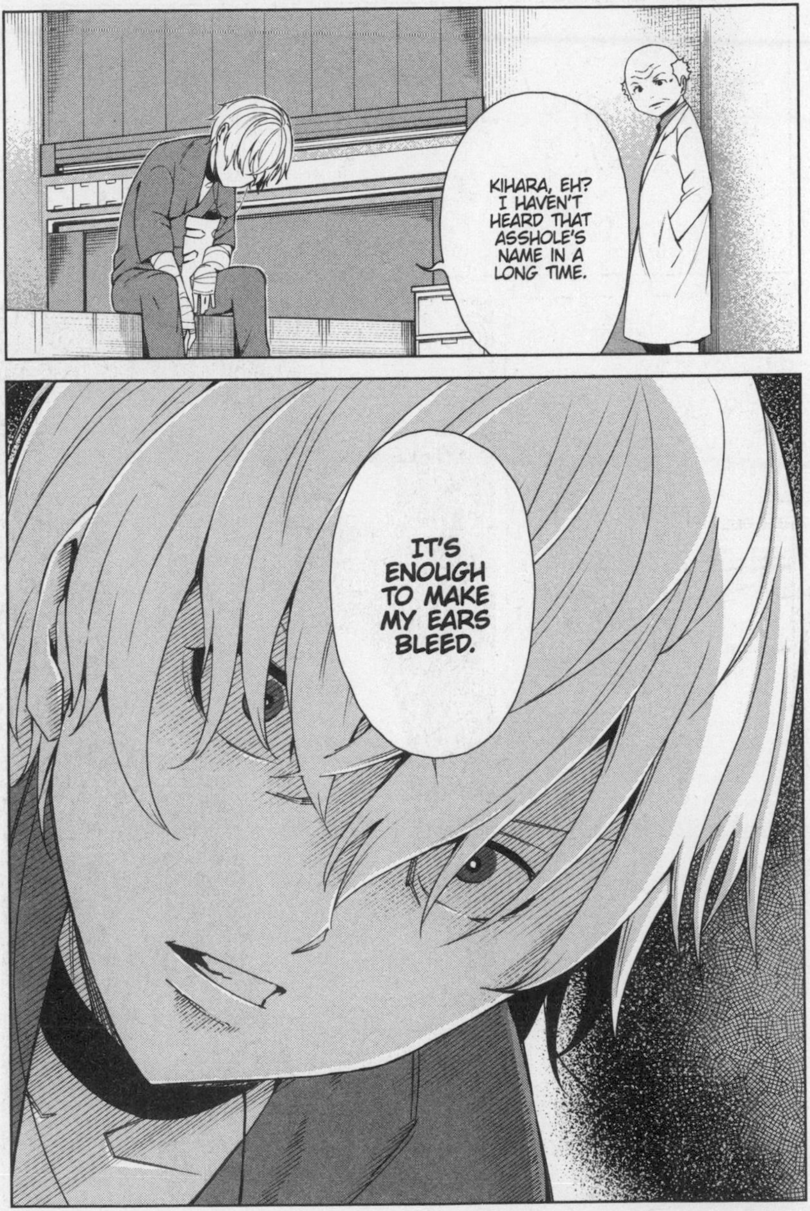
KIHARA, EH? I HAVEN'T HEARD THAT ASSHOLE'S NAME IN A LONG TIME.
IT'S ENOUGH TO MAKE MY EARS BLEED.

とある科学の一方通行

アクセラレータ

とある魔術の禁書目録外伝

CHAPTER 41

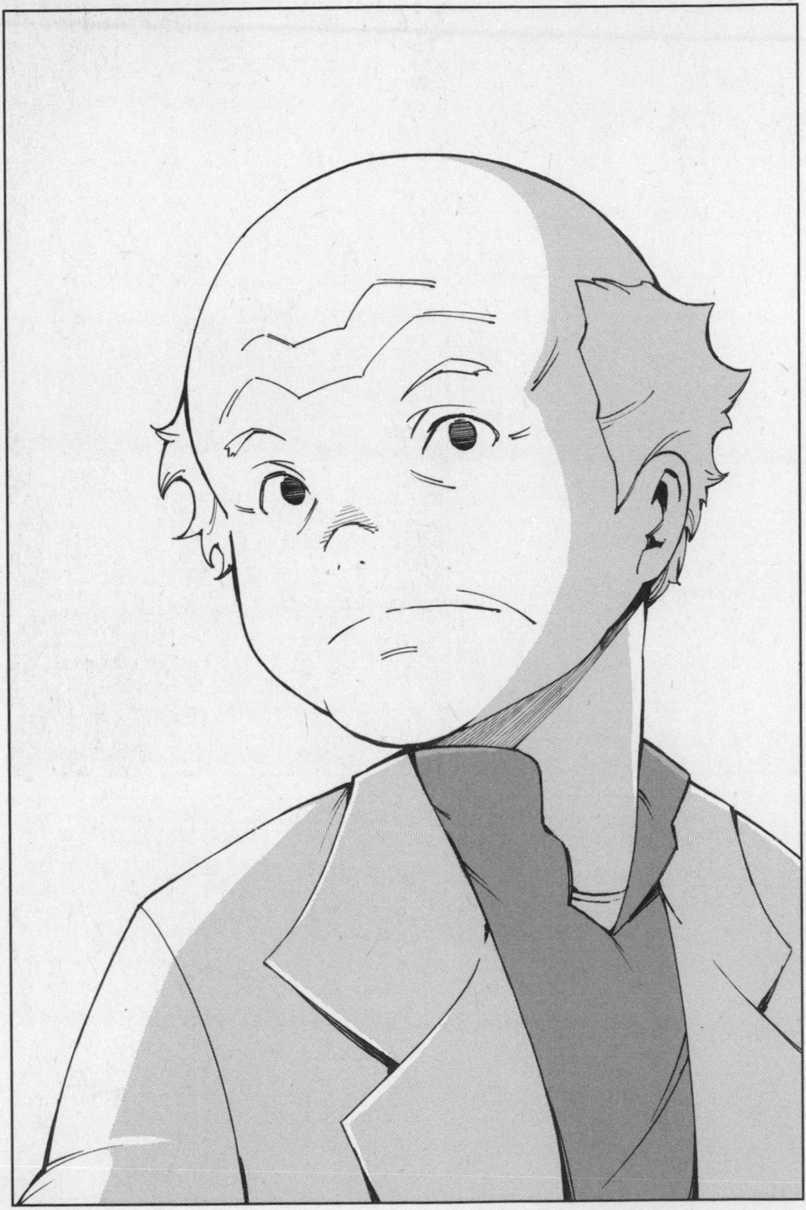

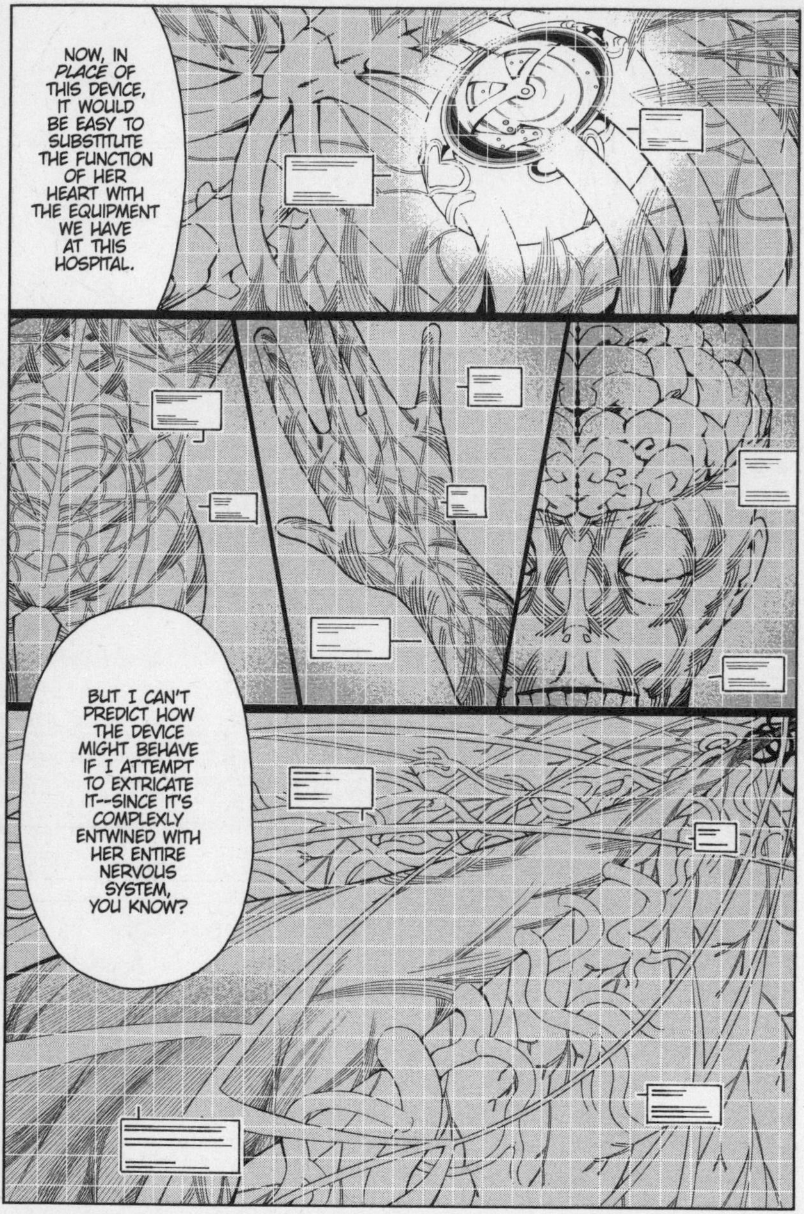
NOW, IN *PLACE* OF THIS DEVICE, IT WOULD BE EASY TO SUBSTITUTE THE FUNCTION OF HER HEART WITH THE EQUIPMENT WE HAVE AT THIS HOSPITAL.
BUT I CAN'T PREDICT HOW THE DEVICE MIGHT BEHAVE IF I ATTEMPT TO EXTRICATE IT--SINCE IT'S COMPLEXLY ENTWINED WITH HER ENTIRE NERVOUS SYSTEM, YOU KNOW?

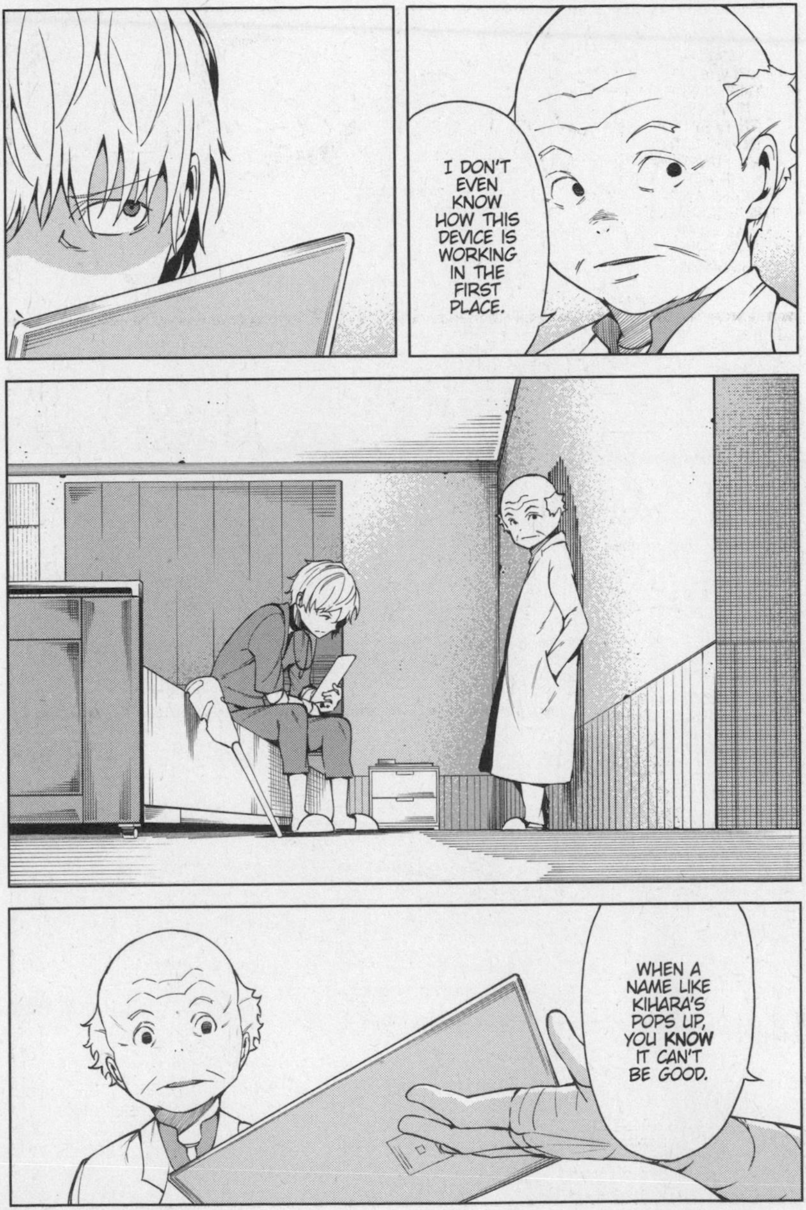
I DON'T EVEN KNOW HOW THIS DEVICE IS WORKING IN THE FIRST PLACE.
WHEN A NAME LIKE KIHARA'S POPS UP, YOU KNOW IT CAN'T BE GOOD.

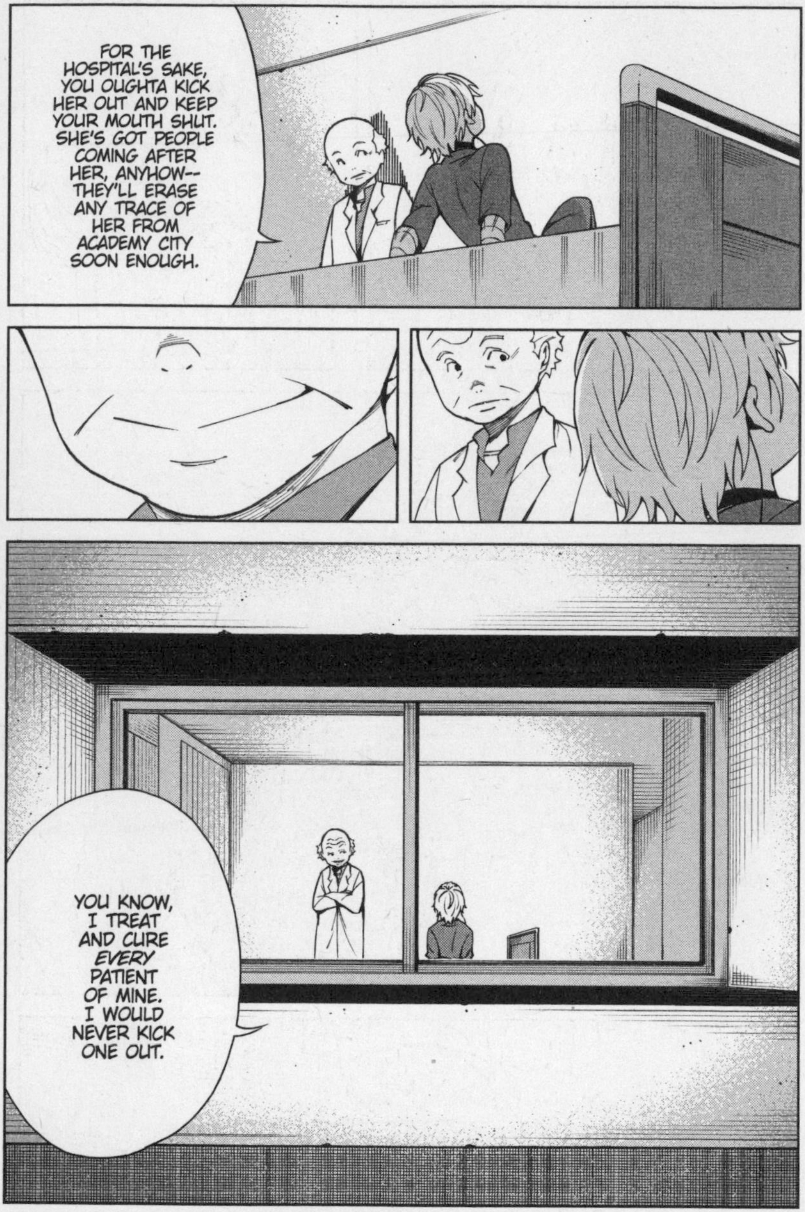
FOR THE HOSPITAL'S SAKE, YOU OUGHTA KICK HER OUT AND KEEP YOUR MOUTH SHUT. SHE'S GOT PEOPLE COMING AFTER HER, ANYHOW-- THEY'LL ERASE ANY TRACE OF HER FROM ACADEMY CITY SOON ENOUGH.
YOU KNOW, I TREAT AND CURE *EVERY* PATIENT OF MINE. I WOULD NEVER KICK ONE OUT.

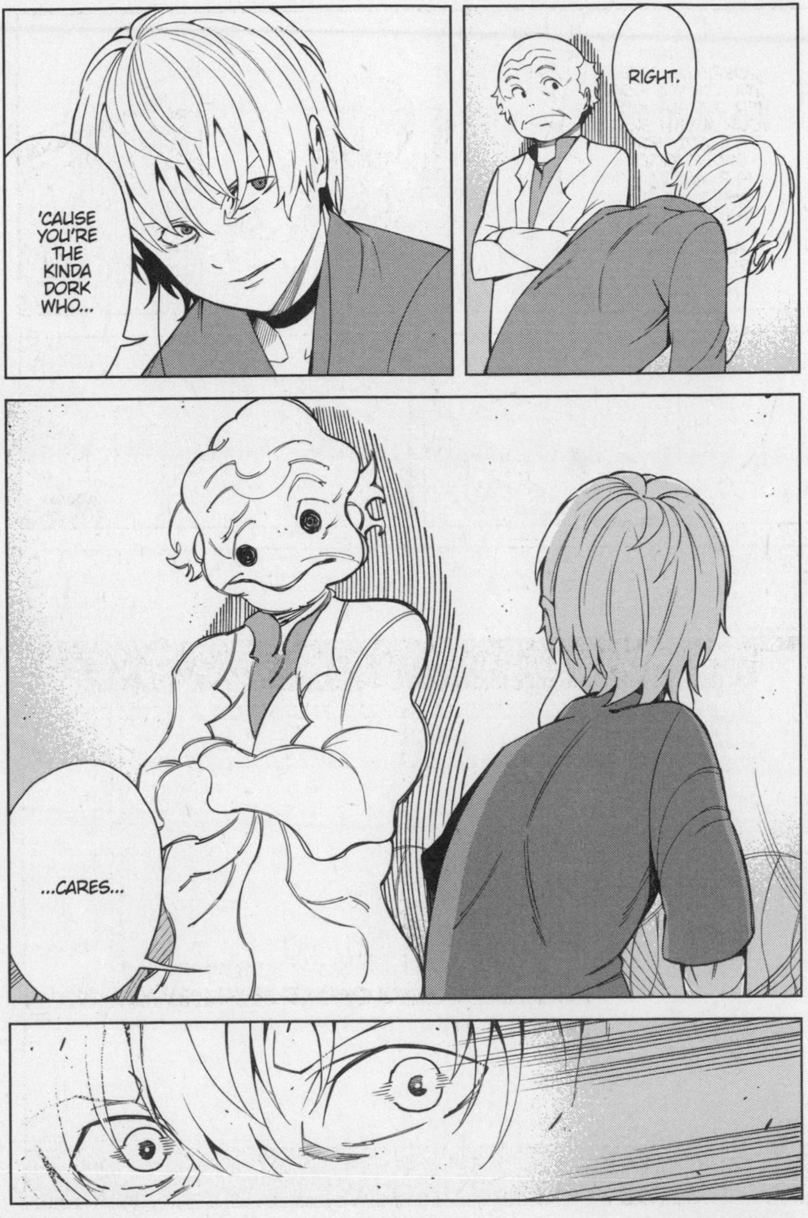
RIGHT.
'CAUSE YOU'RE THE KINDA DORK WHO...
...CARES...

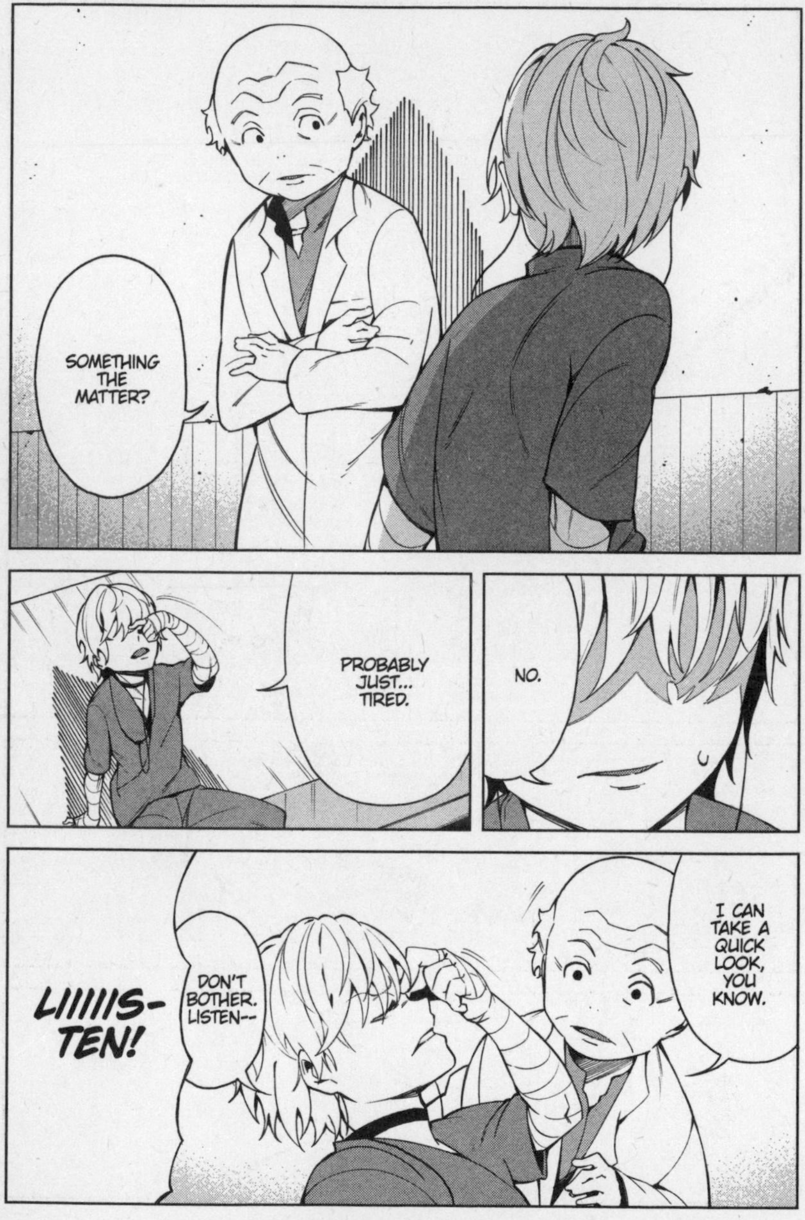
SOMETHING THE MATTER?
NO.
PROBABLY JUST... TIRED.
I CAN TAKE A QUICK LOOK, YOU KNOW.
DON'T BOTHER. LISTEN--
LIIIIIS-TEN!

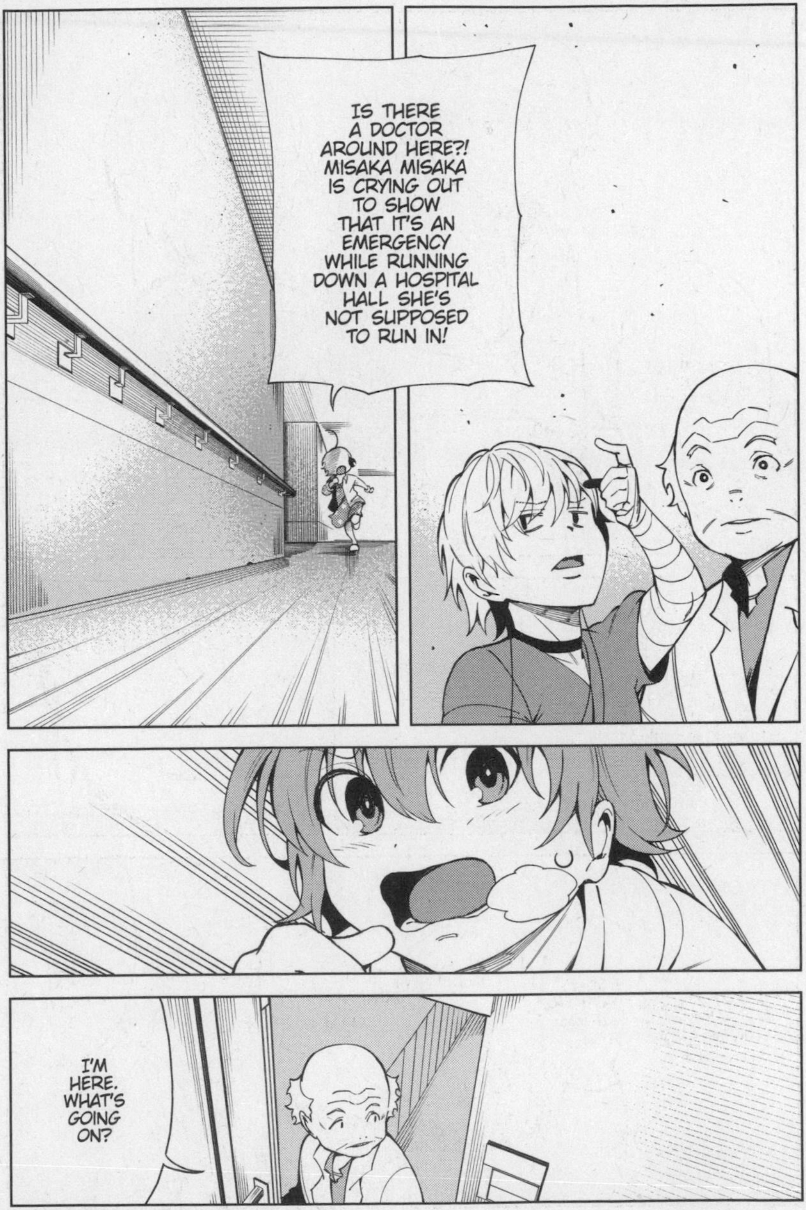
IS THERE A DOCTOR AROUND HERE?! MISAKA MISAKA IS CRYING OUT TO SHOW THAT IT'S AN EMERGENCY WHILE RUNNING DOWN A HOSPITAL HALL SHE'S NOT SUPPOSED TO RUN IN!
I'M HERE. WHAT'S GOING ON?

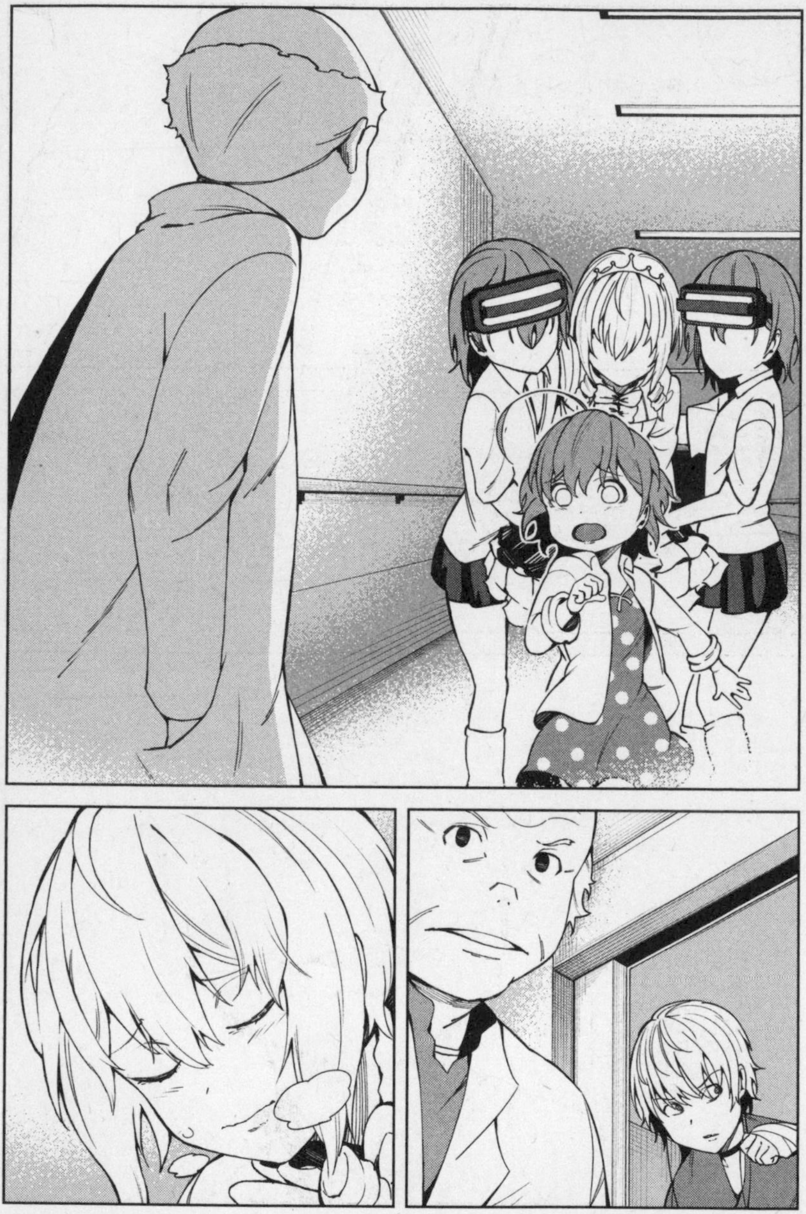

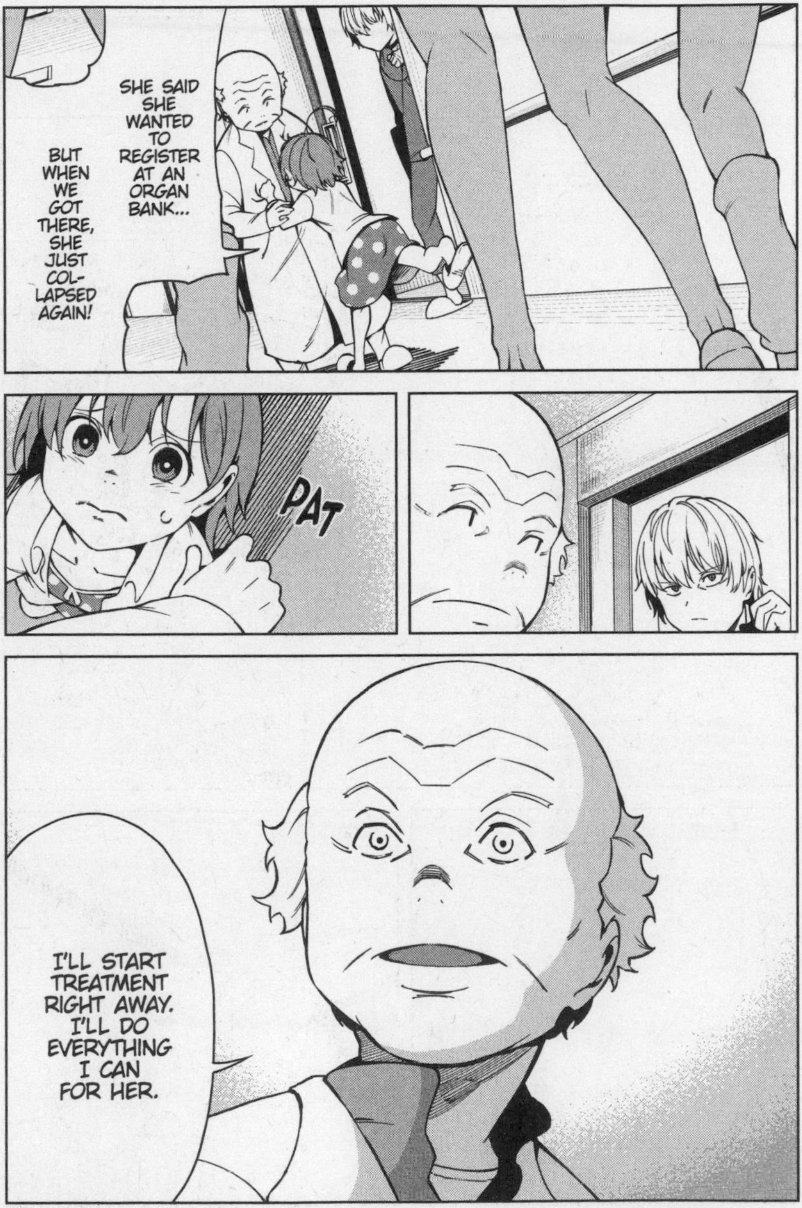
SHE SAID SHE WANTED TO REGISTER AT AN ORGAN BANK...
BUT WHEN WE GOT THERE, SHE JUST COL-LAPSED AGAIN!
PAT
I'LL START TREATMENT RIGHT AWAY. I'LL DO EVERYTHING I CAN FOR HER.

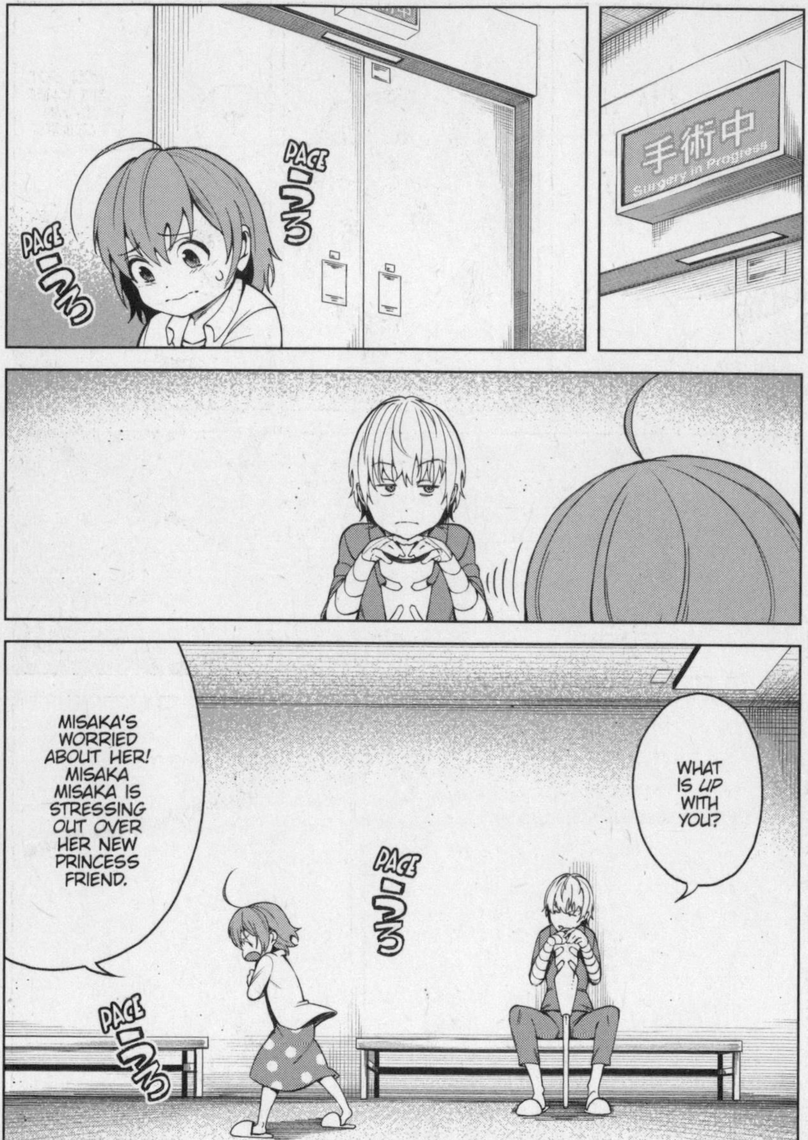
手術中
Surgery in Progress
PACE
PACE
WHAT IS UP WITH YOU?
MISAKA'S WORRIED ABOUT HER! MISAKA MISAKA IS STRESSING OUT OVER HER NEW PRINCESS FRIEND.
PACE
PACE

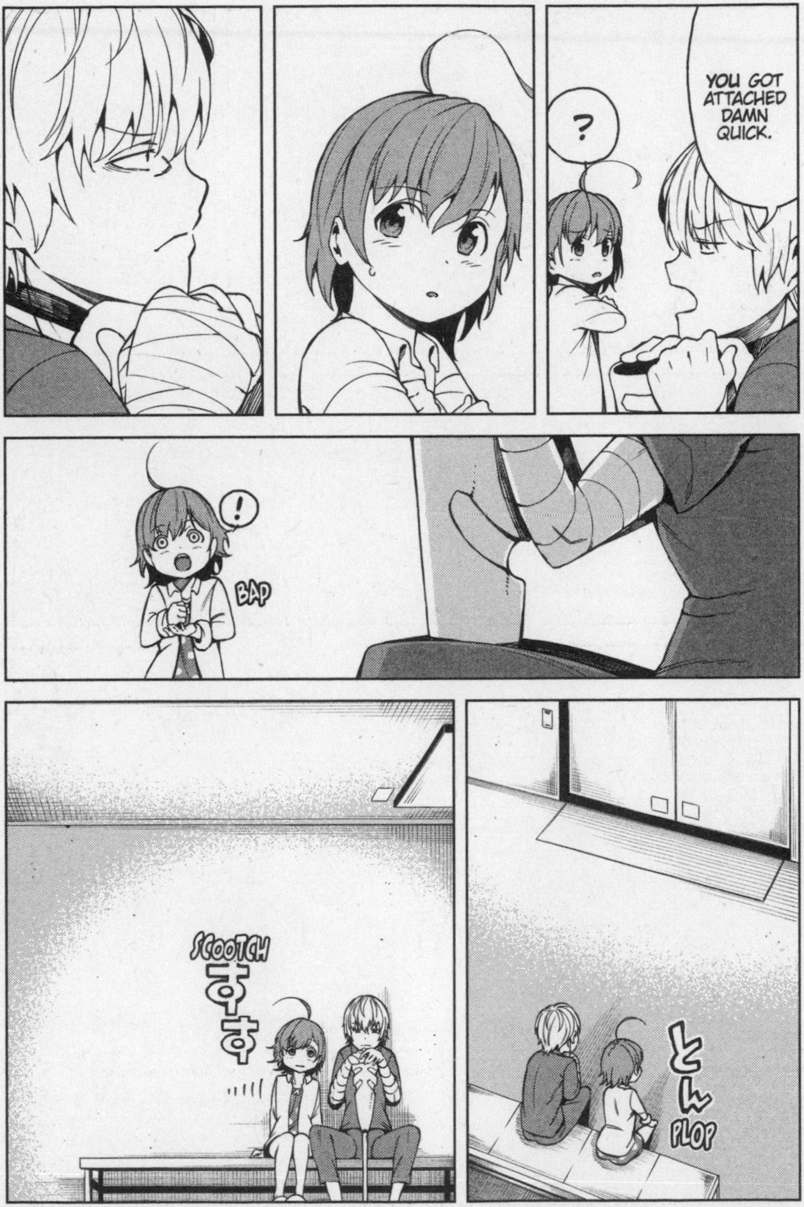
YOU GOT ATTACHED DAMN QUICK.
?
!
BAP
とん
PLOP
SCOOTCH
すす

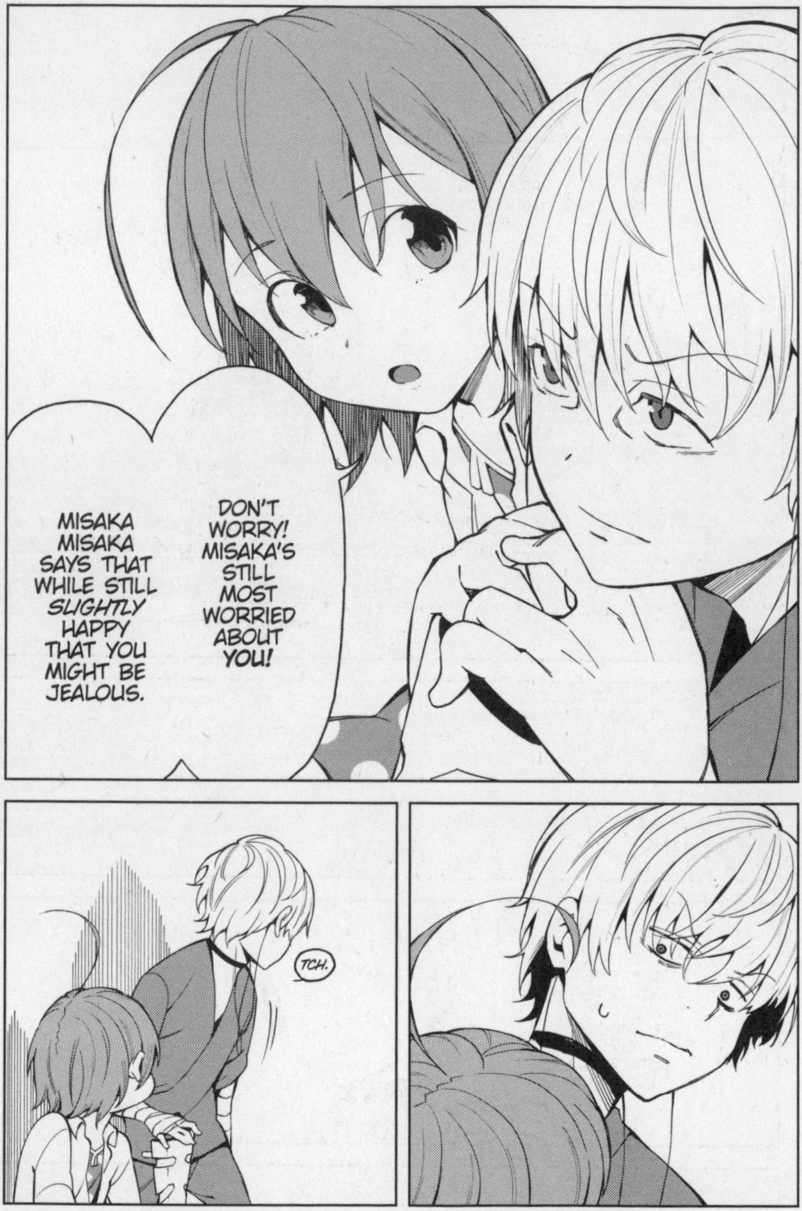
DON'T WORRY! MISAKA'S STILL MOST WORRIED ABOUT YOU!
MISAKA MISAKA SAYS THAT WHILE STILL *SLIGHTLY* HAPPY THAT YOU MIGHT BE JEALOUS.
TCH.

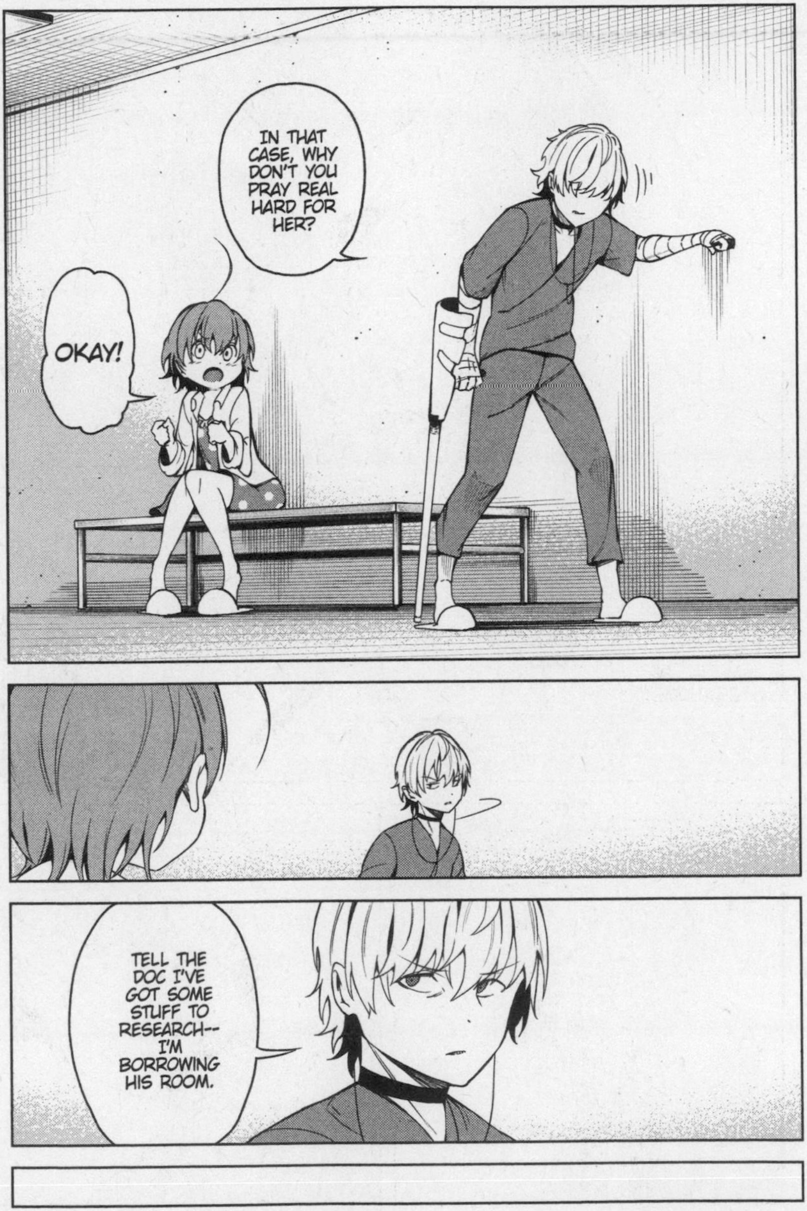
IN THAT CASE, WHY DON'T YOU PRAY REAL HARD FOR HER?
OKAY!
TELL THE DOC I'VE GOT SOME STUFF TO RESEARCH-- I'M BORROWING HIS ROOM.

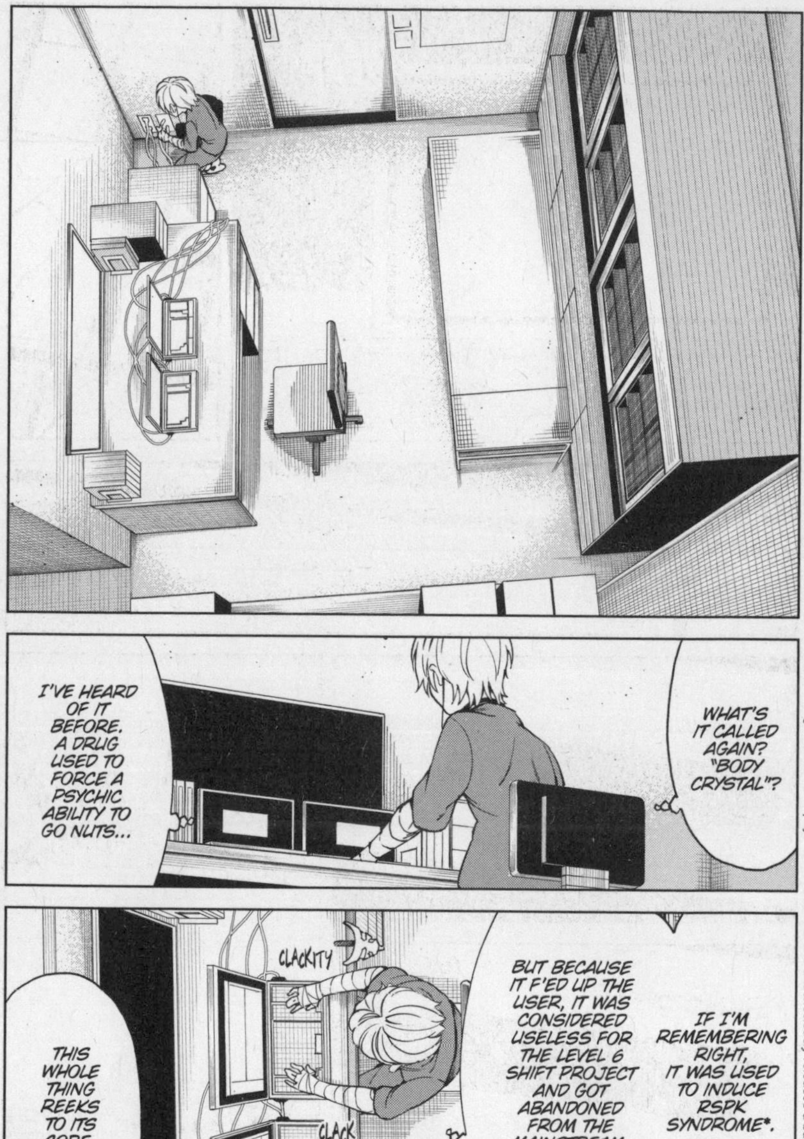
WHAT'S IT CALLED AGAIN? "BODY CRYSTAL"?
I'VE HEARD OF IT BEFORE. A DRUG USED TO FORCE A PSYCHIC ABILITY TO GO NUTS...
IF I'M REMEMBERING RIGHT, IT WAS USED TO INDUCE RSPK SYNDROME*.
BUT BECAUSE IT F'ED UP THE USER, IT WAS CONSIDERED USELESS FOR THE LEVEL 6 SHIFT PROJECT AND GOT ABANDONED FROM THE MAINSTREAM. HN...
CLACKITY
CLACK
THIS WHOLE THING REEKS TO ITS CORE.

*Recurrent Spontaneous PsychoKinesis Syndrome, also called Poltergeist, is when a psychic loses control and unconsciously releases a burst of power.

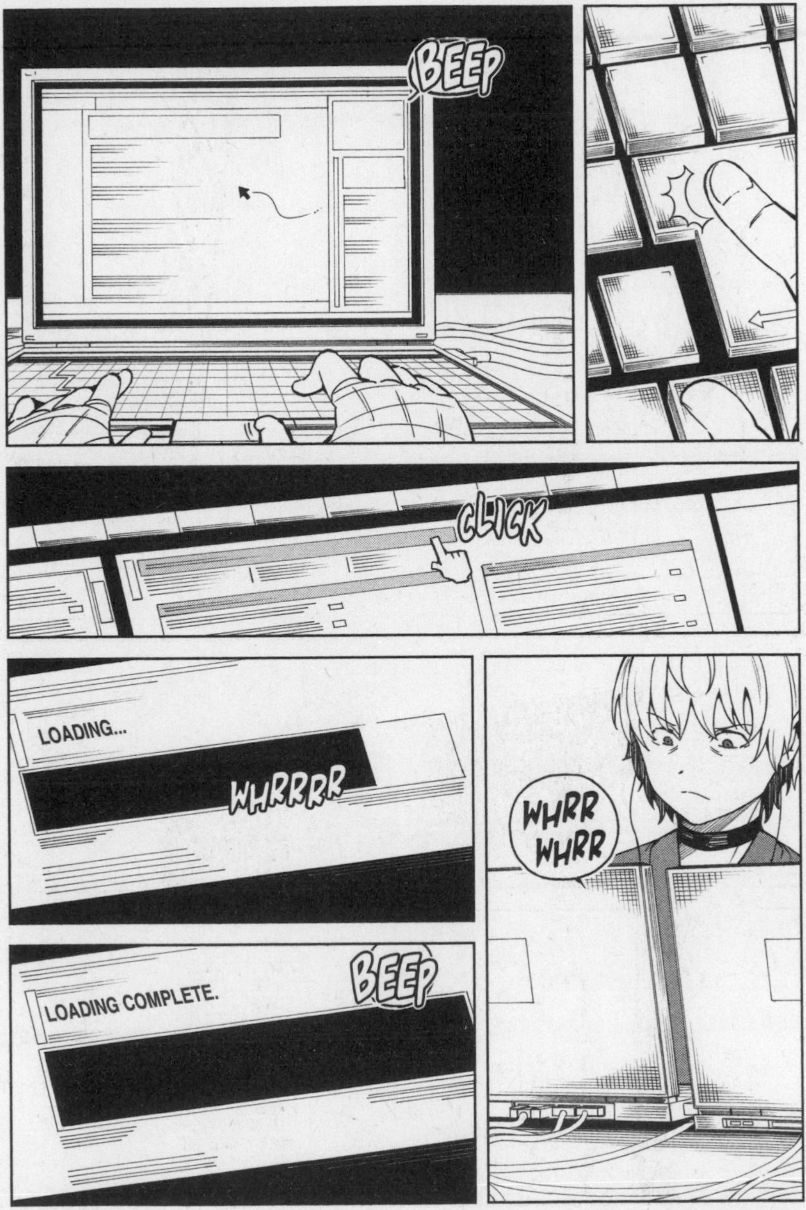
BEEP
CLICK
WHRR WHRR
LOADING...
WHRRRR
BEEP
LOADING COMPLETE.

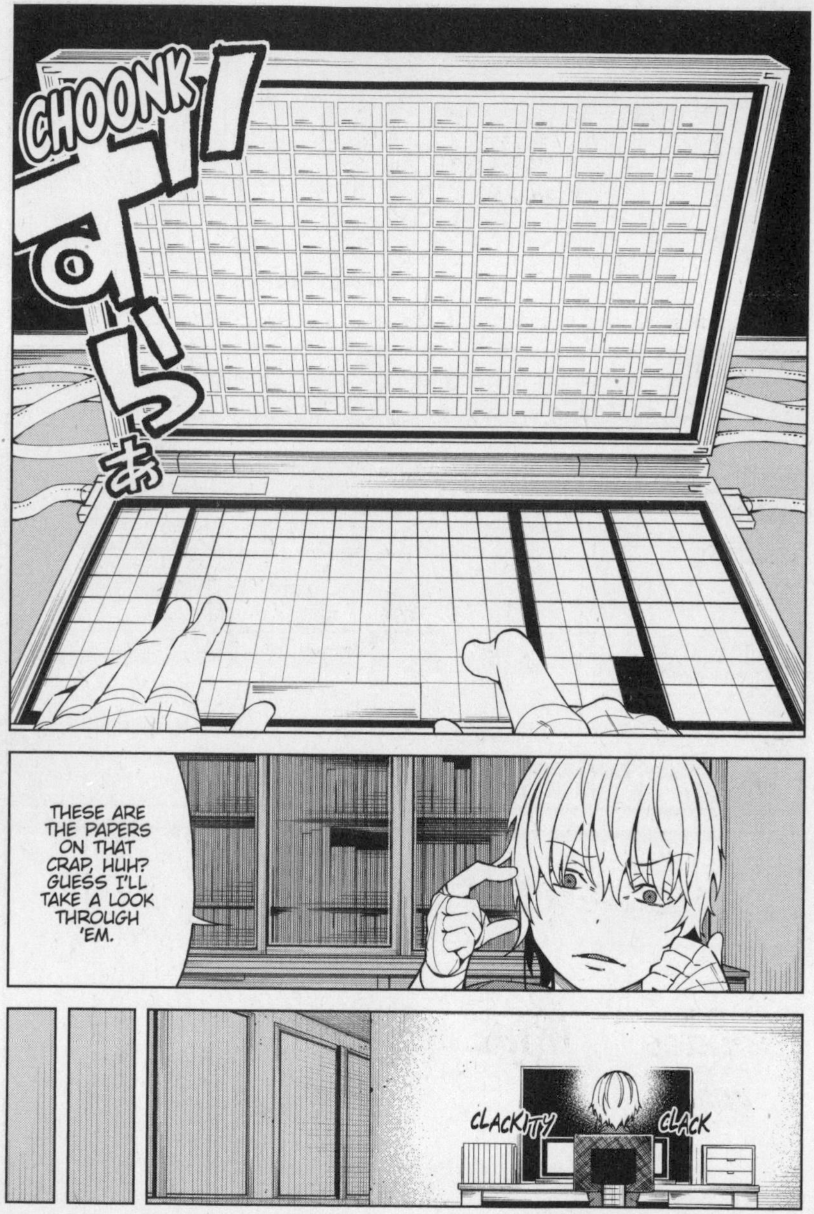
CHOONK
ずらぁ
THESE ARE THE PAPERS ON THAT CRAP, HUH? GUESS I'LL TAKE A LOOK THROUGH 'EM.
CLACKITY
CLACK

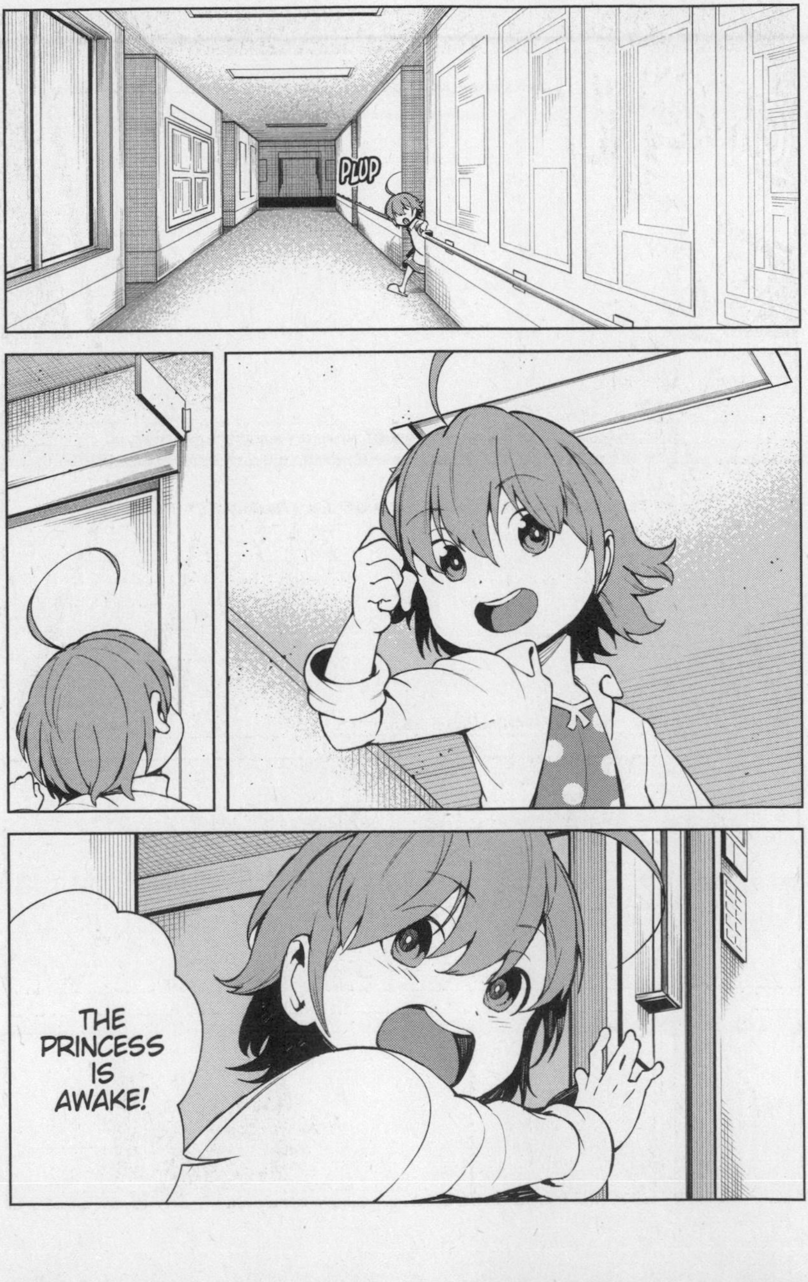
PLUP
THE PRINCESS IS AWAKE!

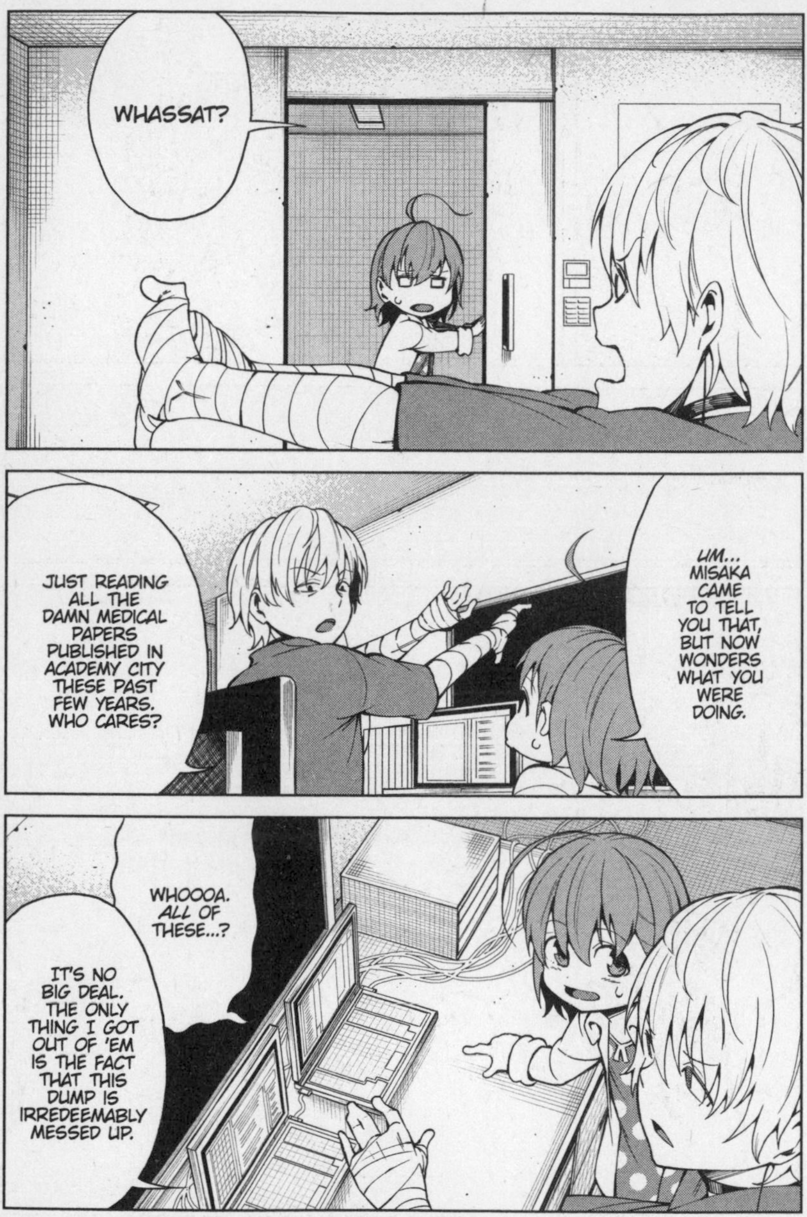
WHASSAT?
UM... MISAKA CAME TO TELL YOU THAT, BUT NOW WONDERS WHAT YOU WERE DOING.
JUST READING ALL THE DAMN MEDICAL PAPERS PUBLISHED IN ACADEMY CITY THESE PAST FEW YEARS. WHO CARES?
WHOOOA. ALL OF THESE...?
IT'S NO BIG DEAL. THE ONLY THING I GOT OUT OF 'EM IS THE FACT THAT THIS DUMP IS IRREDEEMABLY MESSED UP.

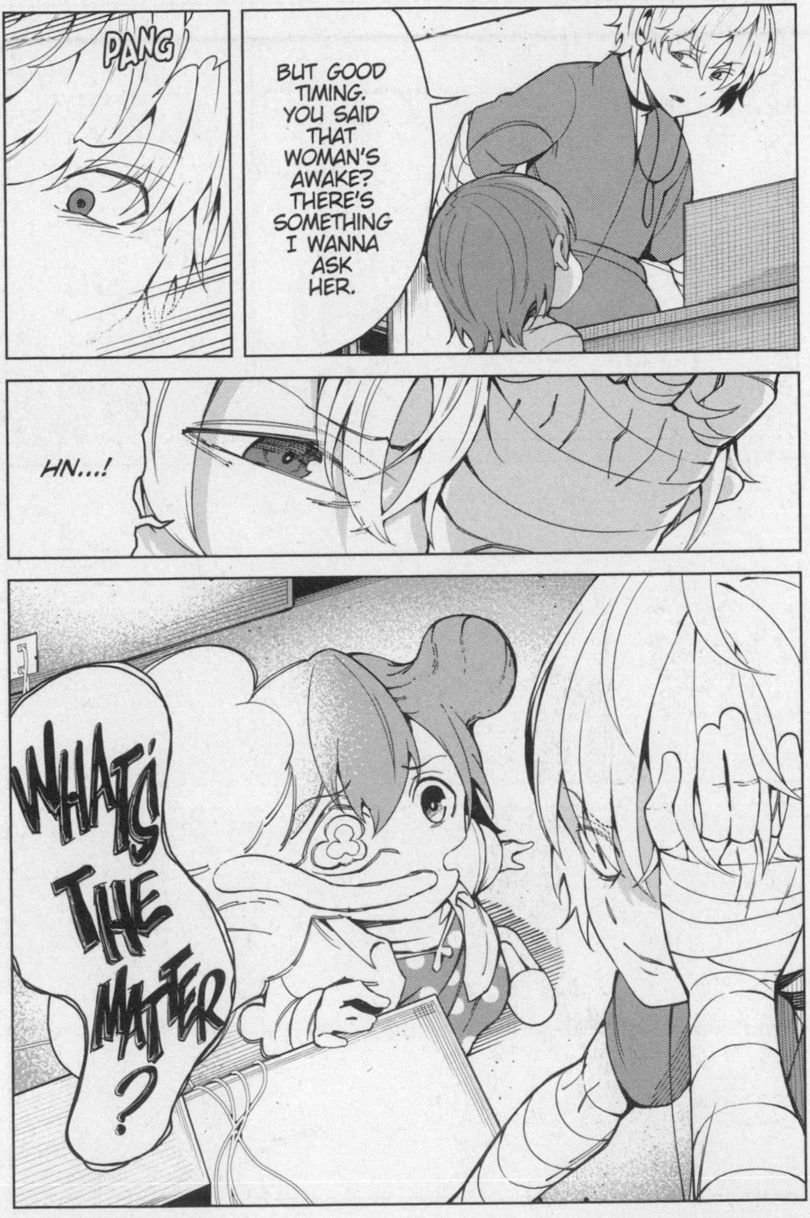
BUT GOOD TIMING. YOU SAID THAT WOMAN'S AWAKE? THERE'S SOMETHING I WANNA ASK HER.
PANG
HN...!
WHAT'S THE MATTER?

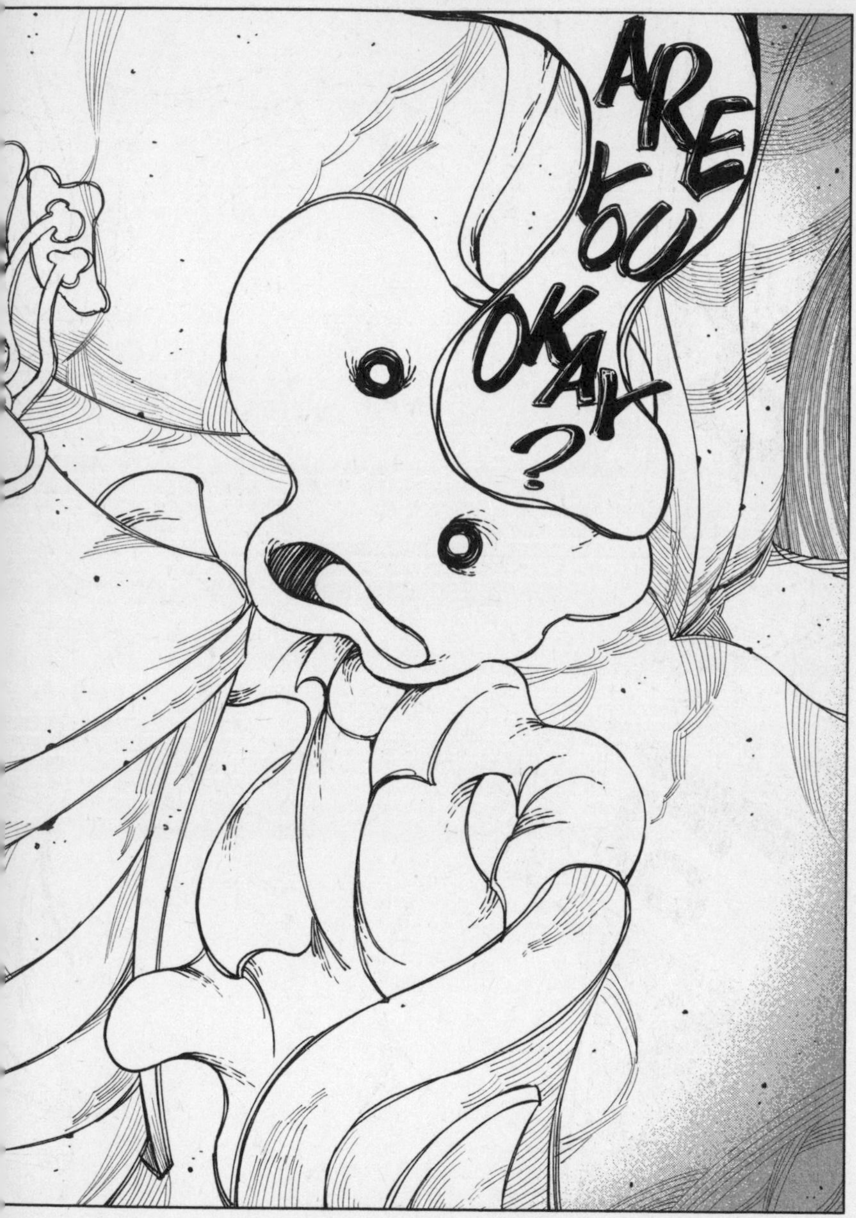
ARE YOU OKAY?

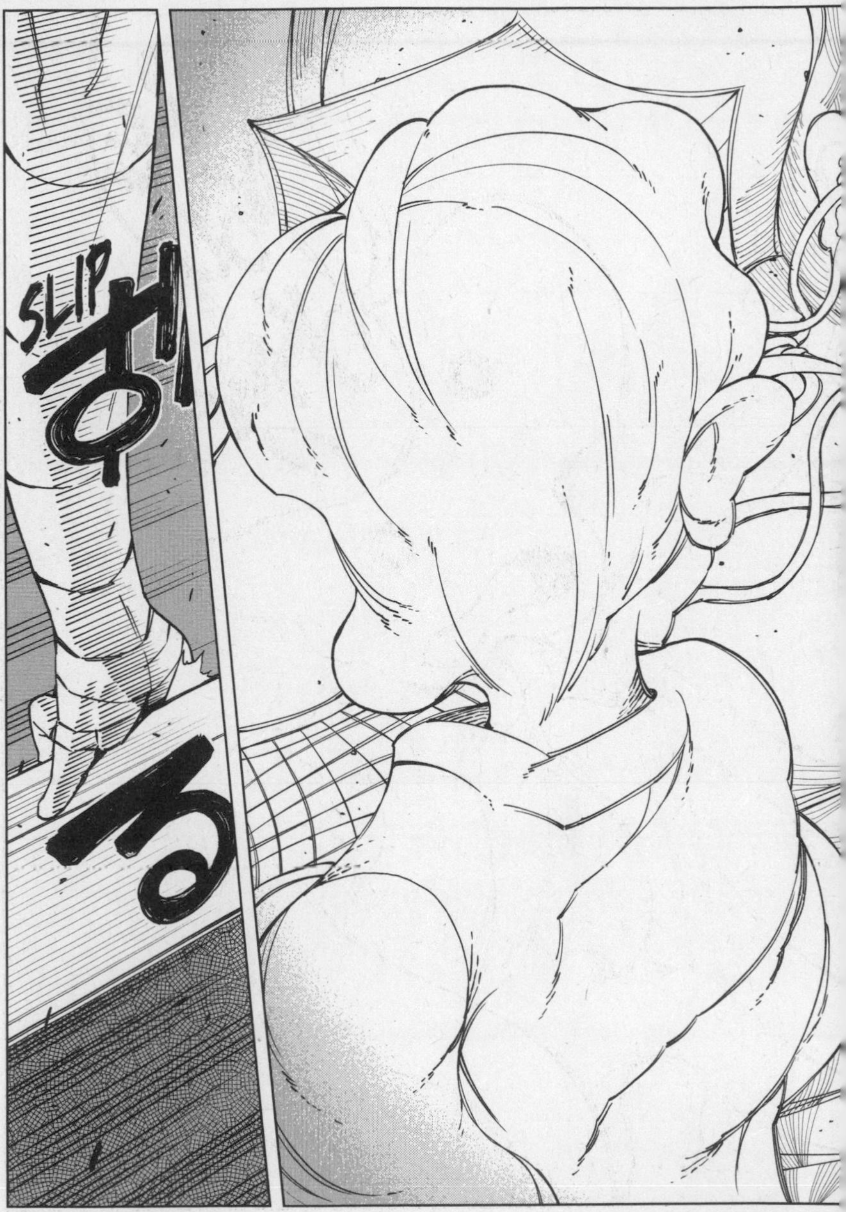
SLIP

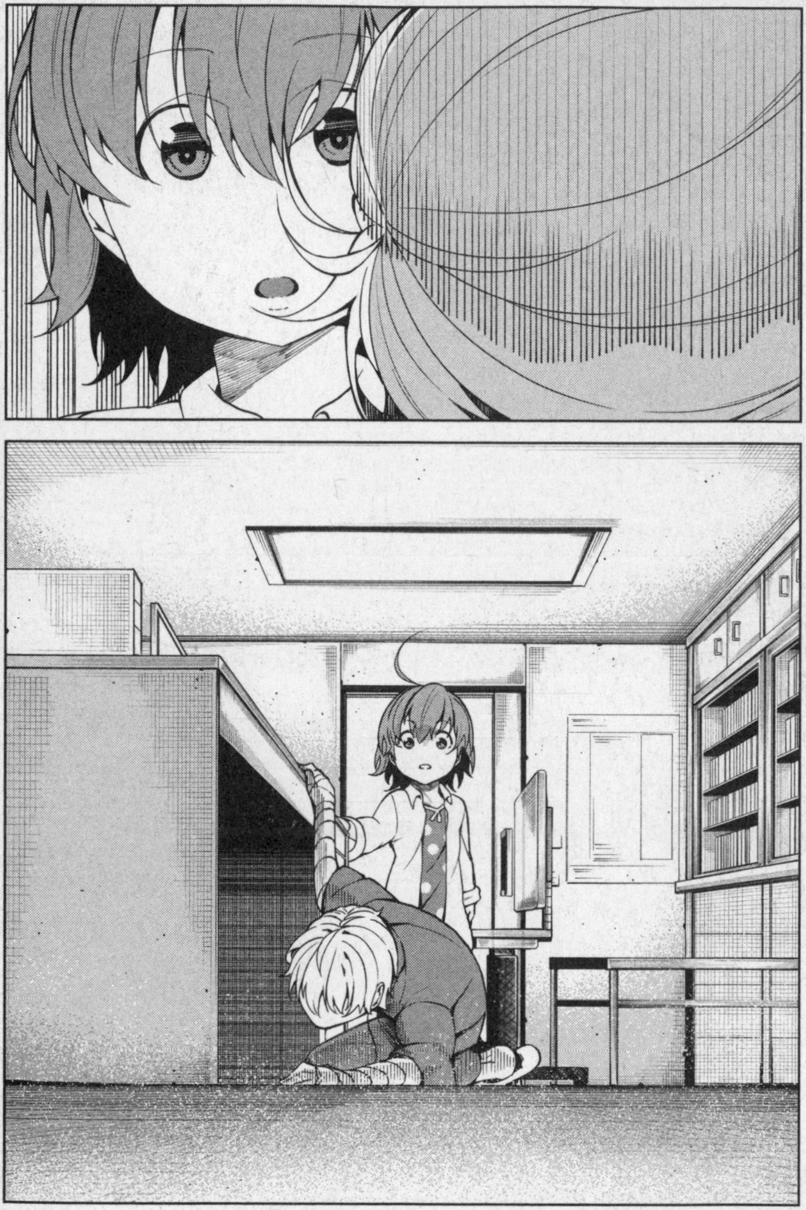

a certain SCIENTIFIC ACCELERATOR

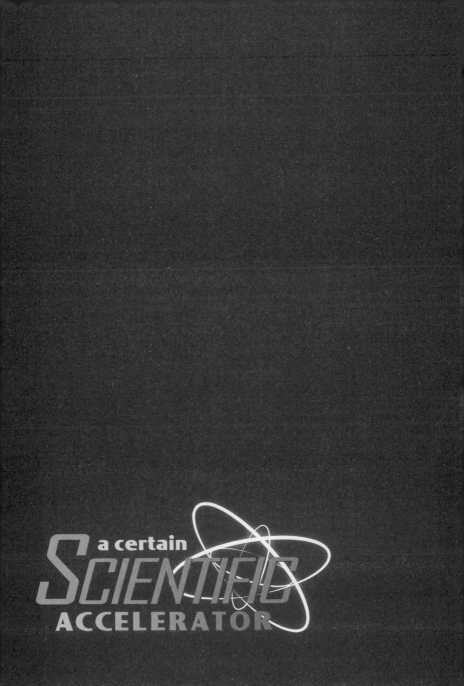

とある科学の一方通行（アクセラレータ）

とある魔術の禁書目録外伝

CHAPTER 42

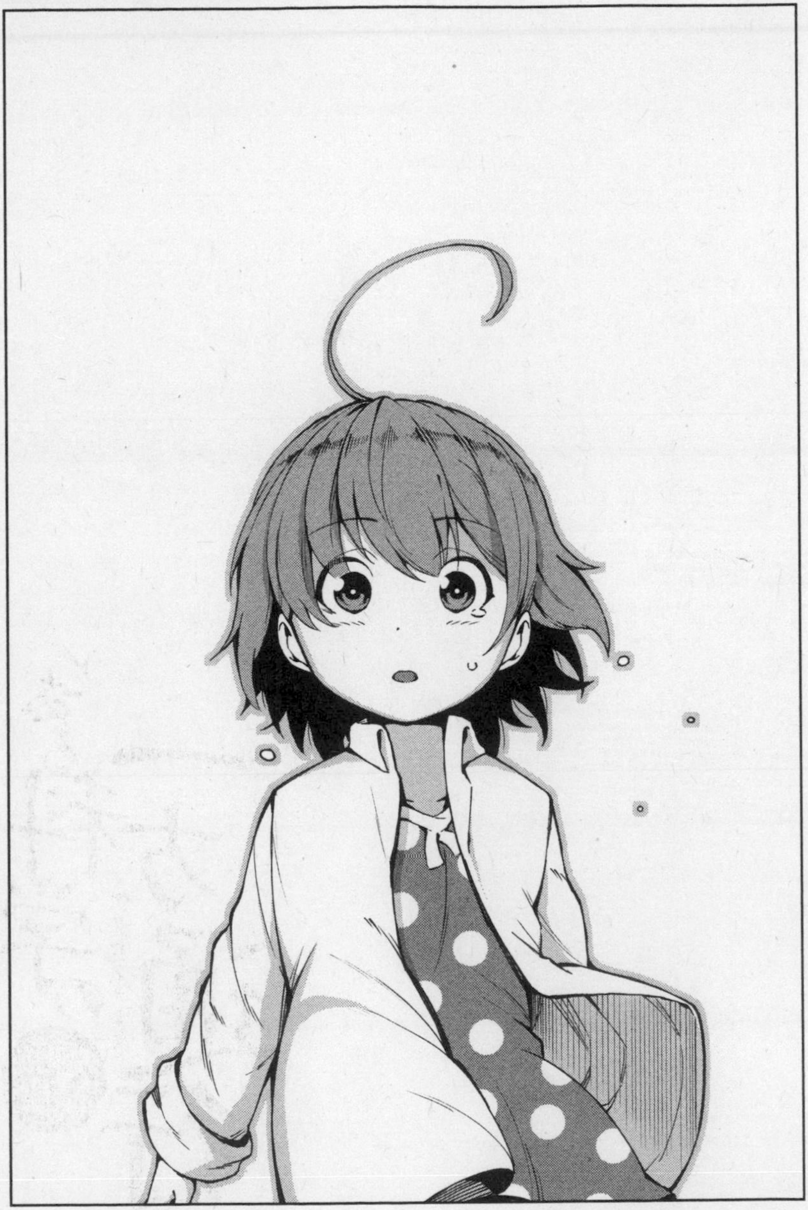

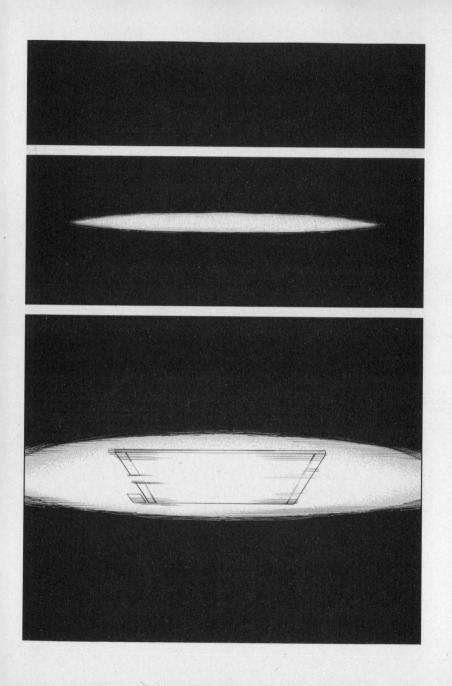

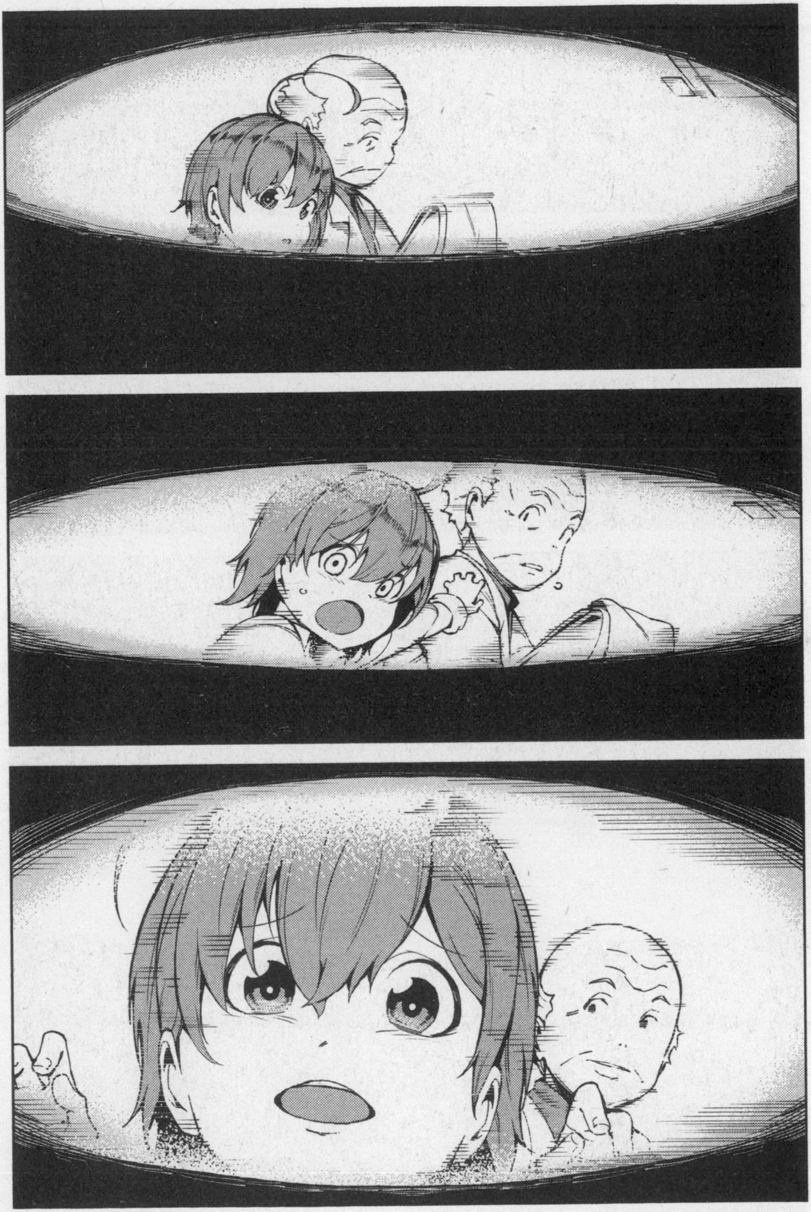

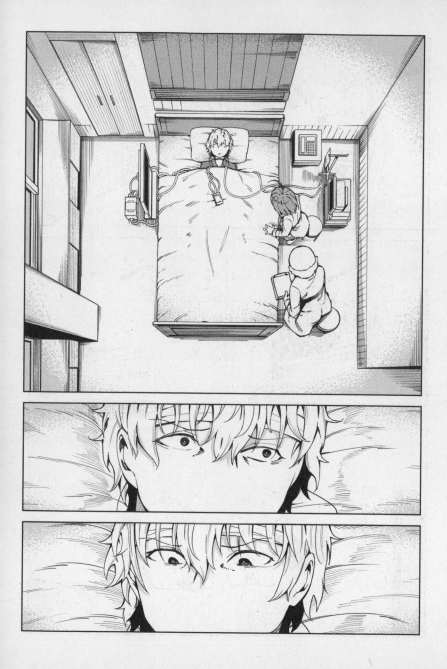

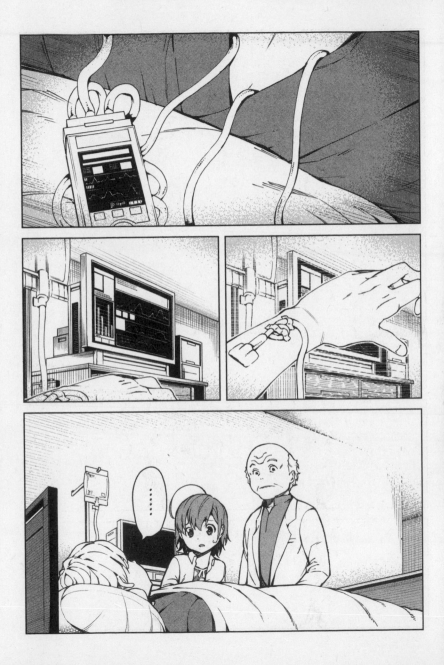

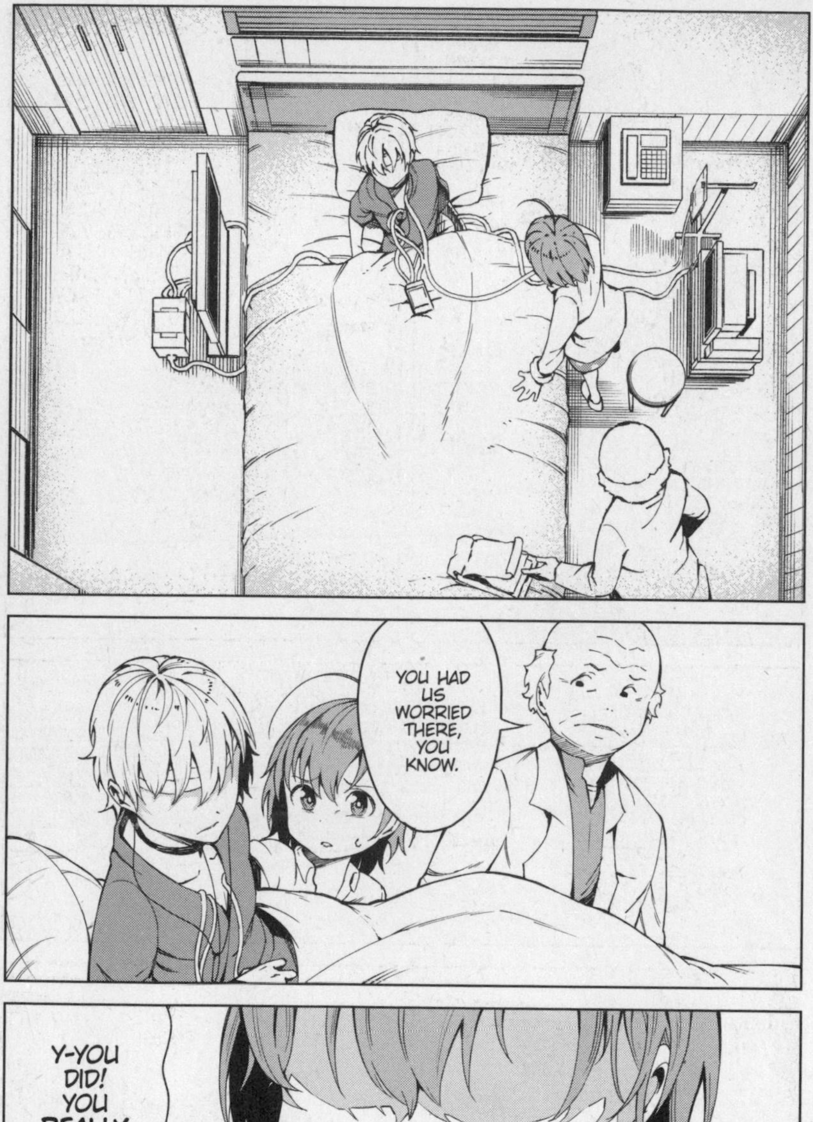
YOU HAD US WORRIED THERE, YOU KNOW.
Y-YOU DID! YOU REALLY DID!

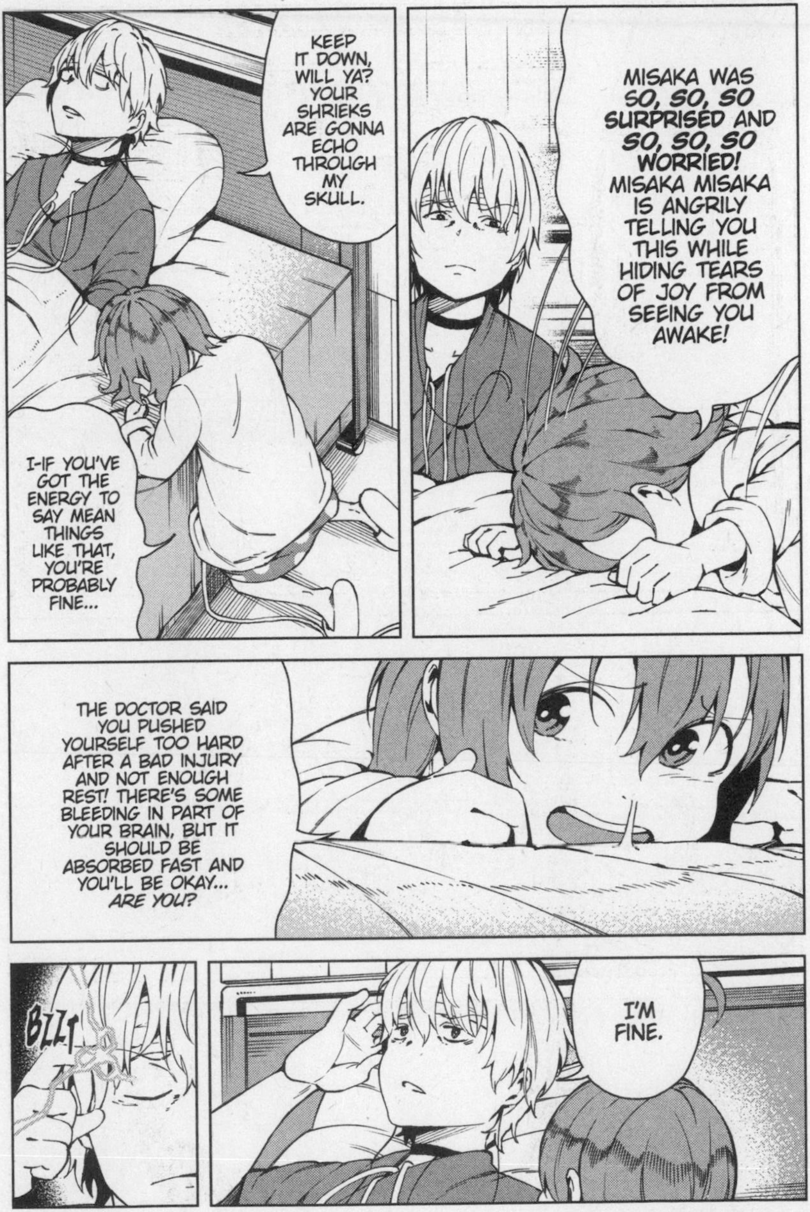
MISAKA WAS SO, SO, SO SURPRISED AND SO, SO, SO WORRIED! MISAKA MISAKA IS ANGRILY TELLING YOU THIS WHILE HIDING TEARS OF JOY FROM SEEING YOU AWAKE!
KEEP IT DOWN, WILL YA? YOUR SHRIEKS ARE GONNA ECHO THROUGH MY SKULL.
I-IF YOU'VE GOT THE ENERGY TO SAY MEAN THINGS LIKE THAT, YOU'RE PROBABLY FINE...
THE DOCTOR SAID YOU PUSHED YOURSELF TOO HARD AFTER A BAD INJURY AND NOT ENOUGH REST! THERE'S SOME BLEEDING IN PART OF YOUR BRAIN, BUT IT SHOULD BE ABSORBED FAST AND YOU'LL BE OKAY... *ARE YOU?*
I'M FINE.
BZZT

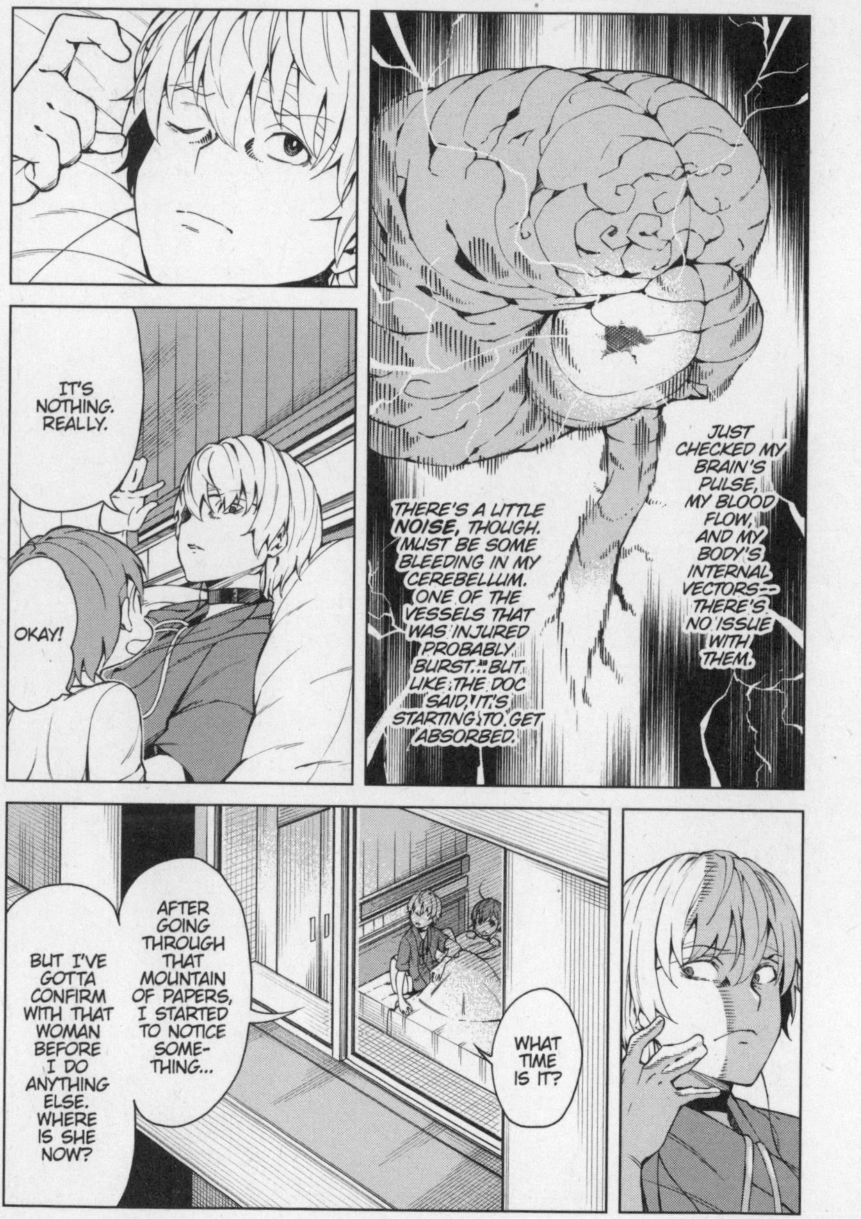
JUST CHECKED MY BRAIN'S PULSE, MY BLOOD FLOW, AND MY BODY'S INTERNAL VECTORS-- THERE'S NO ISSUE WITH THEM.
THERE'S A LITTLE NOISE, THOUGH. MUST BE SOME BLEEDING IN MY CEREBELLUM. ONE OF THE VESSELS THAT WAS INJURED PROBABLY BURST... BUT LIKE THE DOC SAID, IT'S STARTING TO GET ABSORBED.
IT'S NOTHING. REALLY.
OKAY!
WHAT TIME IS IT?
AFTER GOING THROUGH THAT MOUNTAIN OF PAPERS, I STARTED TO NOTICE SOME-THING...
BUT I'VE GOTTA CONFIRM WITH THAT WOMAN BEFORE I DO ANYTHING ELSE. WHERE IS SHE NOW?

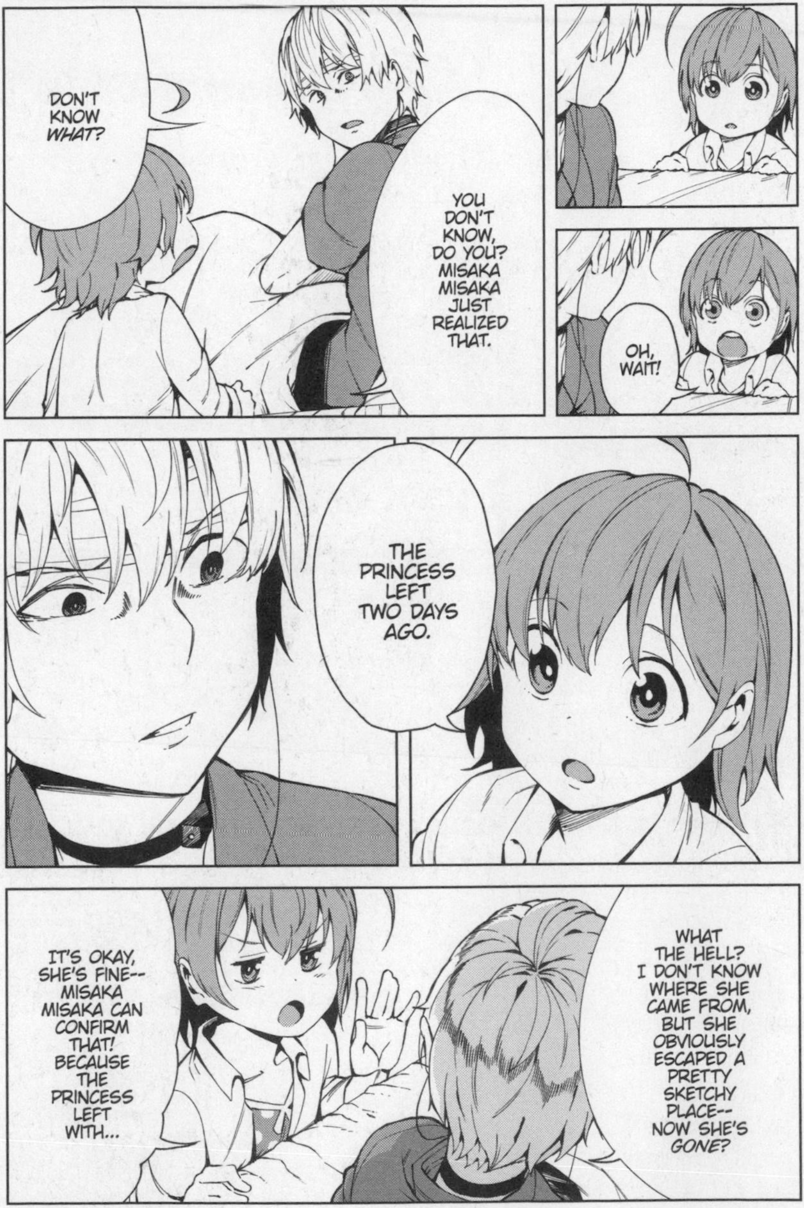
OH, WAIT!
YOU DON'T KNOW, DO YOU? MISAKA MISAKA JUST REALIZED THAT.
DON'T KNOW *WHAT?*
THE PRINCESS LEFT TWO DAYS AGO.
WHAT THE HELL? I DON'T KNOW WHERE SHE CAME FROM, BUT SHE OBVIOUSLY ESCAPED A PRETTY SKETCHY PLACE-- NOW SHE'S *GONE?*
IT'S OKAY, SHE'S FINE-- MISAKA MISAKA CAN CONFIRM THAT! BECAUSE THE PRINCESS LEFT WITH...

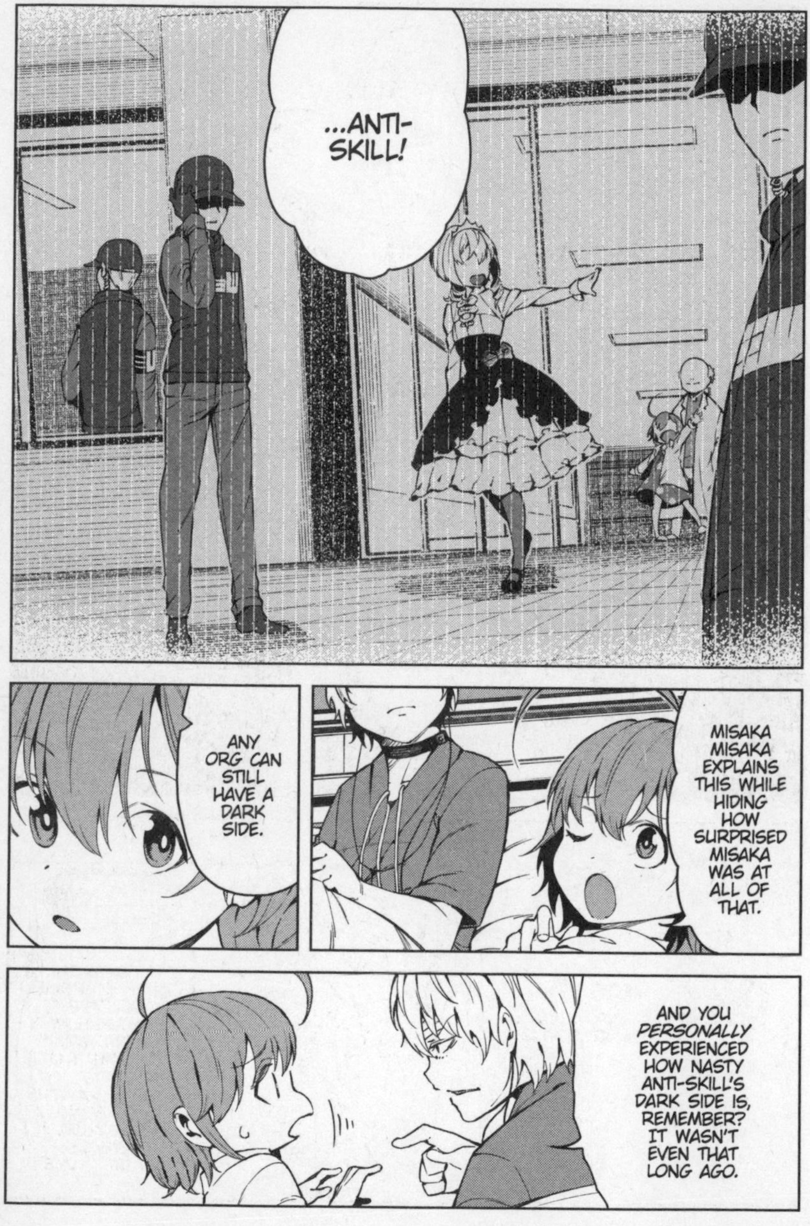
...ANTI-SKILL!
MISAKA MISAKA EXPLAINS THIS WHILE HIDING HOW SURPRISED MISAKA WAS AT ALL OF THAT.
ANY ORG CAN STILL HAVE A DARK SIDE.
AND YOU *PERSONALLY* EXPERIENCED HOW NASTY ANTI-SKILL'S DARK SIDE IS, REMEMBER? IT WASN'T EVEN THAT LONG AGO.

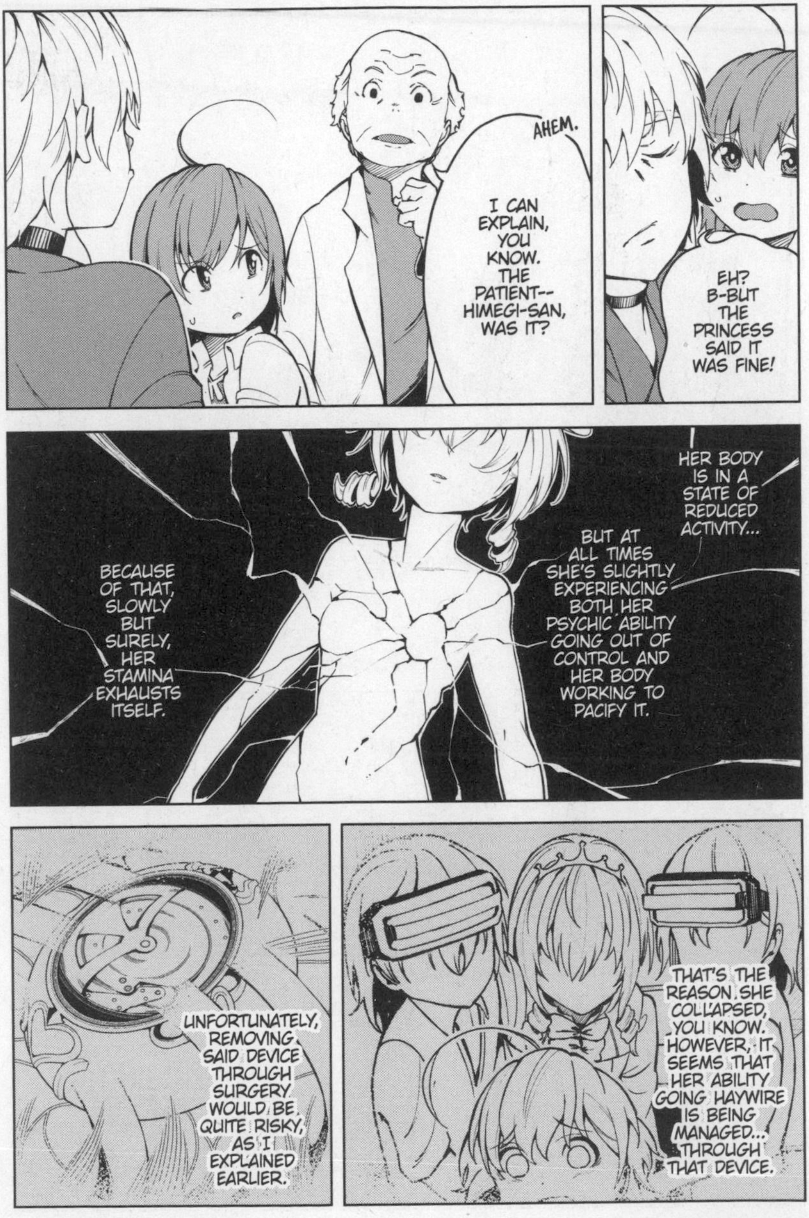
EH? B-BUT THE PRINCESS SAID IT WAS FINE!
AHEM.
I CAN EXPLAIN, YOU KNOW. THE PATIENT-- HIMEGI-SAN, WAS IT?
HER BODY IS IN A STATE OF REDUCED ACTIVITY...
BUT AT ALL TIMES SHE'S SLIGHTLY EXPERIENCING BOTH HER PSYCHIC ABILITY GOING OUT OF CONTROL AND HER BODY WORKING TO PACIFY IT.
BECAUSE OF THAT, SLOWLY BUT SURELY, HER STAMINA EXHAUSTS ITSELF.
THAT'S THE REASON SHE COLLAPSED, YOU KNOW. HOWEVER, IT SEEMS THAT HER ABILITY GOING HAYWIRE IS BEING MANAGED... THROUGH THAT DEVICE.
UNFORTUNATELY, REMOVING SAID DEVICE THROUGH SURGERY WOULD BE QUITE RISKY, AS I EXPLAINED EARLIER.

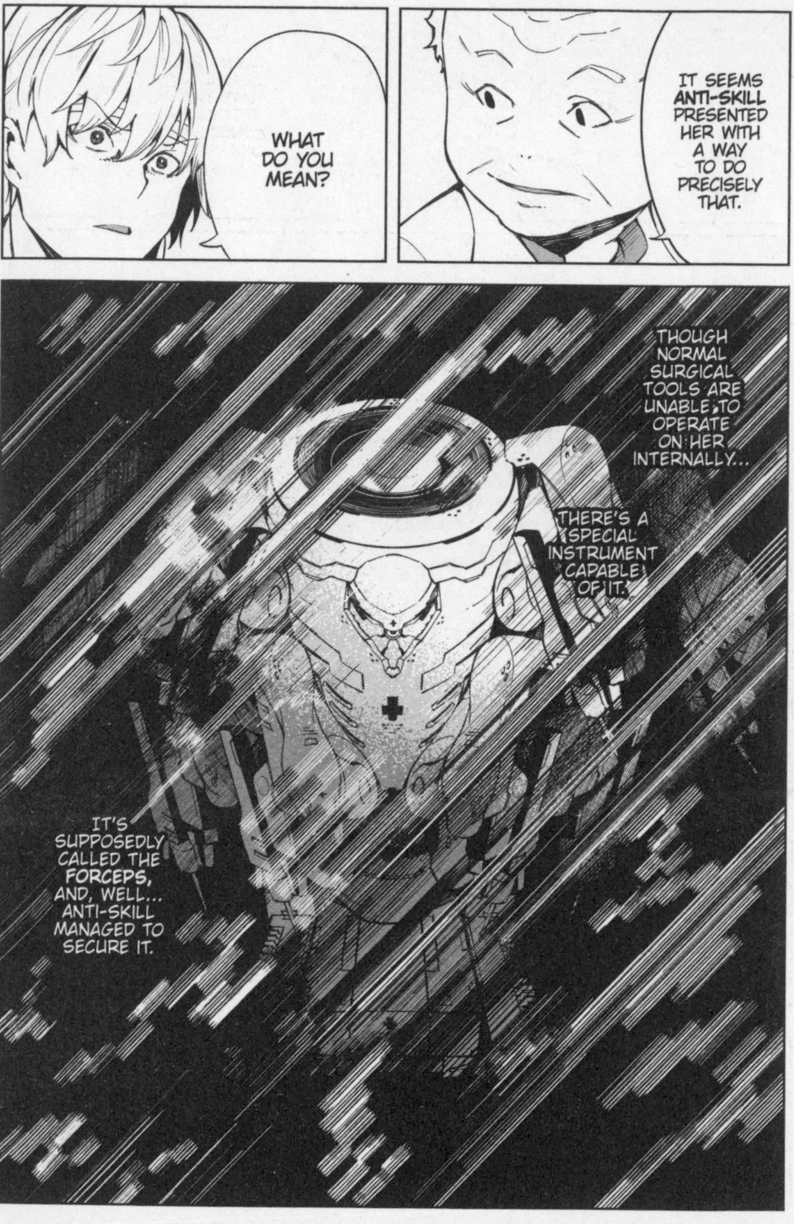
IT SEEMS ANTI-SKILL PRESENTED HER WITH A WAY TO DO PRECISELY THAT.
WHAT DO YOU MEAN?
THOUGH NORMAL SURGICAL TOOLS ARE UNABLE TO OPERATE ON HER INTERNALLY...
THERE'S A SPECIAL INSTRUMENT CAPABLE OF IT.
IT'S SUPPOSEDLY CALLED THE FORCEPS, AND, WELL... ANTI-SKILL MANAGED TO SECURE IT.

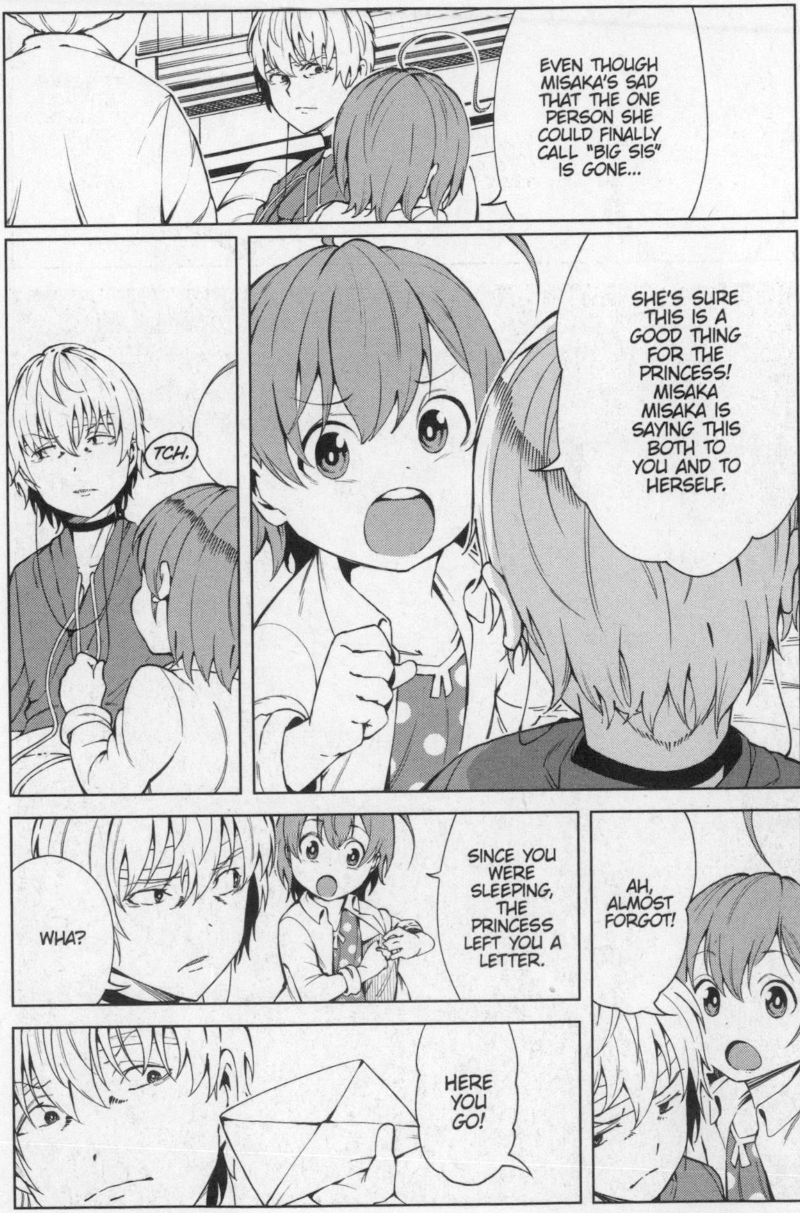
EVEN THOUGH MISAKA'S SAD THAT THE ONE PERSON SHE COULD FINALLY CALL "BIG SIS" IS GONE...
SHE'S SURE THIS IS A GOOD THING FOR THE PRINCESS! MISAKA MISAKA IS SAYING THIS BOTH TO YOU AND TO HERSELF.
TCH.
AH, ALMOST FORGOT!
SINCE YOU WERE SLEEPING, THE PRINCESS LEFT YOU A LETTER.
WHA?
HERE YOU GO!

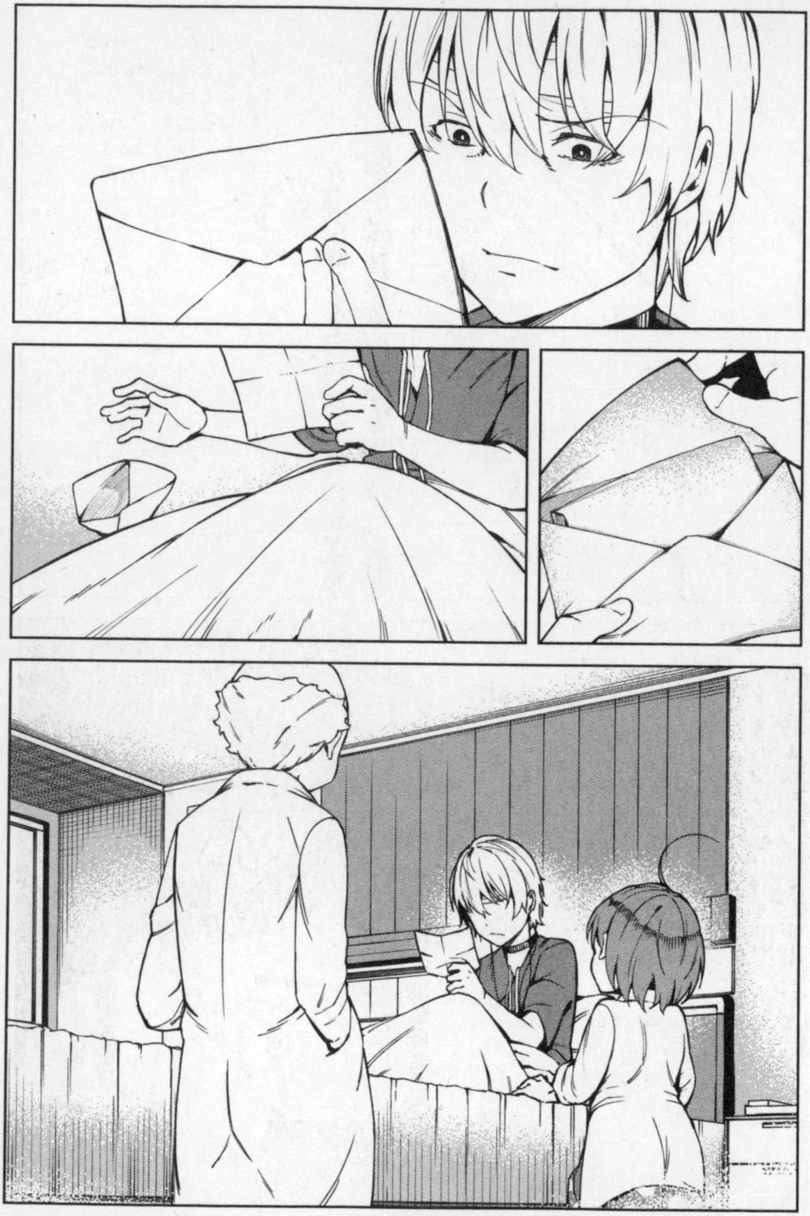

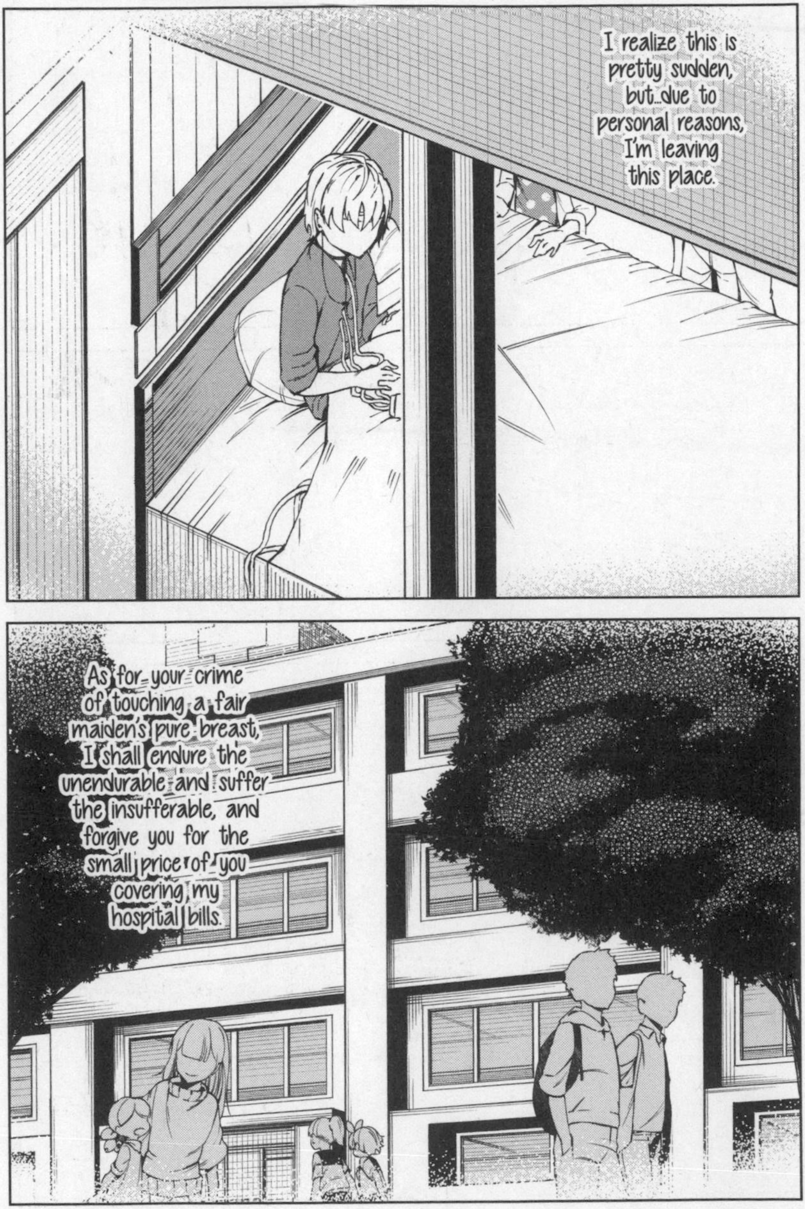
I realize this is pretty sudden, but...due to personal reasons, I'm leaving this place.
As for your crime of touching a fair maiden's pure breast, I shall endure the unendurable and suffer the insufferable, and forgive you for the small price of you covering my hospital bills.

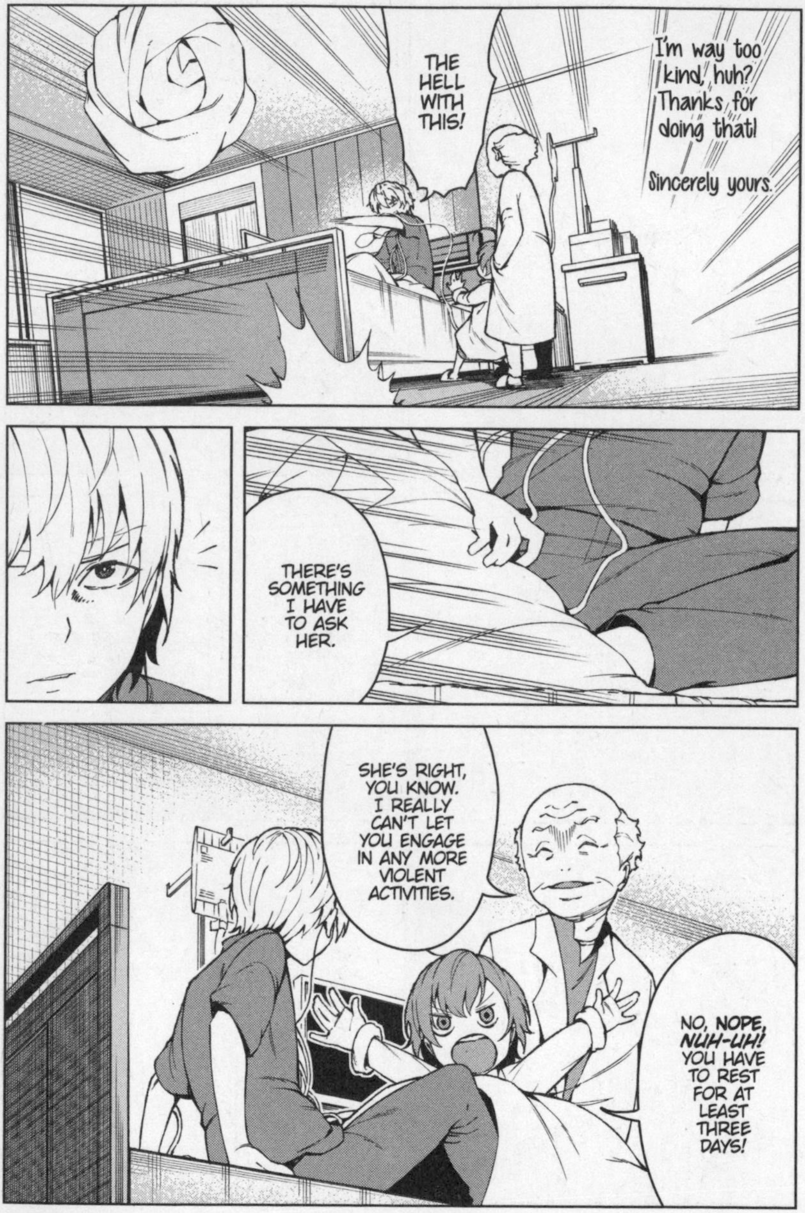

I'm way too kind, huh? Thanks for doing that!
Sincerely yours.
THE HELL WITH THIS!
THERE'S SOMETHING I HAVE TO ASK HER.
NO, NOPE, *NUH-UH!* YOU HAVE TO REST FOR AT LEAST THREE DAYS!
SHE'S RIGHT, YOU KNOW. I REALLY CAN'T LET YOU ENGAGE IN ANY MORE VIOLENT ACTIVITIES.

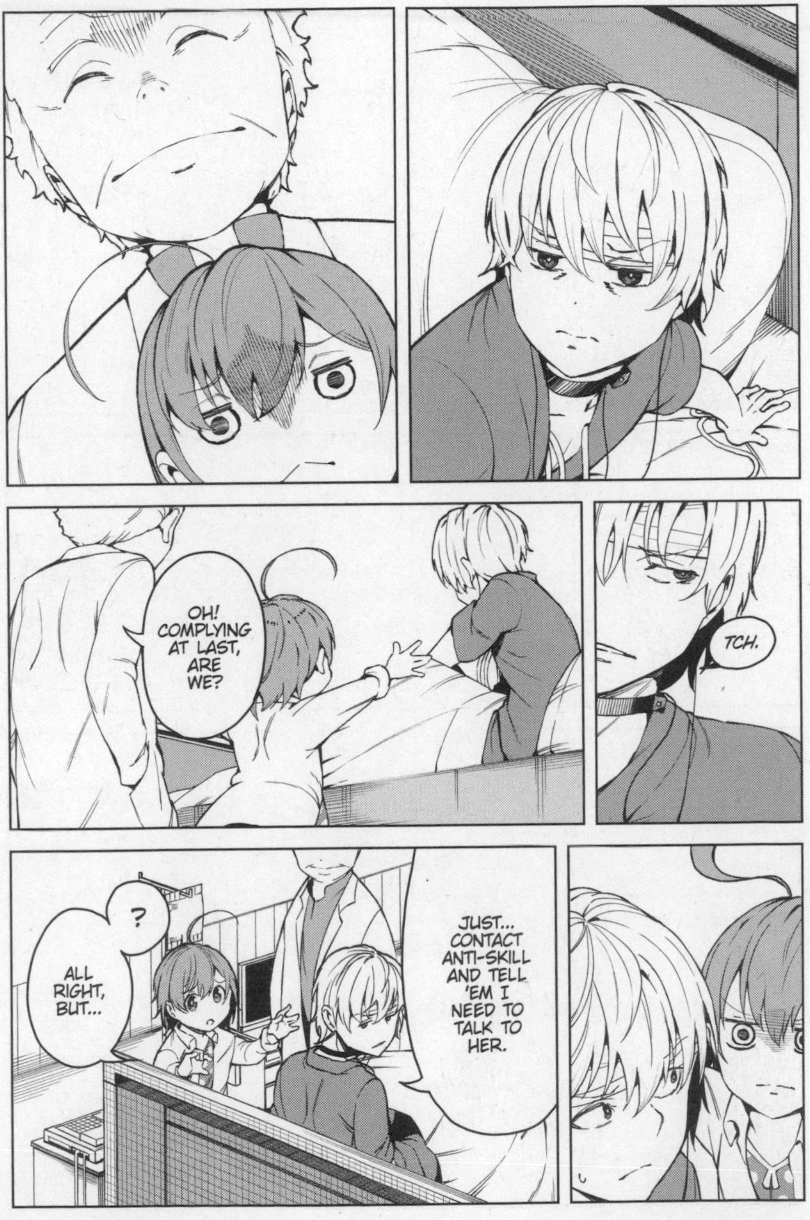
TCH.
OH! COMPLYING AT LAST, ARE WE?
JUST... CONTACT ANTI-SKILL AND TELL 'EM I NEED TO TALK TO HER.
?
ALL RIGHT, BUT...

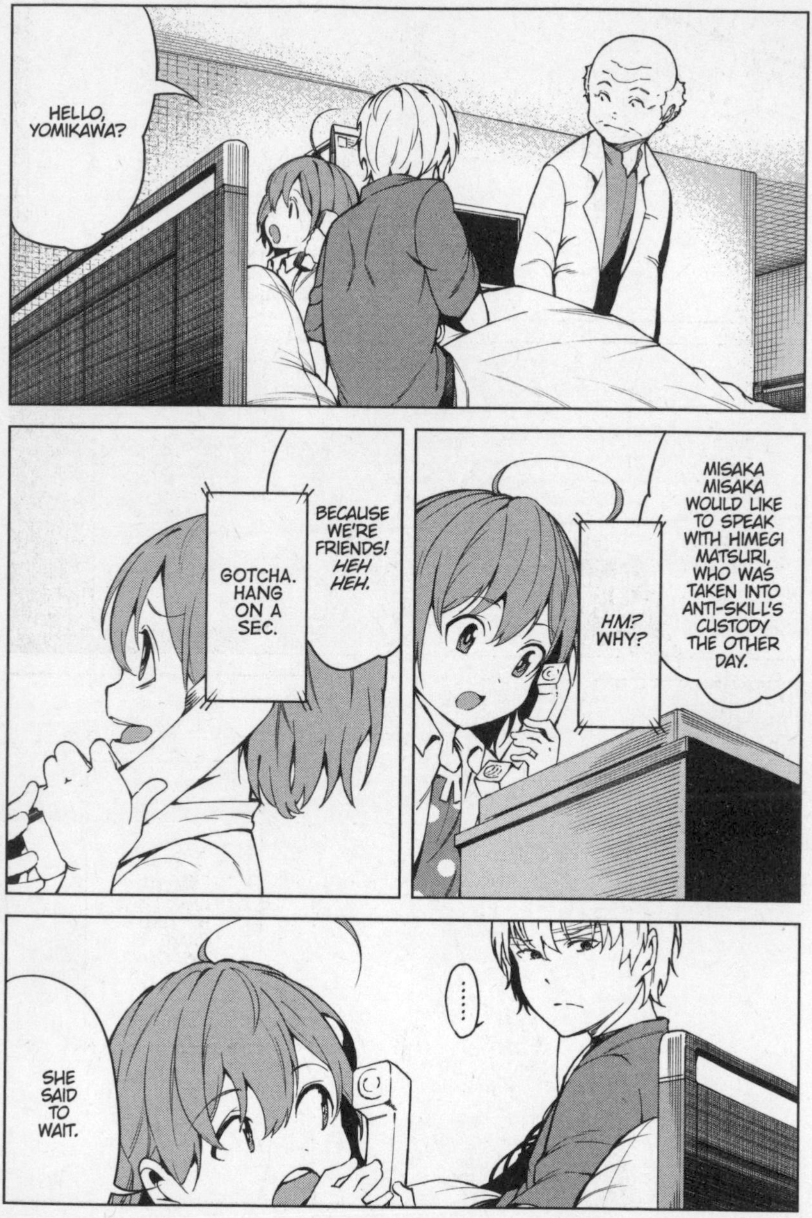
HELLO, YOMIKAWA?
MISAKA MISAKA WOULD LIKE TO SPEAK WITH HIMEGI MATSURI, WHO WAS TAKEN INTO ANTI-SKILL'S CUSTODY THE OTHER DAY.
HM? WHY?
BECAUSE WE'RE FRIENDS! HEH HEH.
GOTCHA. HANG ON A SEC.
......
SHE SAID TO WAIT.

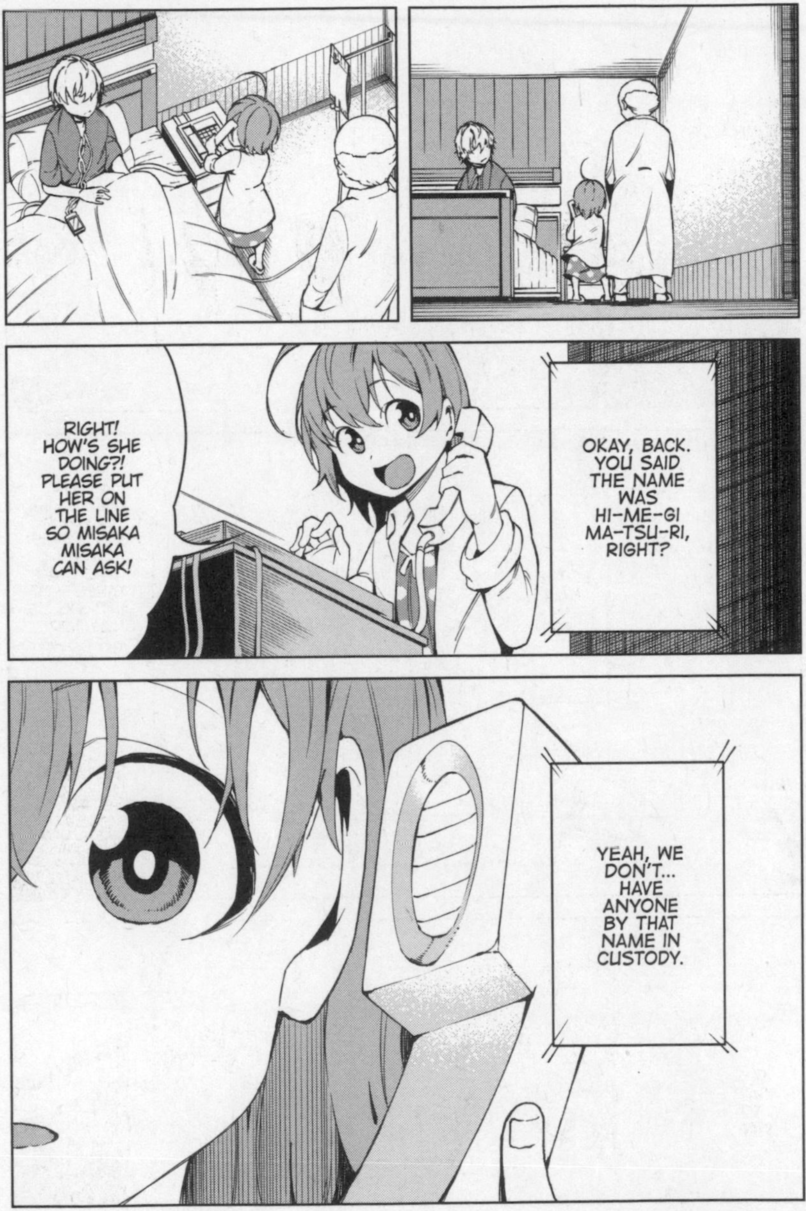
OKAY, BACK. YOU SAID THE NAME WAS HI-ME-GI MA-TSU-RI, RIGHT?
RIGHT! HOW'S SHE DOING?! PLEASE PUT HER ON THE LINE SO MISAKA MISAKA CAN ASK!
YEAH, WE DON'T... HAVE ANYONE BY THAT NAME IN CUSTODY.

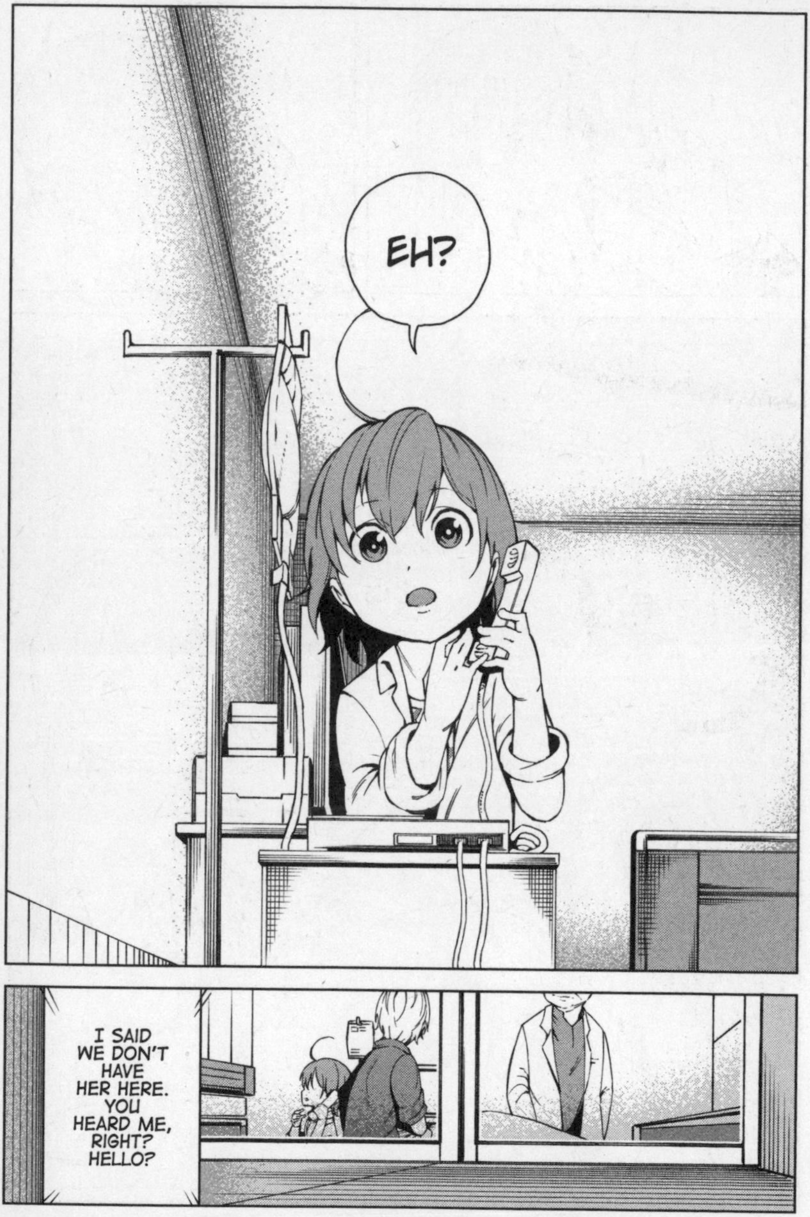
EH?
I SAID WE DON'T HAVE HER HERE. YOU HEARD ME, RIGHT? HELLO?

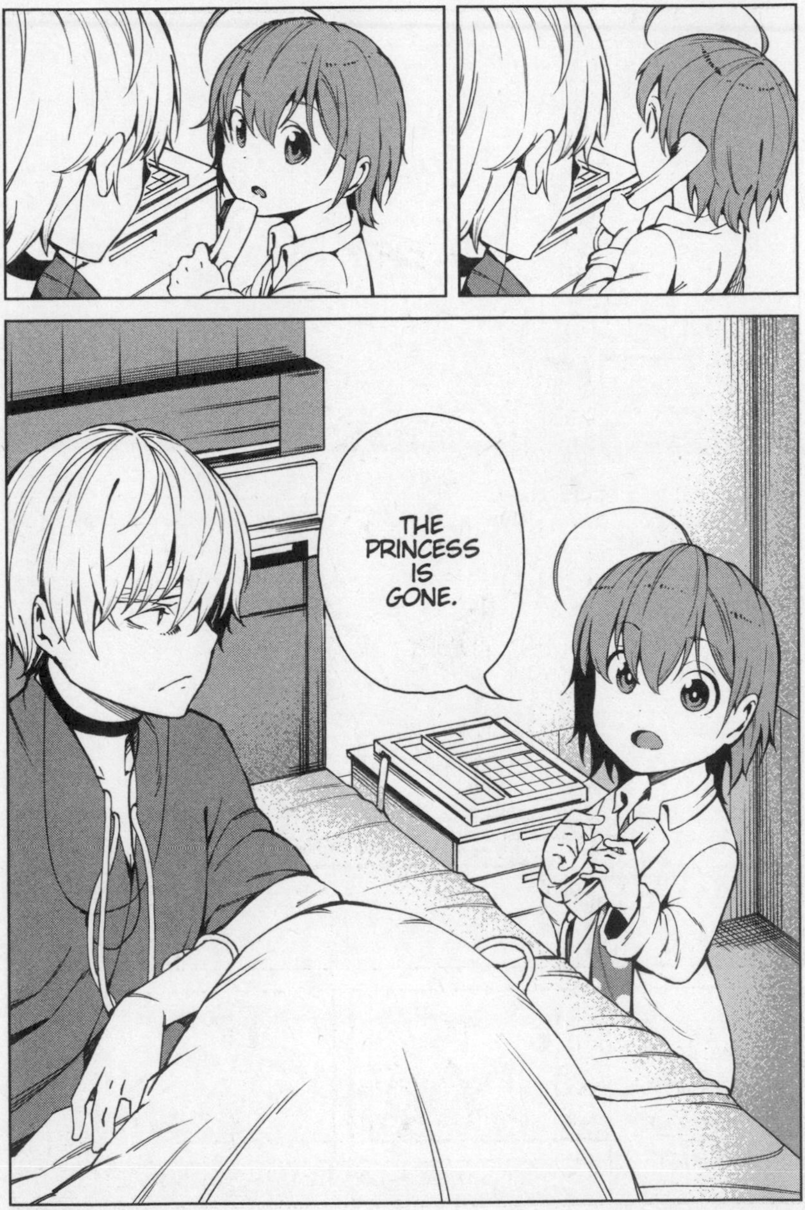
THE PRINCESS IS GONE.

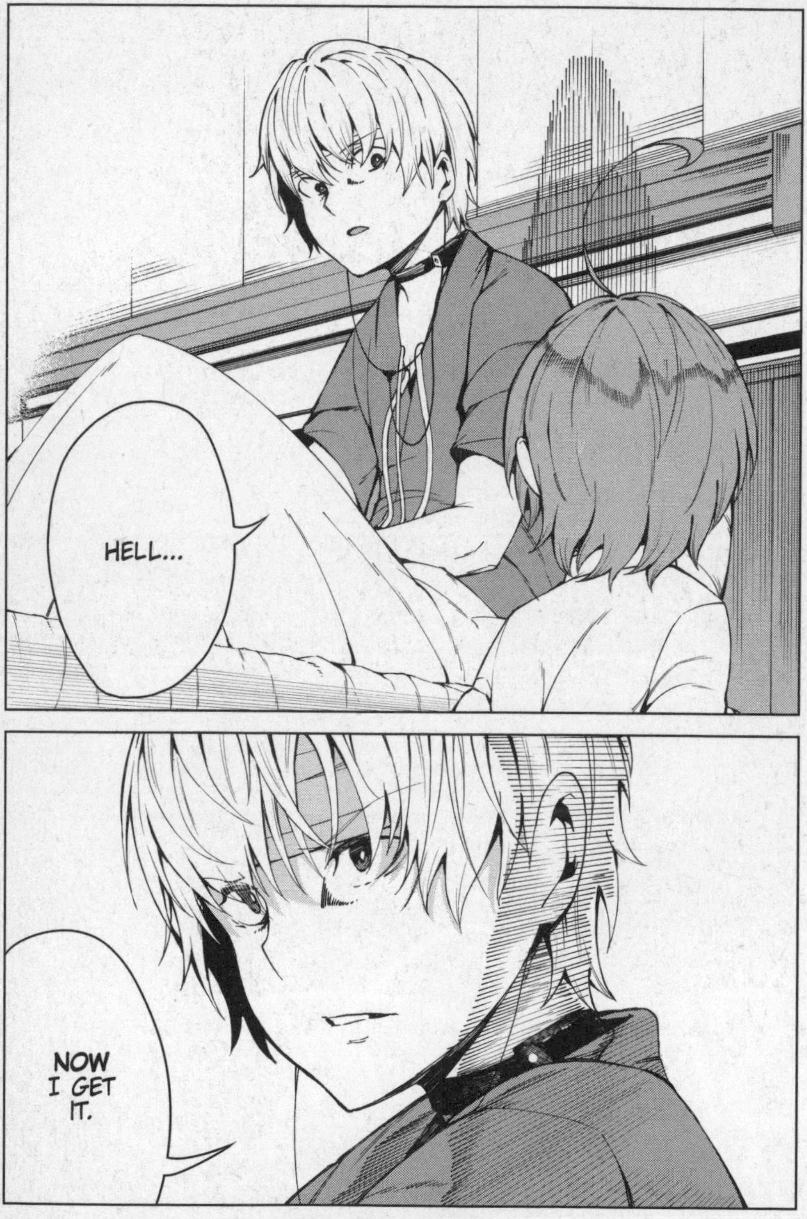
HELL...
NOW I GET IT.

a certain SCIENTIFIC ACCELERATOR

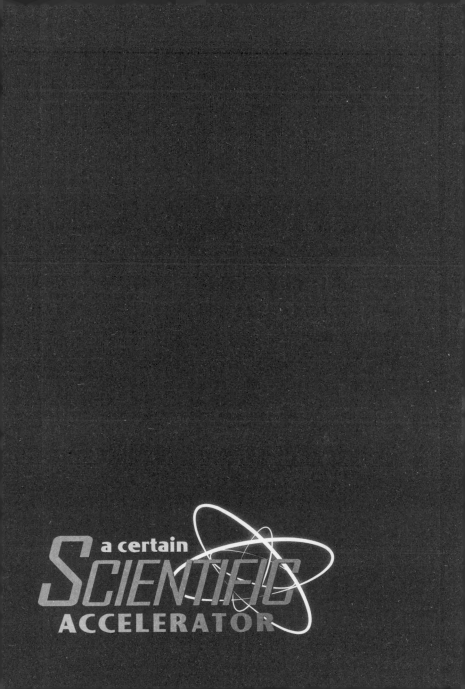

とある科学の一方通行（アクセラレータ）

とある魔術の禁書目録 外伝

CHAPTER 43

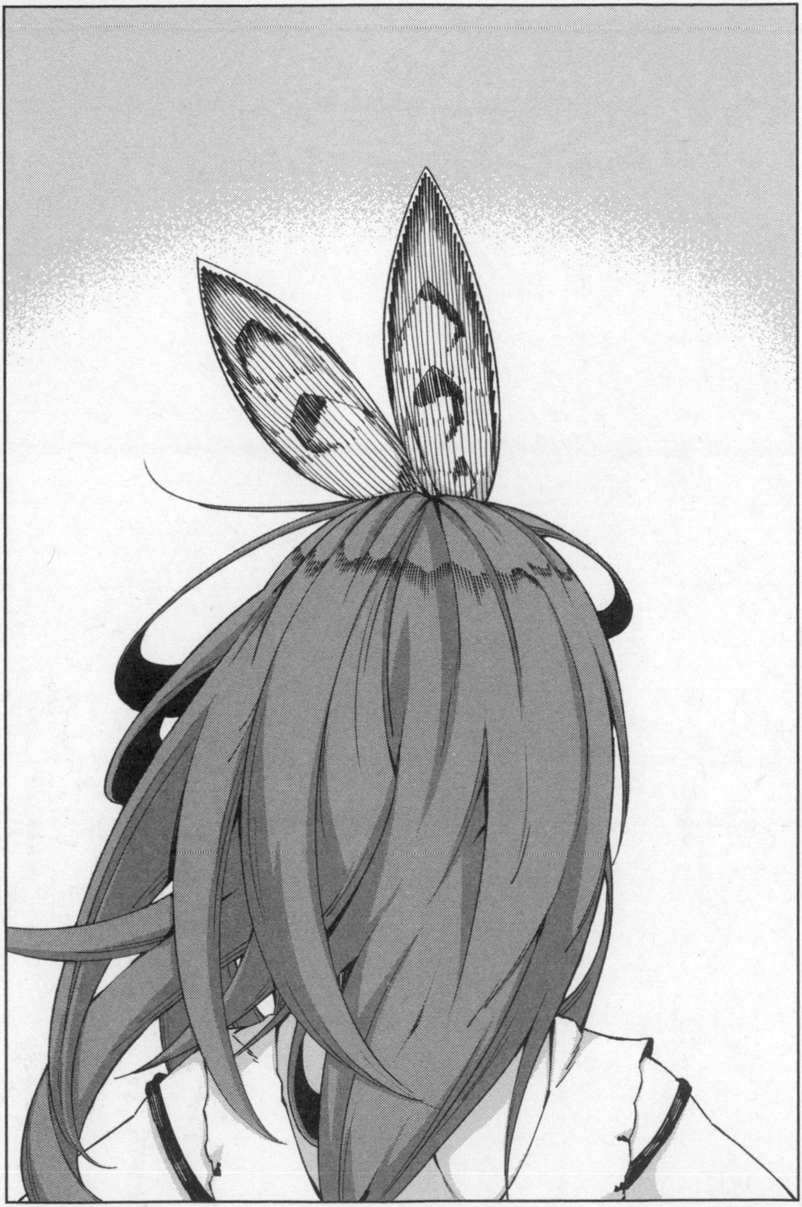

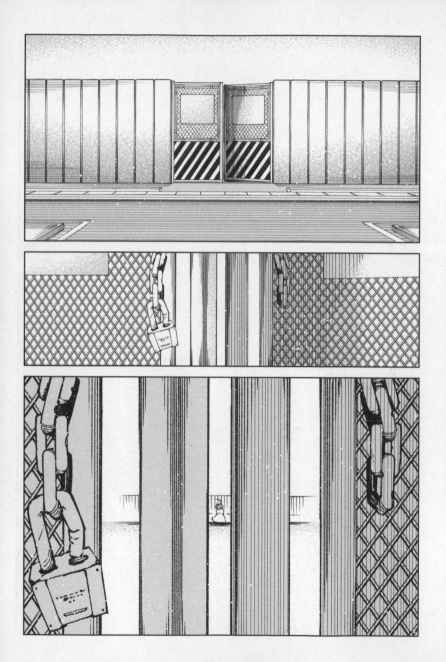

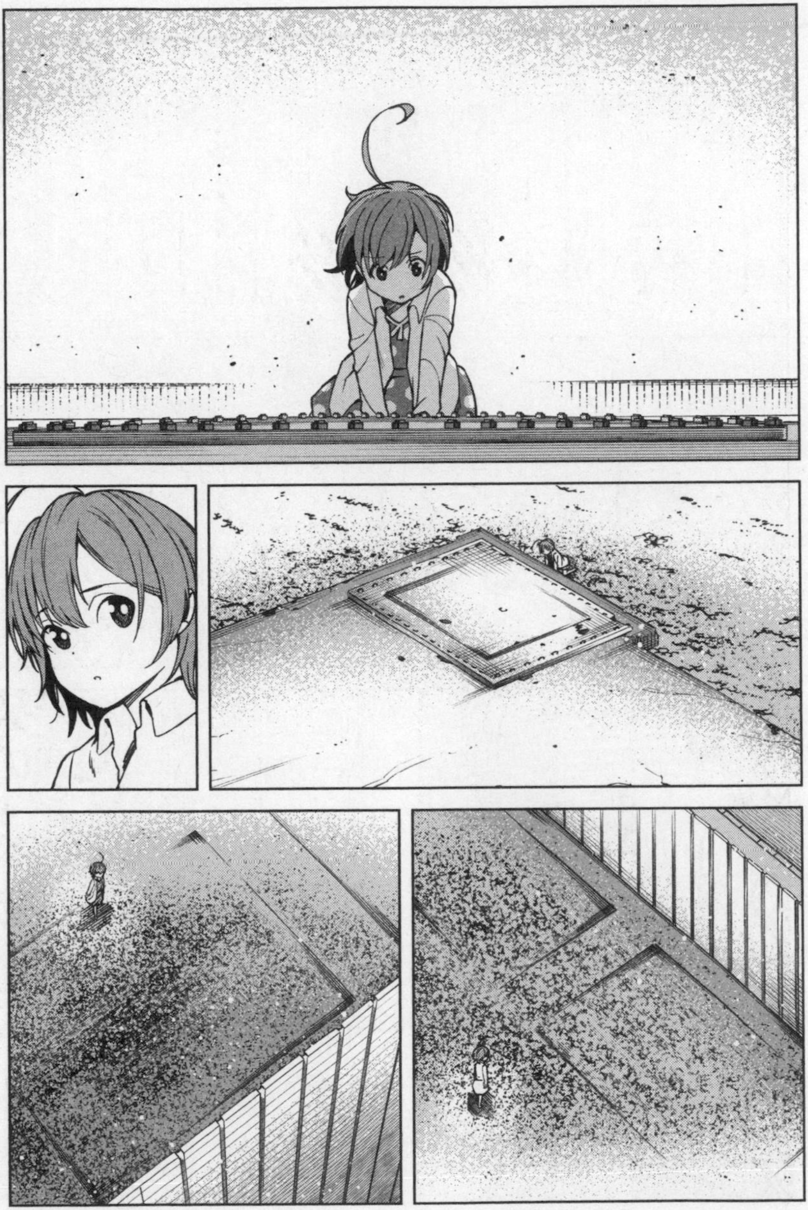

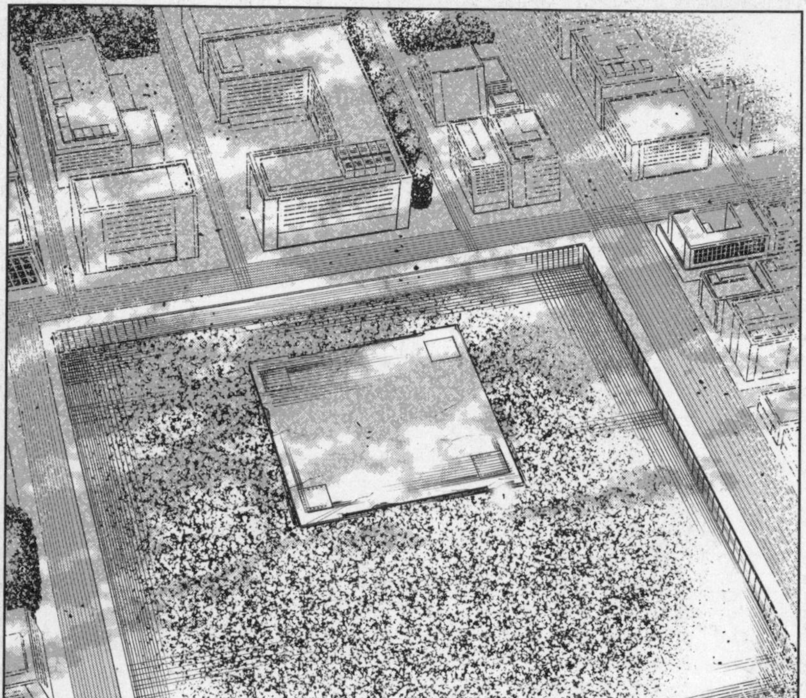

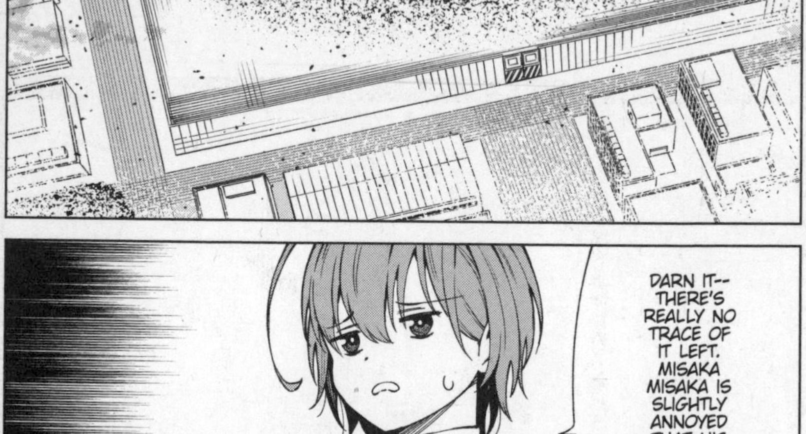
DARN IT-- THERE'S REALLY NO TRACE OF IT LEFT. MISAKA MISAKA IS SLIGHTLY ANNOYED THAT HIS GUESS WAS RIGHT...

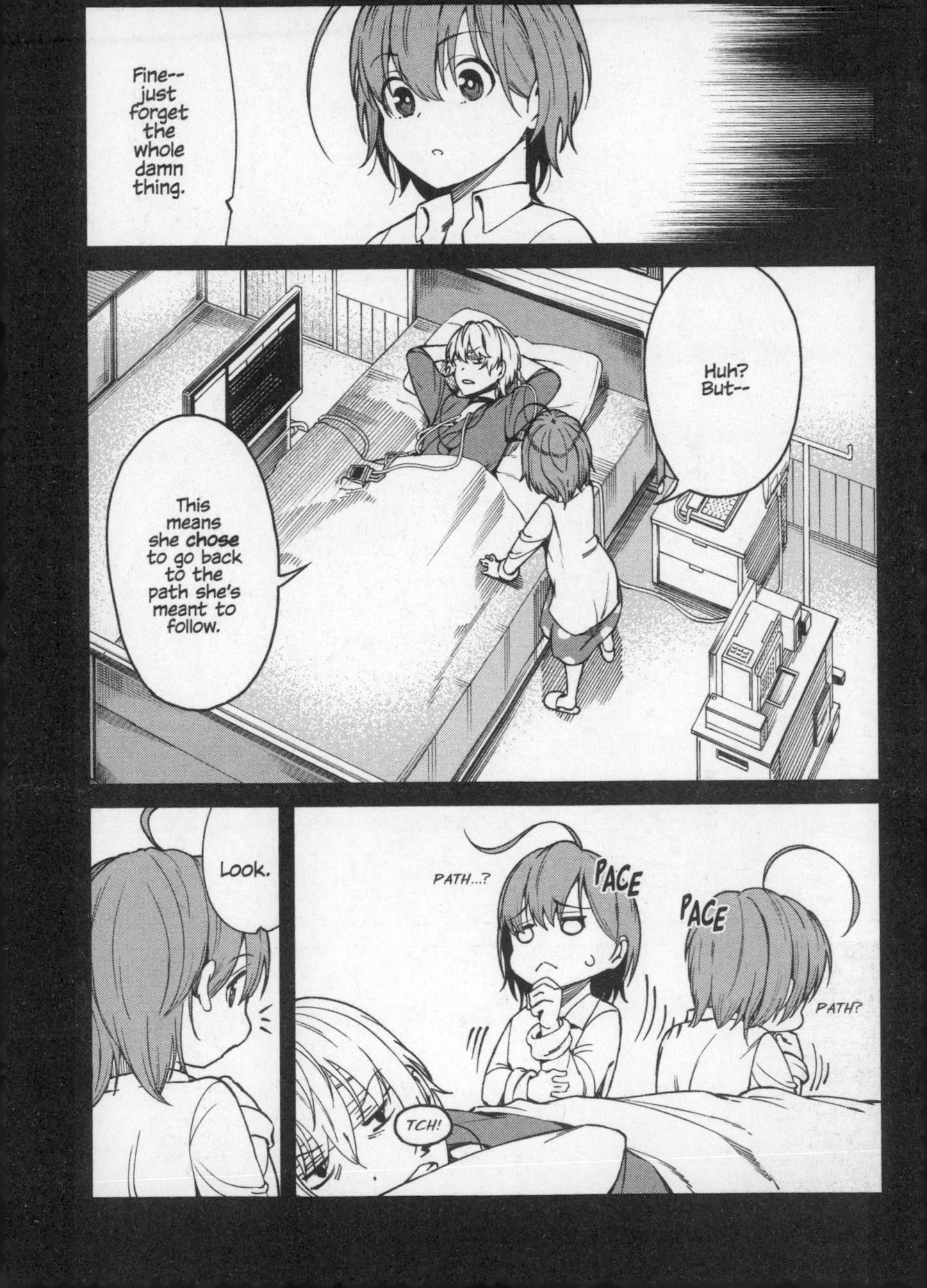

Fine-- just forget the whole damn thing.
Huh? But--
This means she **chose** to go back to the path she's meant to follow.
PACE
PACE
PATH?
PATH...?
TCH!
Look.

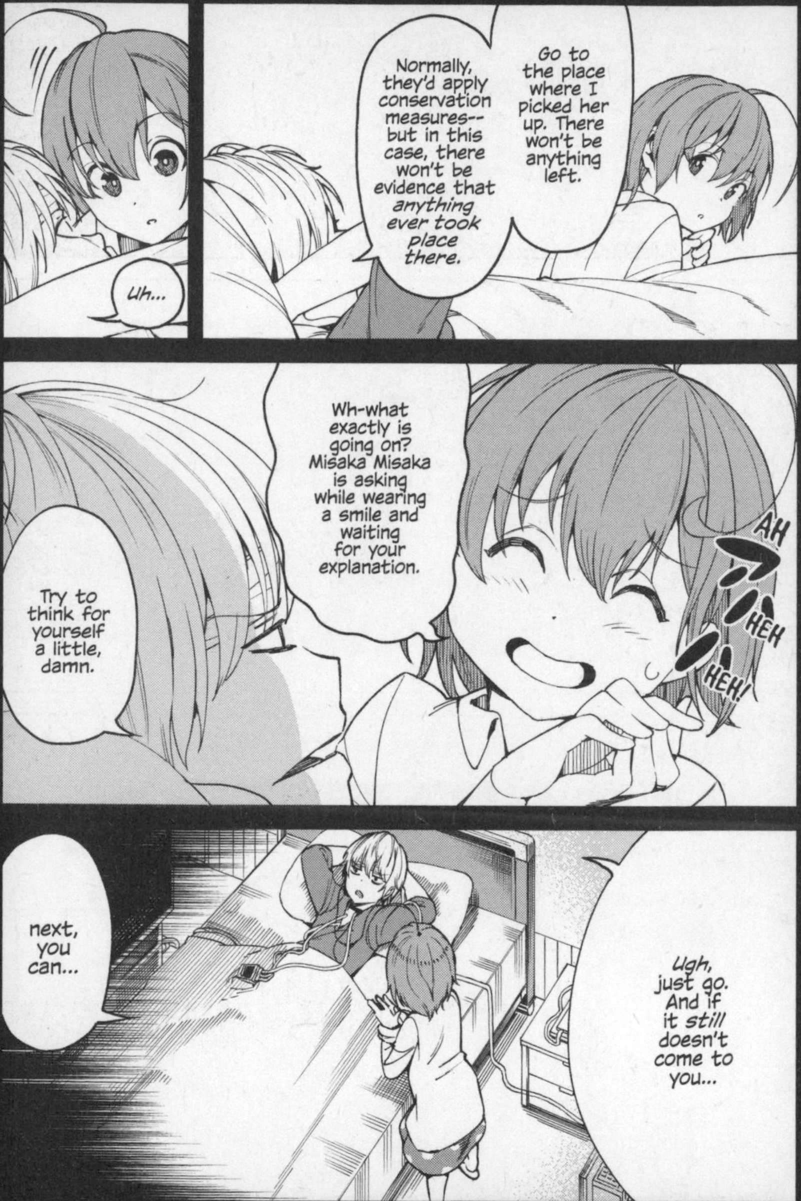
Go to the place where I picked her up. There won't be anything left.
Normally, they'd apply conservation measures-- but in this case, there won't be evidence that *anything ever took place there.*
Uh...
Wh-what exactly is going on? Misaka Misaka is asking while wearing a smile and waiting for your explanation.
AH HEH HEH!
Try to think for yourself a little, damn.
Ugh, just go. And if it *still* doesn't come to you...
next, you can...

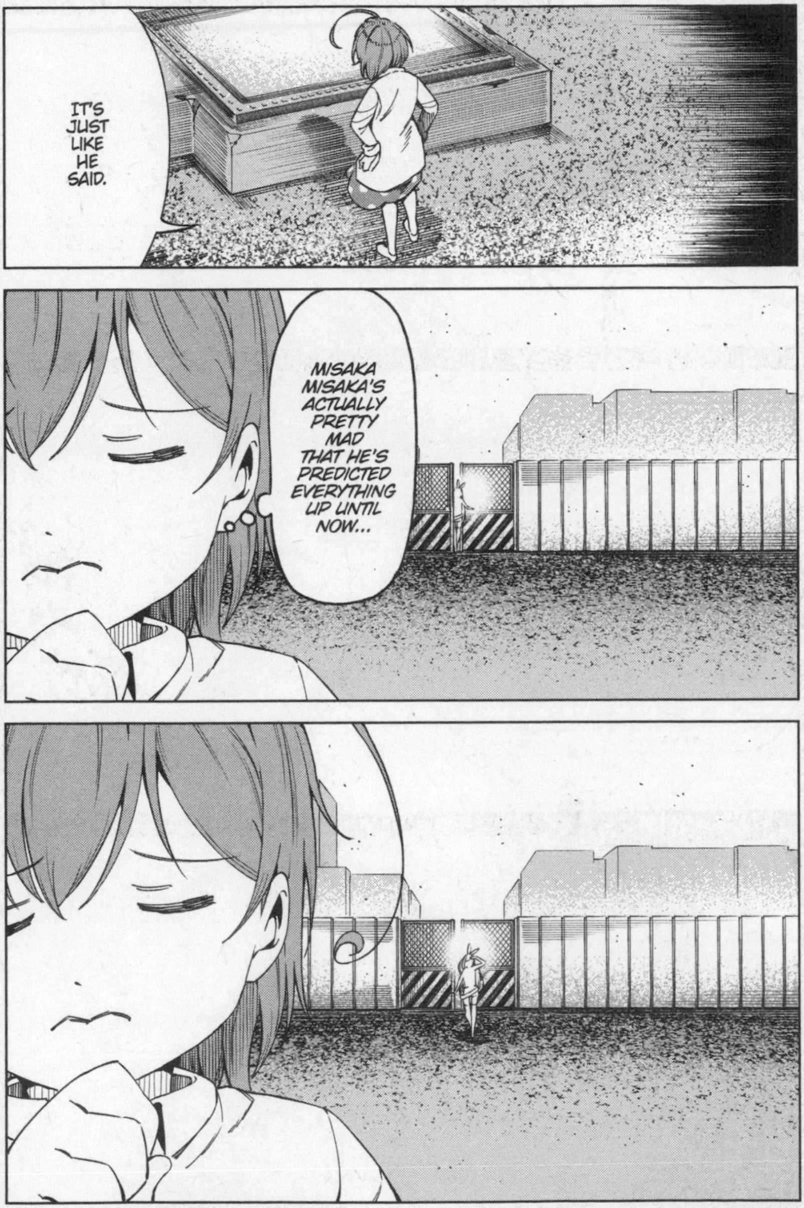
IT'S JUST LIKE HE SAID.
MISAKA MISAKA'S ACTUALLY PRETTY MAD THAT HE'S PREDICTED EVERYTHING UP UNTIL NOW...

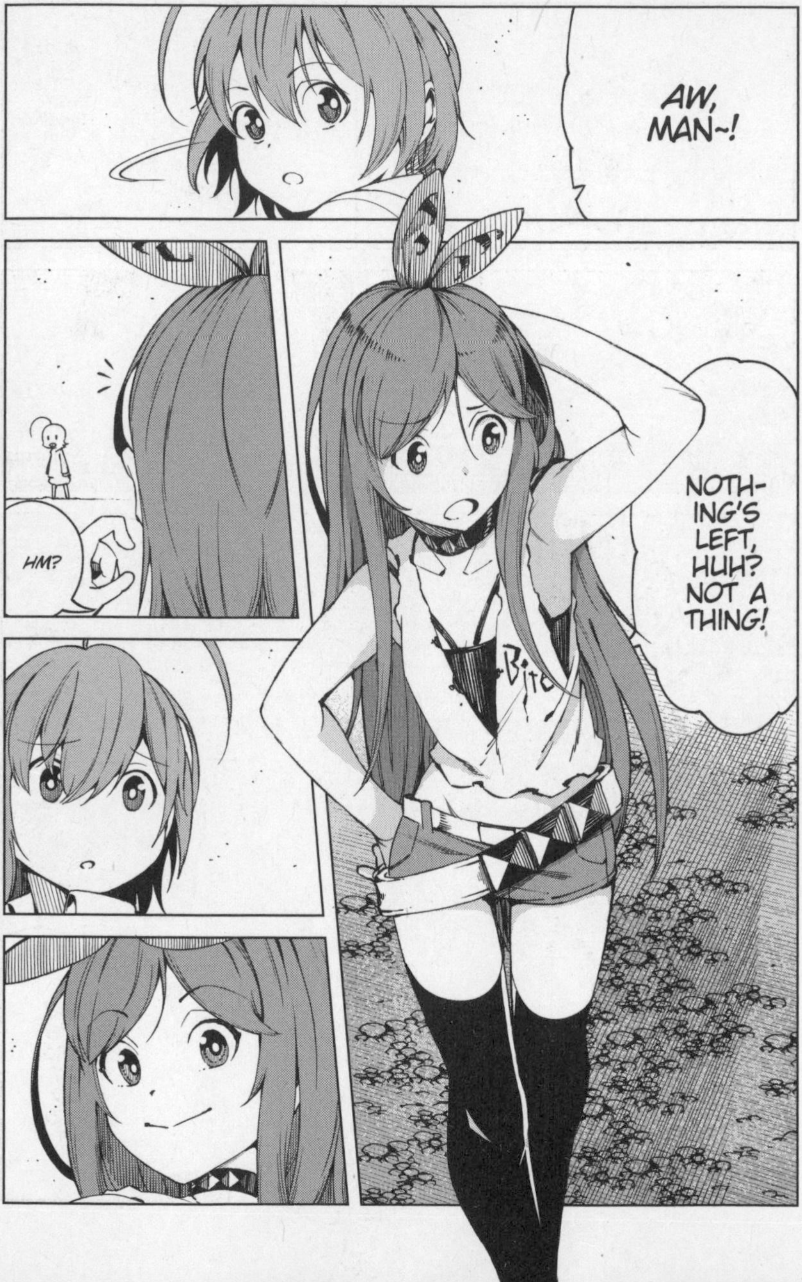
AW, MAN~!
NOTH-ING'S LEFT, HUH? NOT A THING!
HM?

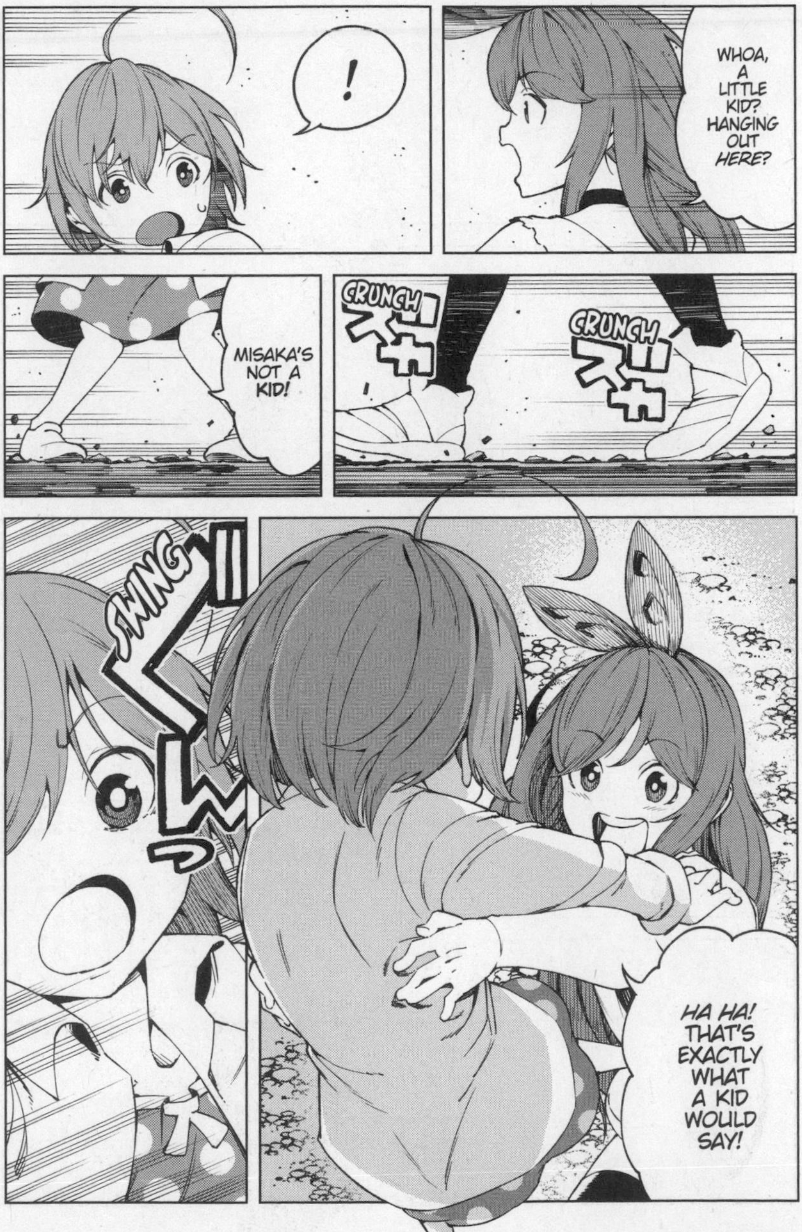
WHOA, A LITTLE KID? HANGING OUT HERE?
!
CRUNCH
CRUNCH
MISAKA'S NOT A KID!
HA HA! THAT'S EXACTLY WHAT A KID WOULD SAY!
SWING

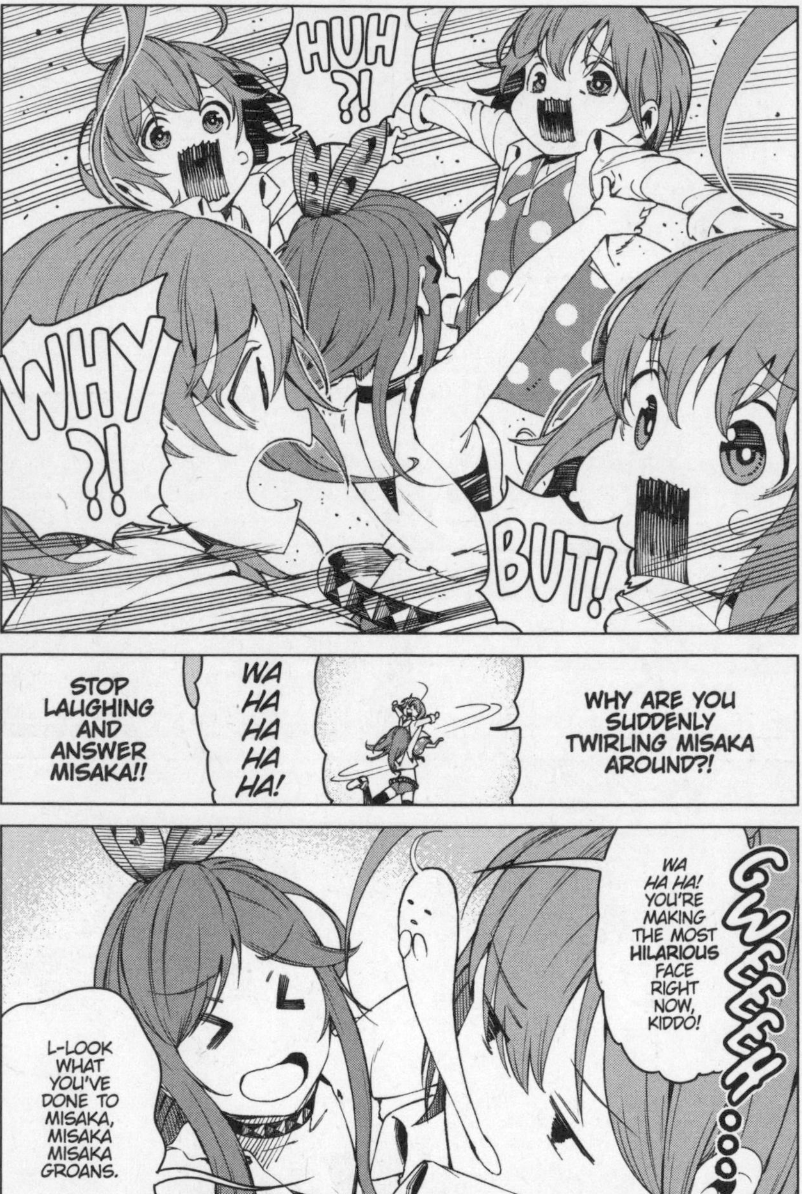
HUH ?!
BUT!
WHY ?!
WHY ARE YOU SUDDENLY TWIRLING MISAKA AROUND?!
WA HA HA HA HA HA!
STOP LAUGHING AND ANSWER MISAKA!!
GWEEEEHooo
WA HA HA! YOU'RE MAKING THE MOST HILARIOUS FACE RIGHT NOW, KIDDO!
L-LOOK WHAT YOU'VE DONE TO MISAKA, MISAKA MISAKA GROANS.

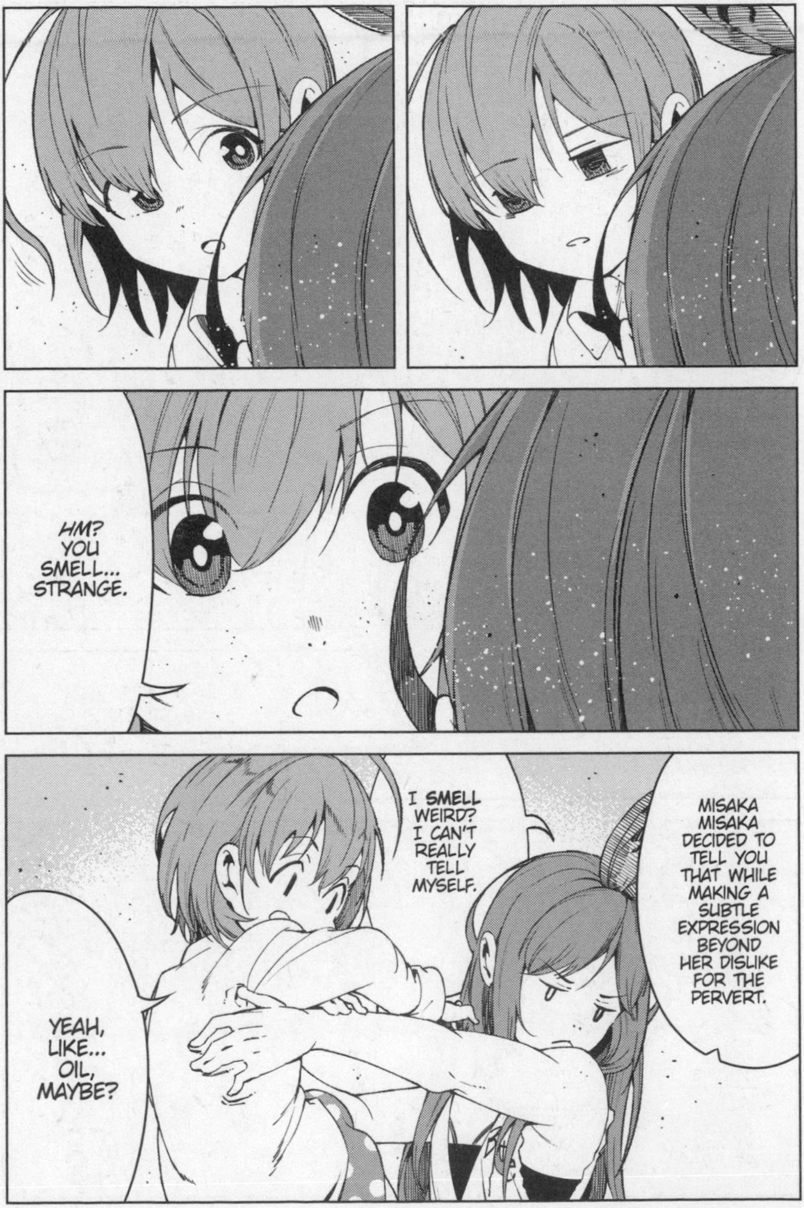
HM? YOU SMELL... STRANGE.
MISAKA MISAKA DECIDED TO TELL YOU THAT WHILE MAKING A SUBTLE EXPRESSION BEYOND HER DISLIKE FOR THE PERVERT.
I SMELL WEIRD? I CAN'T REALLY TELL MYSELF.
YEAH, LIKE... OIL, MAYBE?

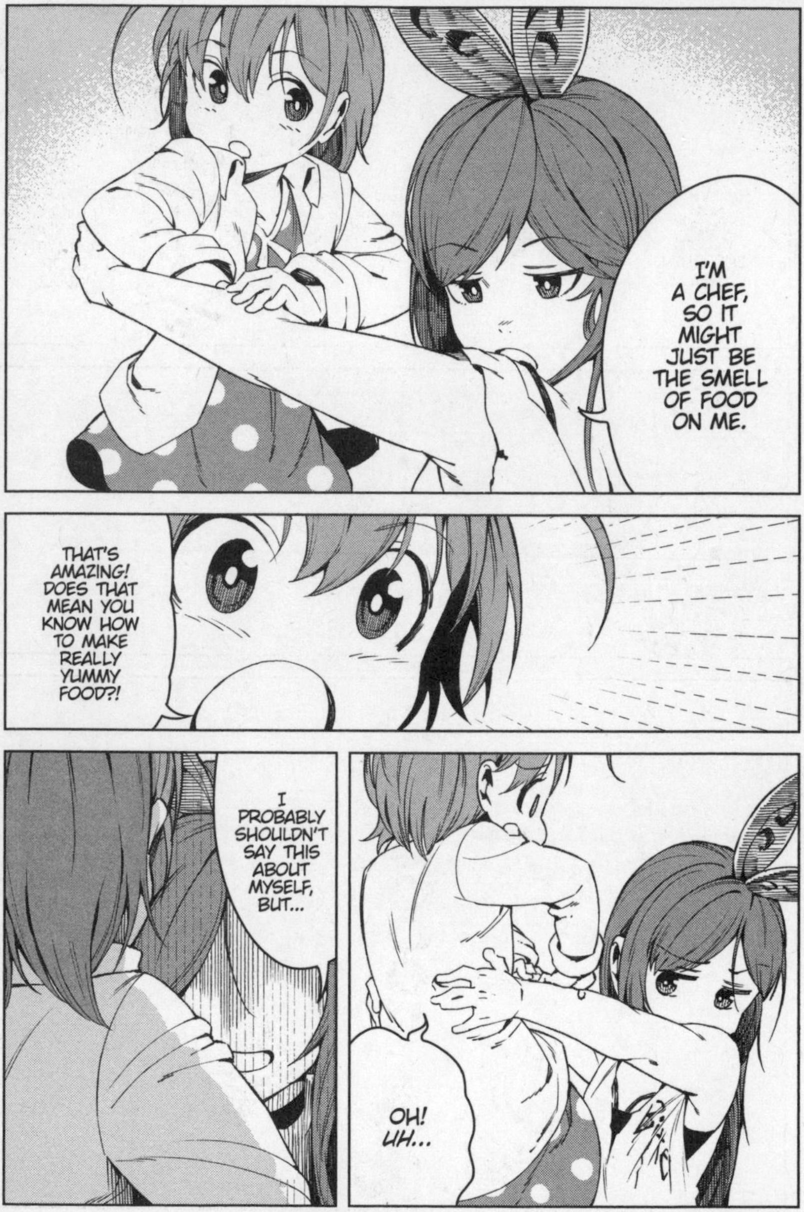
I'M A CHEF, SO IT MIGHT JUST BE THE SMELL OF FOOD ON ME.
THAT'S AMAZING! DOES THAT MEAN YOU KNOW HOW TO MAKE REALLY YUMMY FOOD?!
OH! UH...
I PROBABLY SHOULDN'T SAY THIS ABOUT MYSELF, BUT...

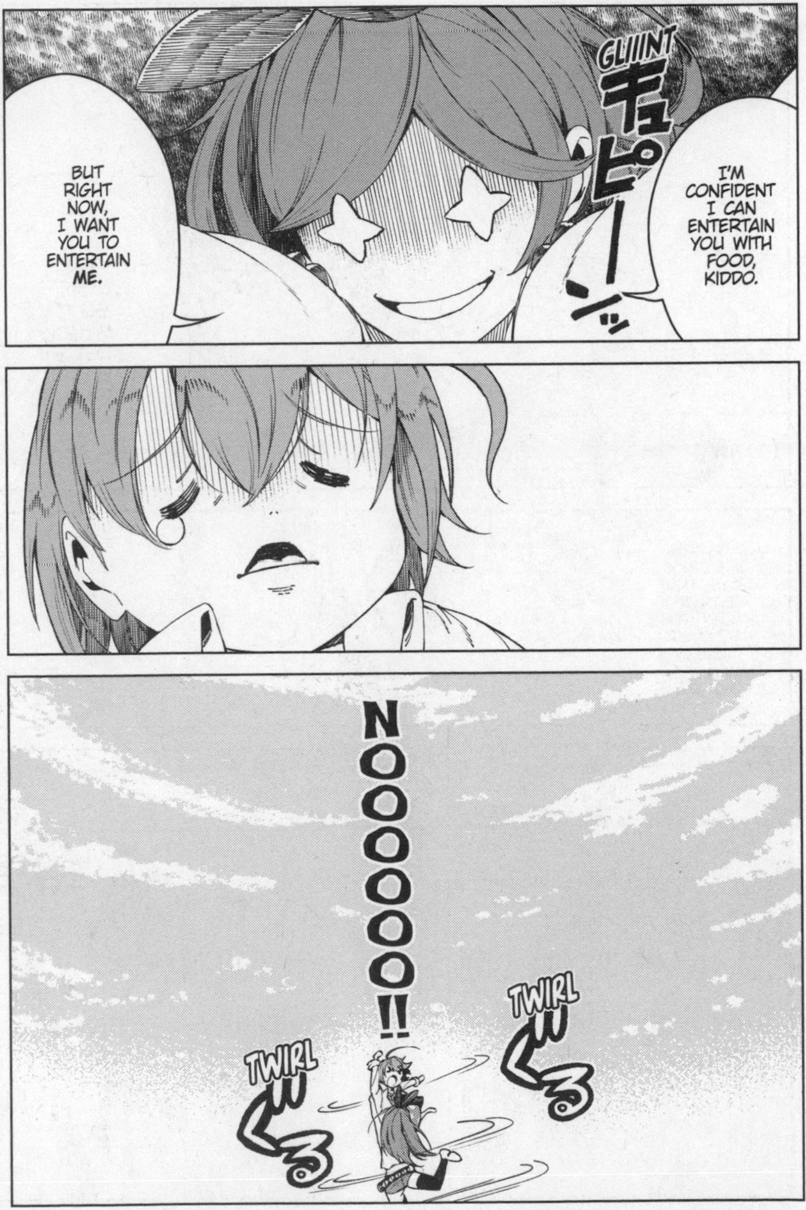
I'M CONFIDENT I CAN ENTERTAIN YOU WITH FOOD, KIDDO.
GLIIINT
キュピーンッ
BUT RIGHT NOW, I WANT YOU TO ENTERTAIN ME.
NOOOOOO!!
TWIRL
くる
TWIRL
くる

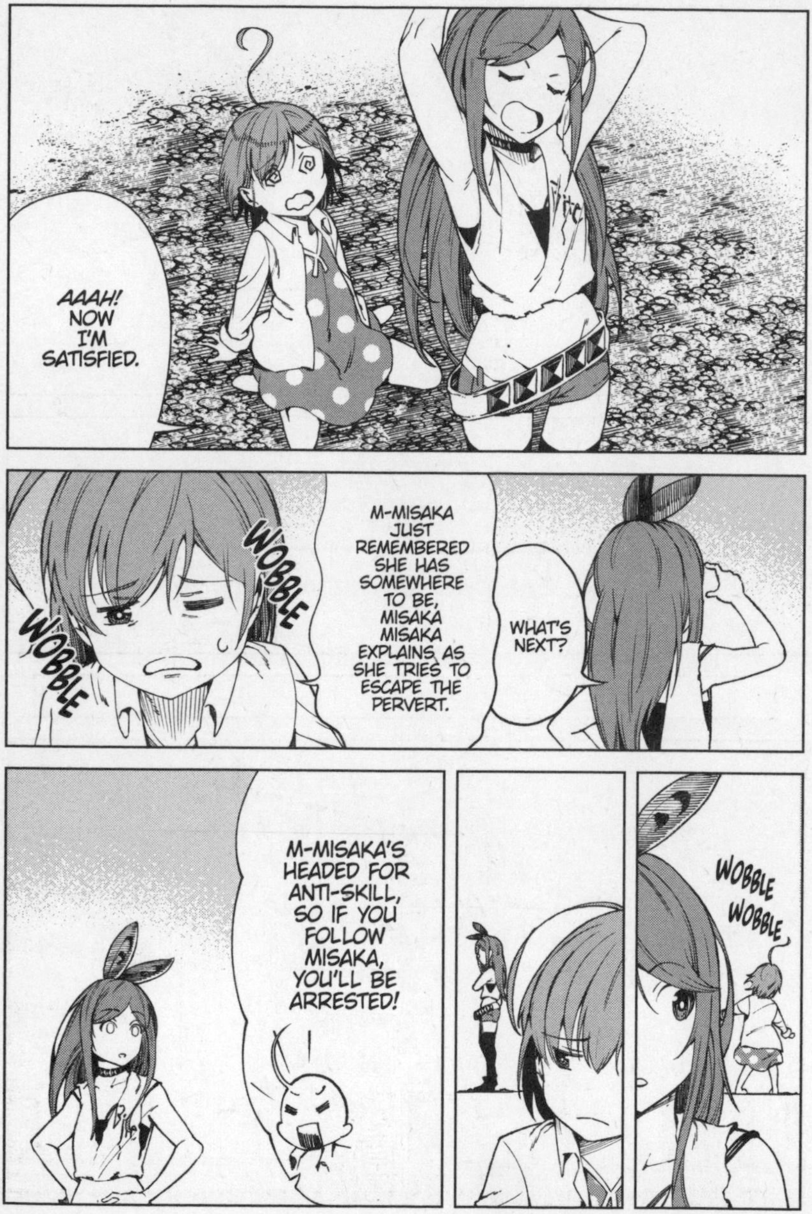
AAAH! NOW I'M SATISFIED.
WHAT'S NEXT?
M-MISAKA JUST REMEMBERED SHE HAS SOMEWHERE TO BE, MISAKA MISAKA EXPLAINS AS SHE TRIES TO ESCAPE THE PERVERT.
WOBBLE WOBBLE
WOBBLE WOBBLE
M-MISAKA'S HEADED FOR ANTI-SKILL, SO IF YOU FOLLOW MISAKA, YOU'LL BE ARRESTED!

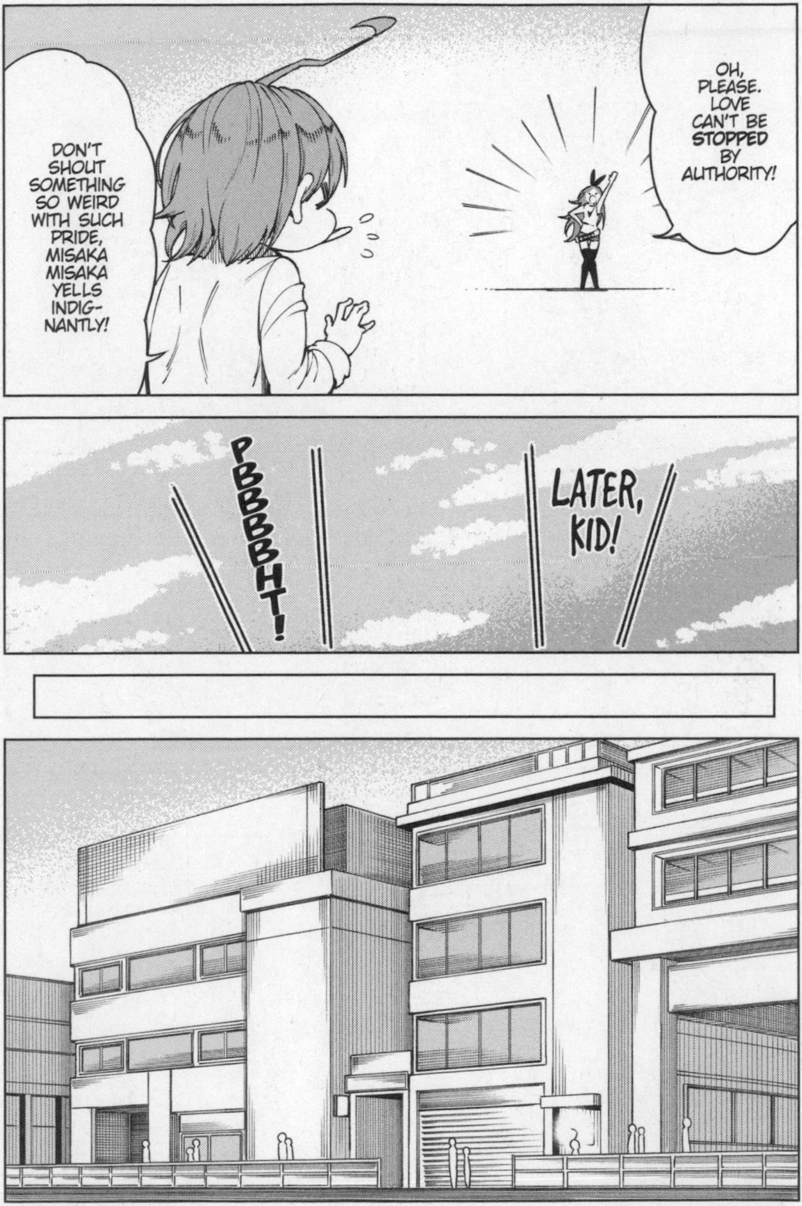
OH, PLEASE. LOVE CAN'T BE STOPPED BY AUTHORITY!
DON'T SHOUT SOMETHING SO WEIRD WITH SUCH PRIDE, MISAKA MISAKA YELLS INDIG-NANTLY!
LATER, KID!
PBBBBHT!

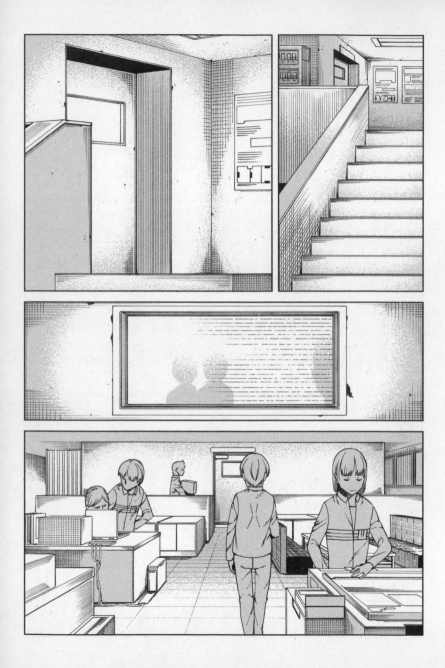

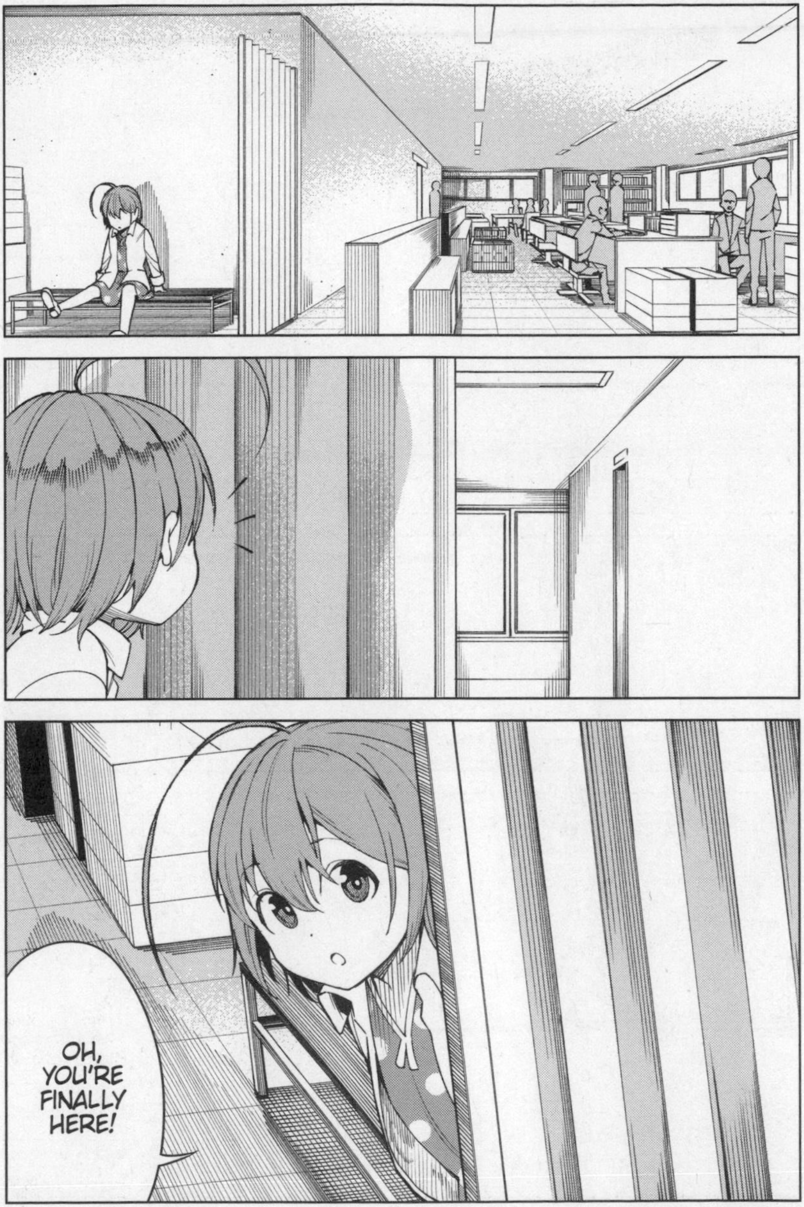
OH, YOU'RE FINALLY HERE!

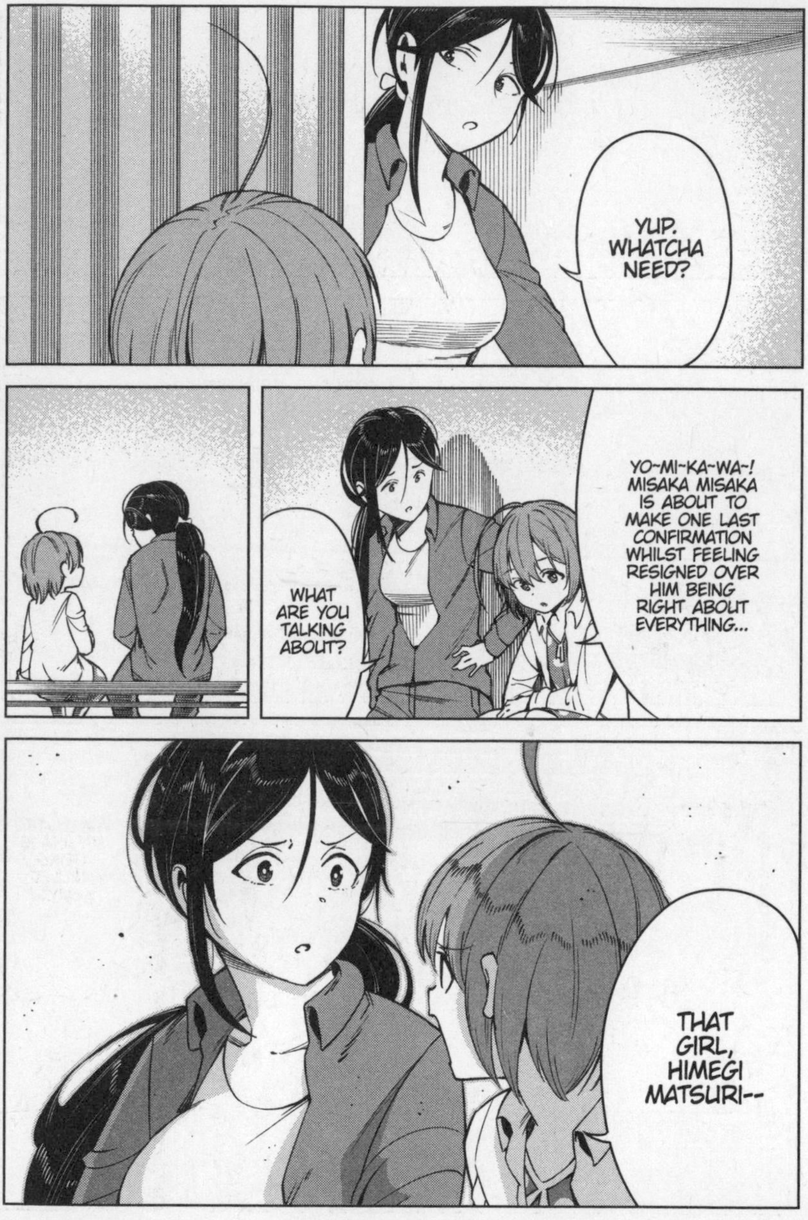
YUP. WHATCHA NEED?
YO~MI~KA~WA~! MISAKA MISAKA IS ABOUT TO MAKE ONE LAST CONFIRMATION WHILST FEELING RESIGNED OVER HIM BEING RIGHT ABOUT EVERYTHING...
WHAT ARE YOU TALKING ABOUT?
THAT GIRL, HIMEGI MATSURI--

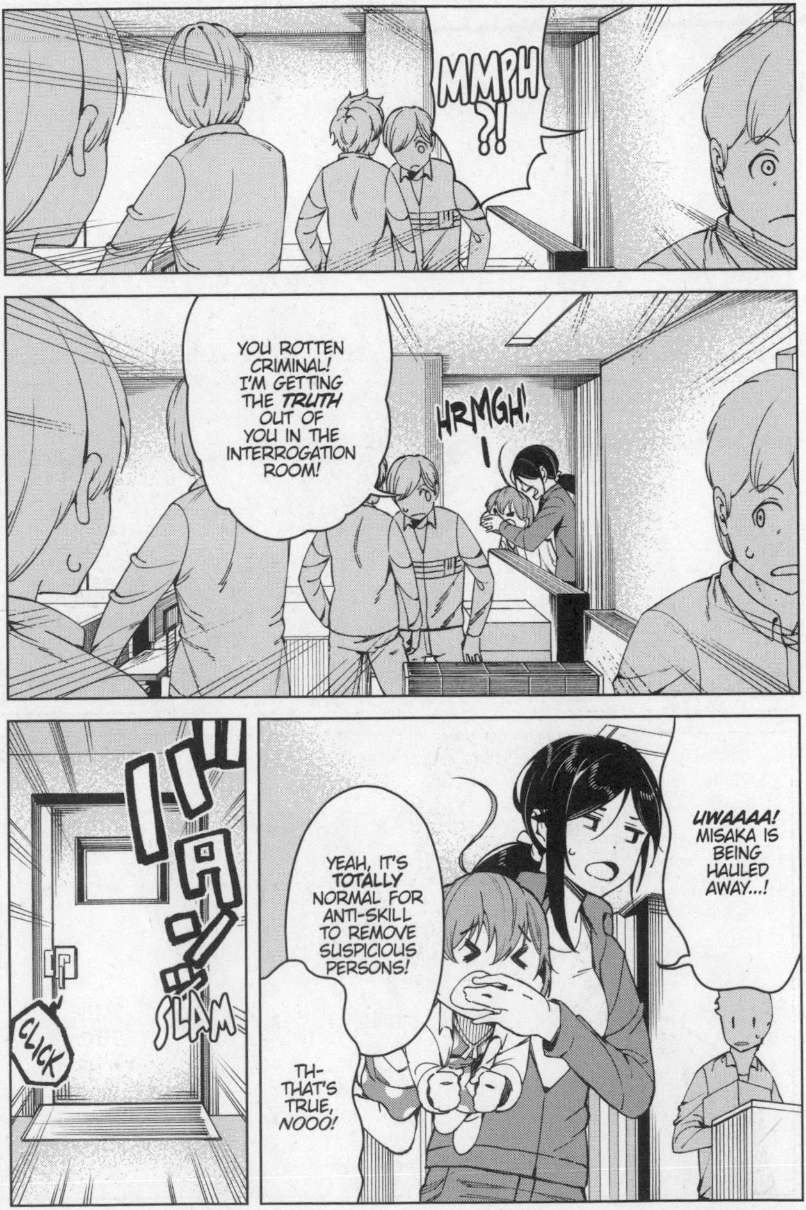
MMPH ?!
HRMGH!
YOU ROTTEN CRIMINAL! I'M GETTING THE *TRUTH* OUT OF YOU IN THE INTERROGATION ROOM!
UWAAAA! MISAKA IS BEING HAULED AWAY...!
YEAH, IT'S **TOTALLY** NORMAL FOR ANTI-SKILL TO REMOVE SUSPICIOUS PERSONS!
TH- THAT'S TRUE, *NOOO!*
SLAM
CLICK

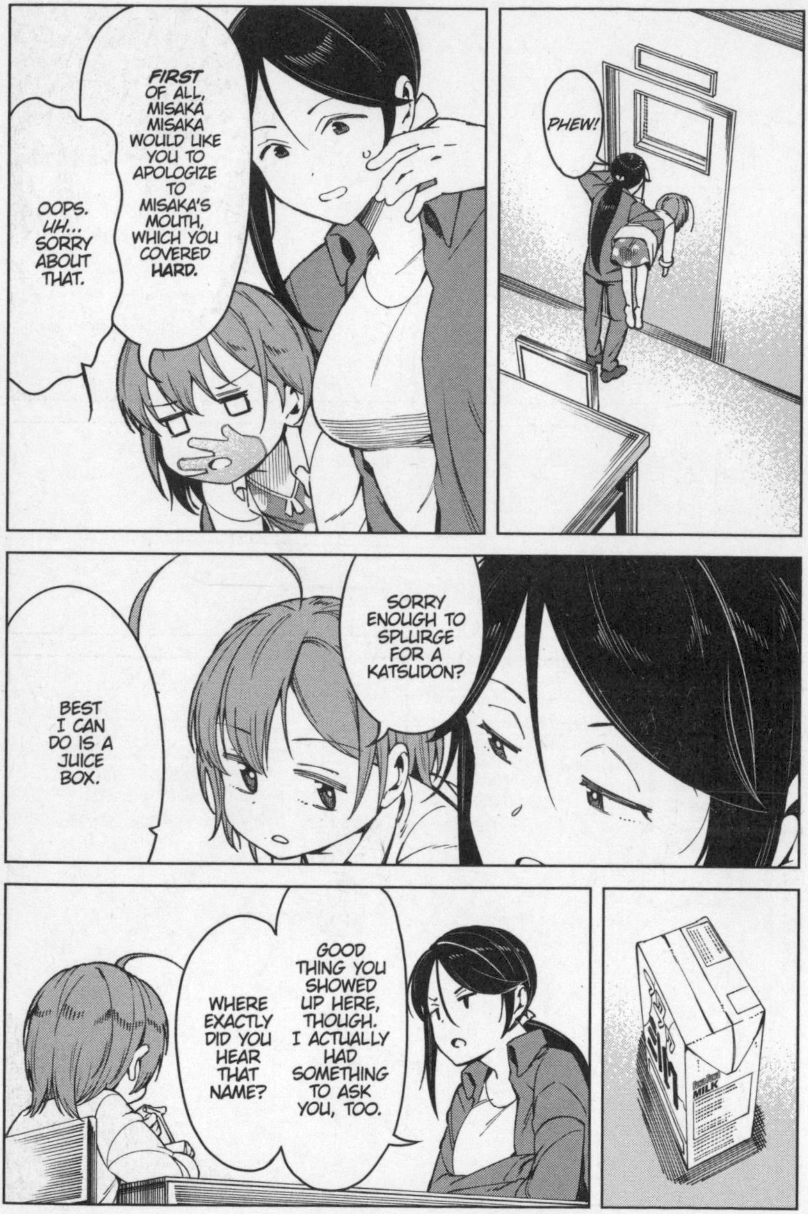
PHEW!
FIRST OF ALL, MISAKA MISAKA WOULD LIKE YOU TO APOLOGIZE TO MISAKA'S MOUTH, WHICH YOU COVERED HARD.
OOPS. UH... SORRY ABOUT THAT.
SORRY ENOUGH TO SPLURGE FOR A KATSUDON?
BEST I CAN DO IS A JUICE BOX.
MILK
GOOD THING YOU SHOWED UP HERE, THOUGH. I ACTUALLY HAD SOMETHING TO ASK YOU, TOO.
WHERE EXACTLY DID YOU HEAR THAT NAME?

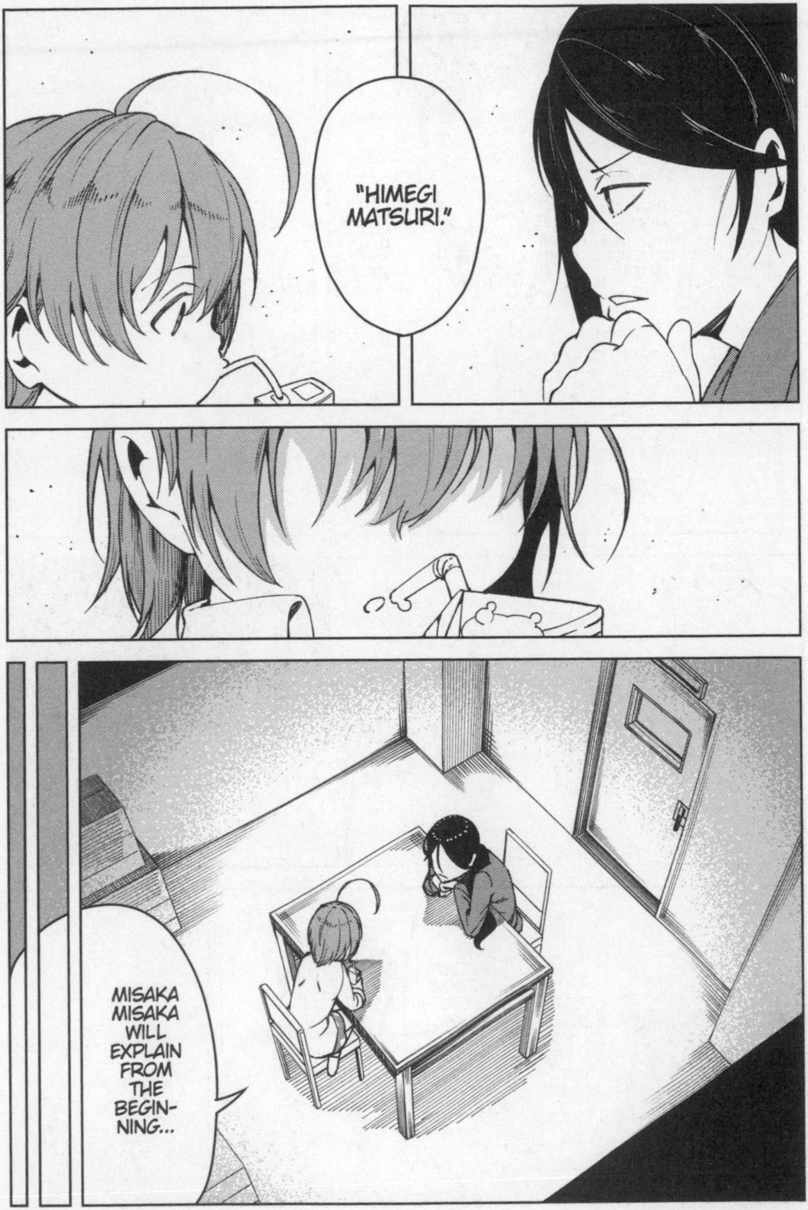
"HIMEGI MATSURI."
MISAKA MISAKA WILL EXPLAIN FROM THE BEGIN-NING...

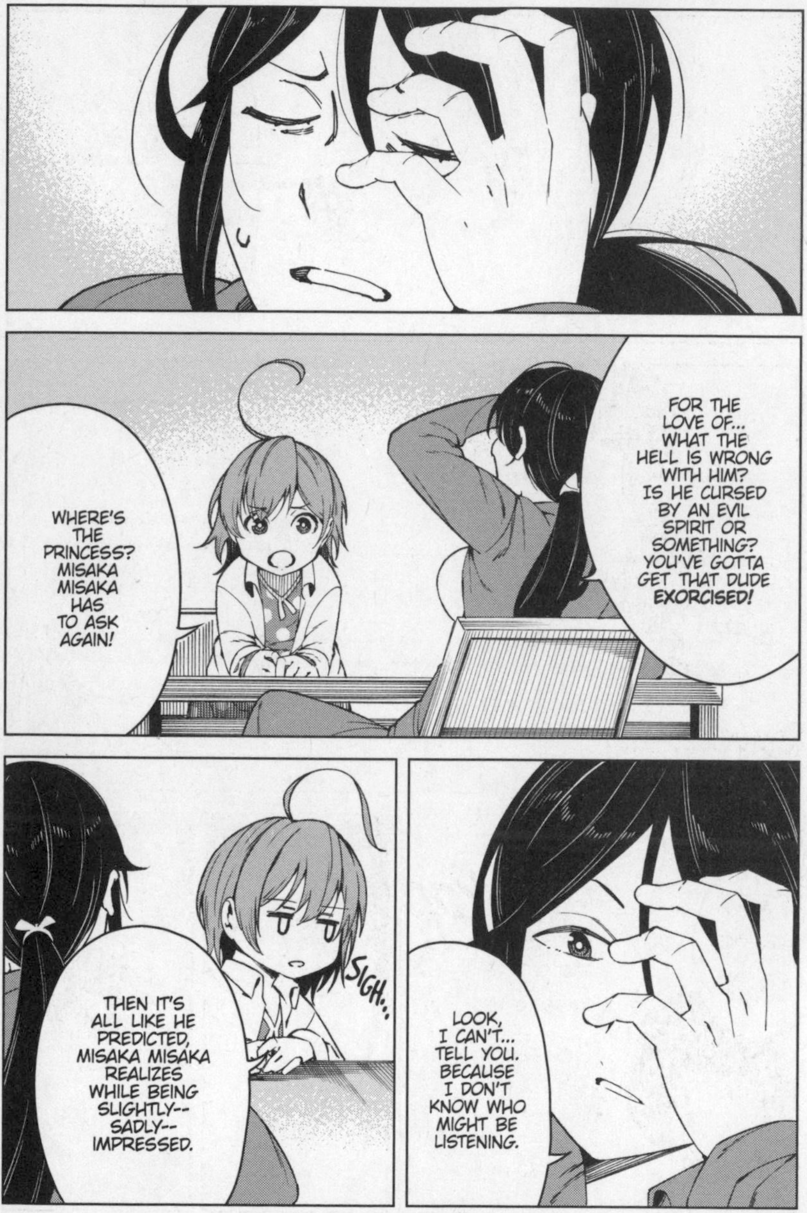
FOR THE LOVE OF... WHAT THE HELL IS WRONG WITH HIM? IS HE CURSED BY AN EVIL SPIRIT OR SOMETHING? YOU'VE GOTTA GET THAT DUDE **EXORCISED!**
WHERE'S THE PRINCESS? MISAKA MISAKA HAS TO ASK AGAIN!
LOOK, I CAN'T... TELL YOU. BECAUSE I DON'T KNOW WHO MIGHT BE LISTENING.
SIGH...
THEN IT'S ALL LIKE HE PREDICTED, MISAKA MISAKA REALIZES WHILE BEING SLIGHTLY-- SADLY-- IMPRESSED.

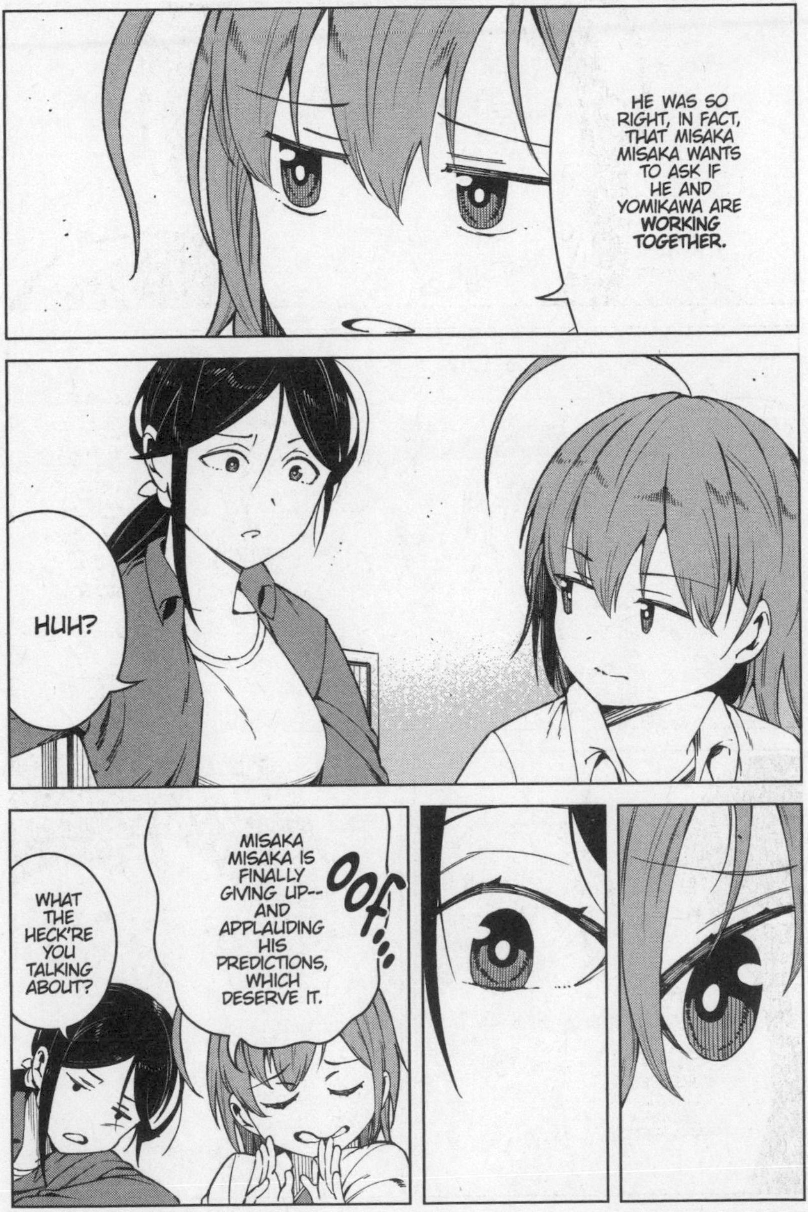
HE WAS SO RIGHT, IN FACT, THAT MISAKA MISAKA WANTS TO ASK IF HE AND YOMIKAWA ARE **WORKING TOGETHER.**
HUH?
MISAKA MISAKA IS FINALLY GIVING UP-- AND APPLAUDING HIS PREDICTIONS, WHICH DESERVE IT.
OOF...
WHAT THE HECK'RE YOU TALKING ABOUT?

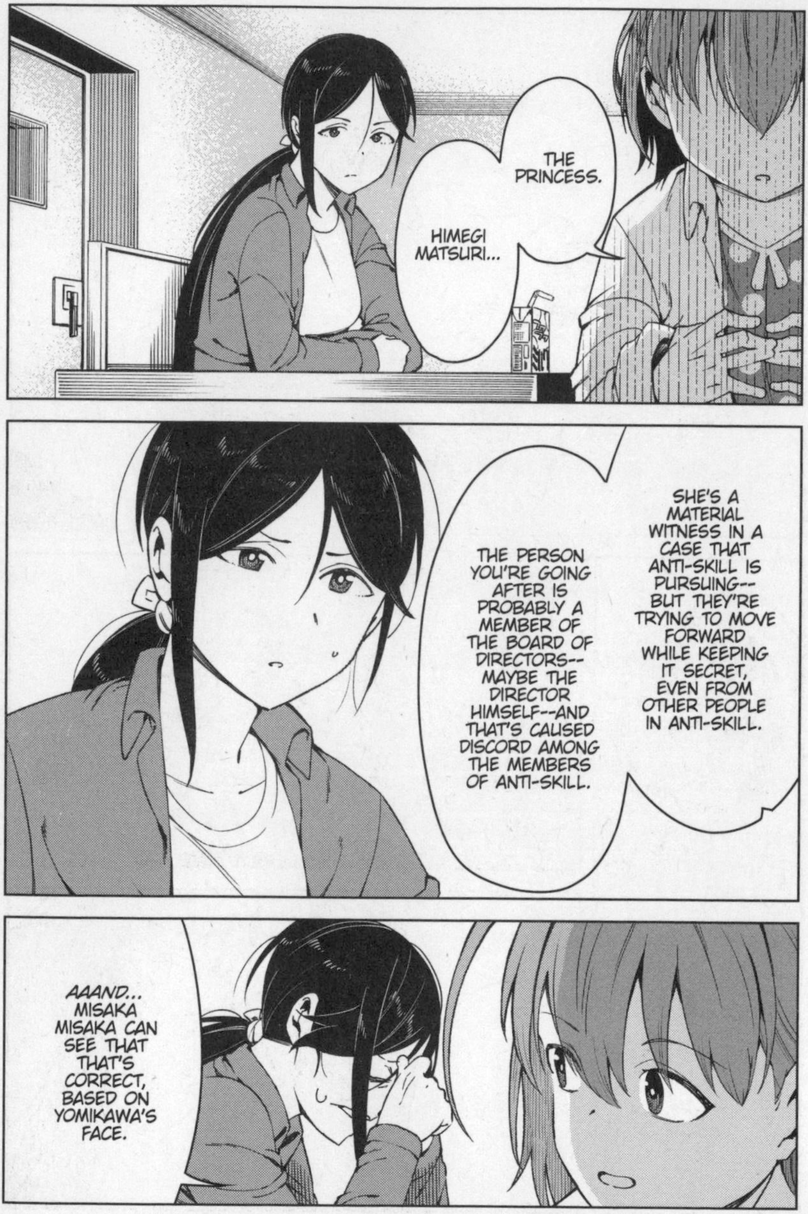
THE PRINCESS.
HIMEGI MATSURI...
SHE'S A MATERIAL WITNESS IN A CASE THAT ANTI-SKILL IS PURSUING--BUT THEY'RE TRYING TO MOVE FORWARD WHILE KEEPING IT SECRET, EVEN FROM OTHER PEOPLE IN ANTI-SKILL.
THE PERSON YOU'RE GOING AFTER IS PROBABLY A MEMBER OF THE BOARD OF DIRECTORS--MAYBE THE DIRECTOR HIMSELF--AND THAT'S CAUSED DISCORD AMONG THE MEMBERS OF ANTI-SKILL.
AAAND... MISAKA MISAKA CAN SEE THAT THAT'S CORRECT, BASED ON YOMIKAWA'S FACE.

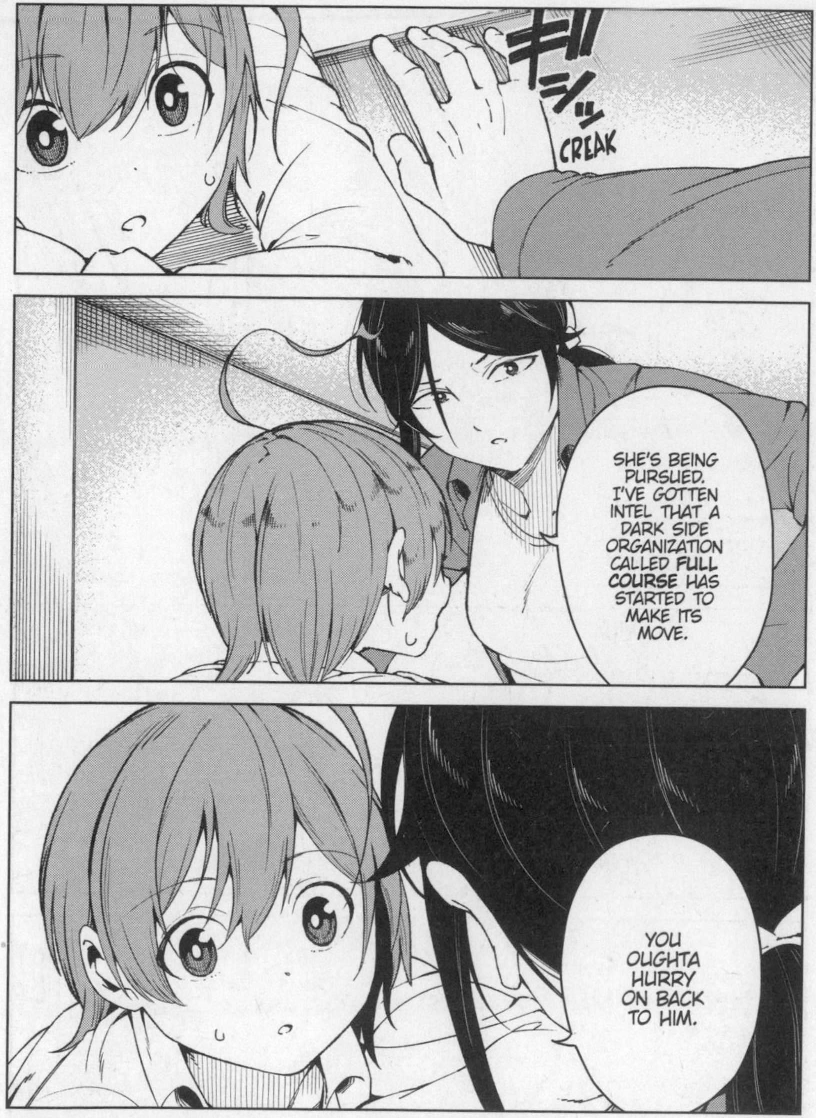
ギシッ
CREAK
SHE'S BEING PURSUED. I'VE GOTTEN INTEL THAT A DARK SIDE ORGANIZATION CALLED **FULL COURSE** HAS STARTED TO MAKE ITS MOVE.
YOU OUGHTA HURRY ON BACK TO HIM.

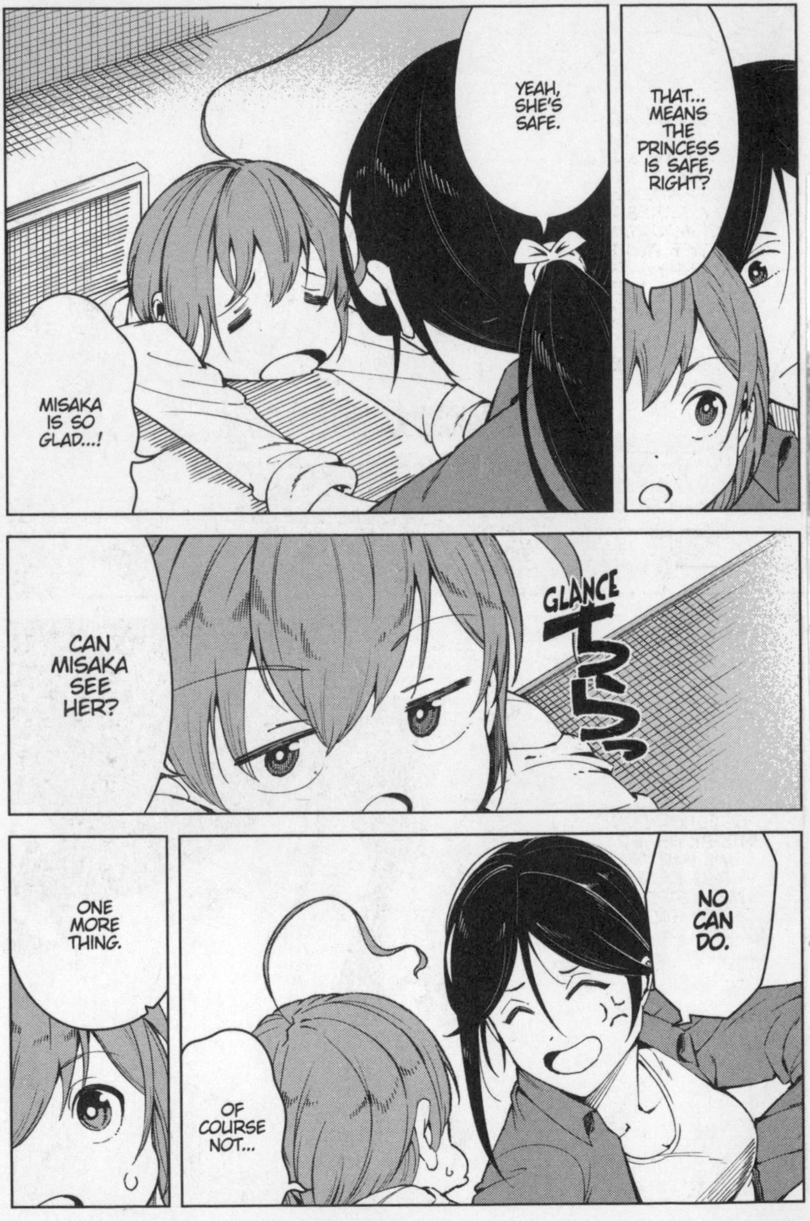
THAT... MEANS THE PRINCESS IS SAFE, RIGHT?
YEAH, SHE'S SAFE.
MISAKA IS SO GLAD...!
GLANCE
CAN MISAKA SEE HER?
NO CAN DO.
OF COURSE NOT...
ONE MORE THING.

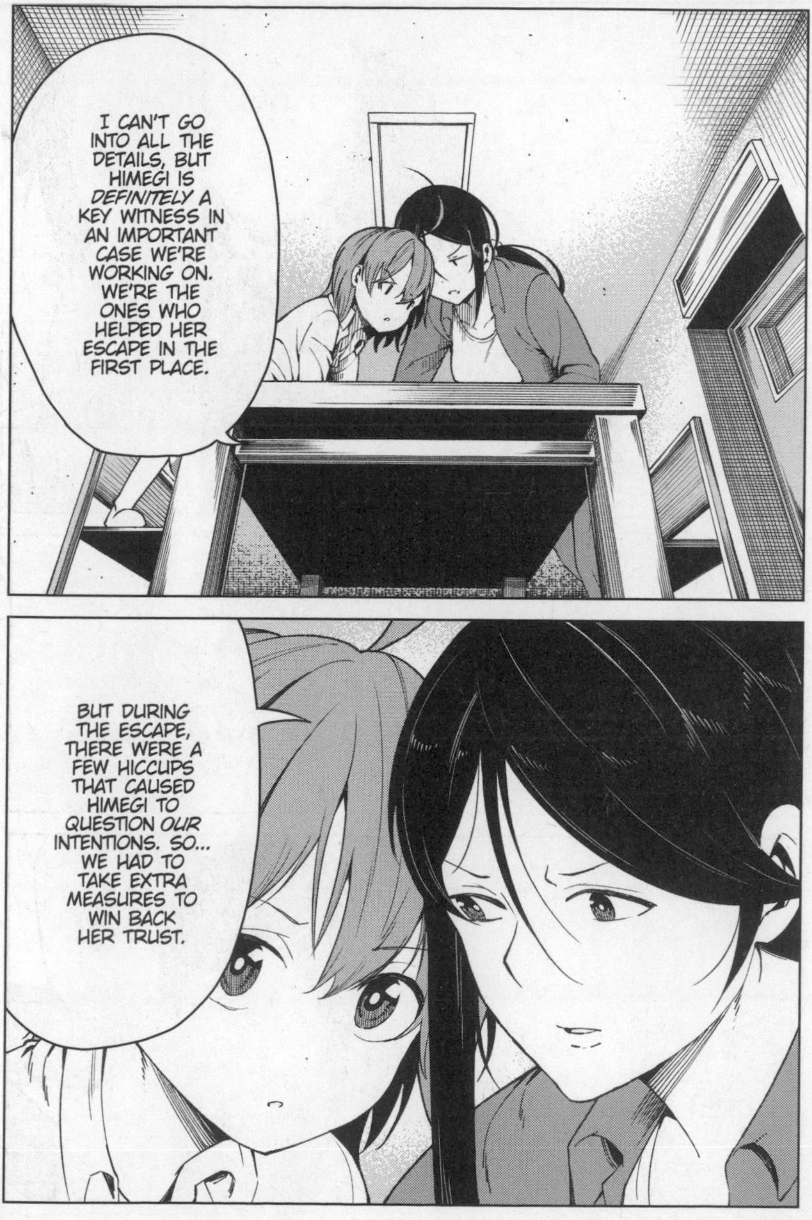
I CAN'T GO INTO ALL THE DETAILS, BUT HIMEGI IS *DEFINITELY* A KEY WITNESS IN AN IMPORTANT CASE WE'RE WORKING ON. WE'RE THE ONES WHO HELPED HER ESCAPE IN THE FIRST PLACE.
BUT DURING THE ESCAPE, THERE WERE A FEW HICCUPS THAT CAUSED HIMEGI TO QUESTION *OUR* INTENTIONS. SO... WE HAD TO TAKE EXTRA MEASURES TO WIN BACK HER TRUST.

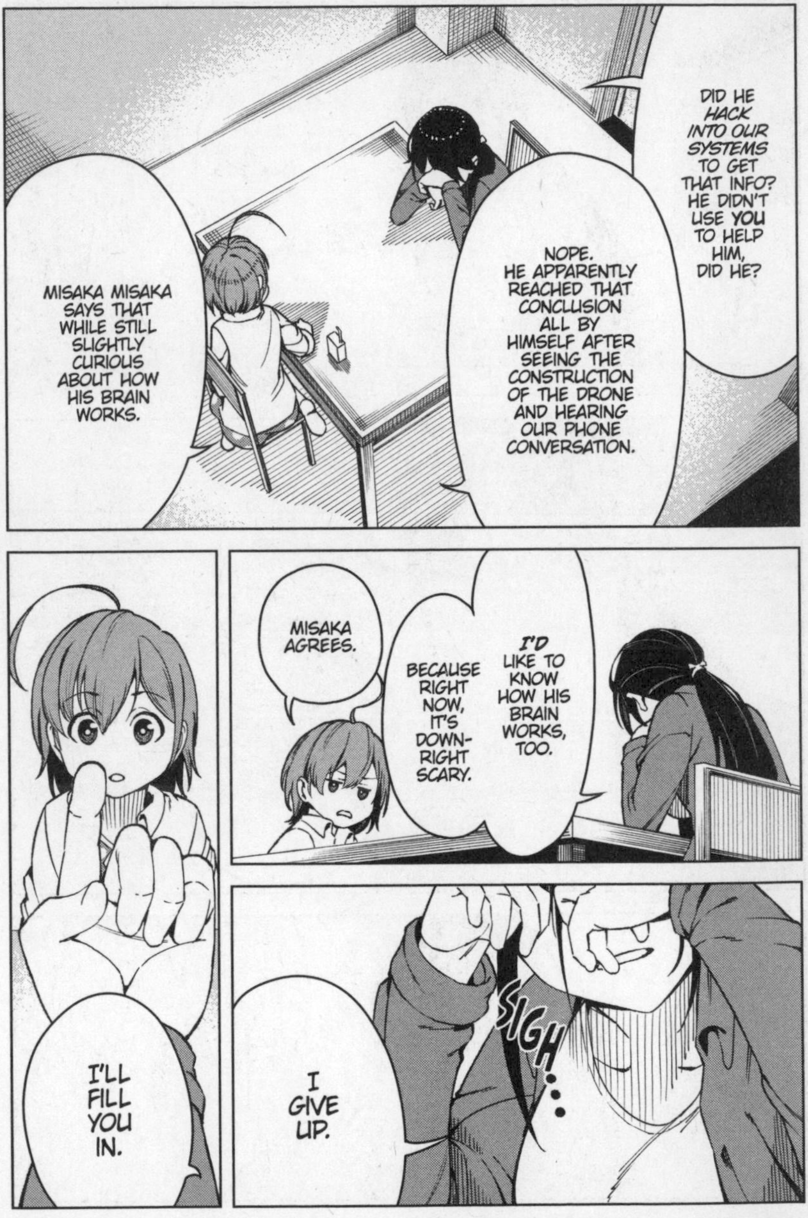
DID HE HACK INTO OUR SYSTEMS TO GET THAT INFO? HE DIDN'T USE YOU TO HELP HIM, DID HE?
NOPE. HE APPARENTLY REACHED THAT CONCLUSION ALL BY HIMSELF AFTER SEEING THE CONSTRUCTION OF THE DRONE AND HEARING OUR PHONE CONVERSATION.
MISAKA MISAKA SAYS THAT WHILE STILL SLIGHTLY CURIOUS ABOUT HOW HIS BRAIN WORKS.
I'D LIKE TO KNOW HOW HIS BRAIN WORKS, TOO.
BECAUSE RIGHT NOW, IT'S DOWN-RIGHT SCARY.
MISAKA AGREES.
SIGH...
I GIVE UP.
I'LL FILL YOU IN.

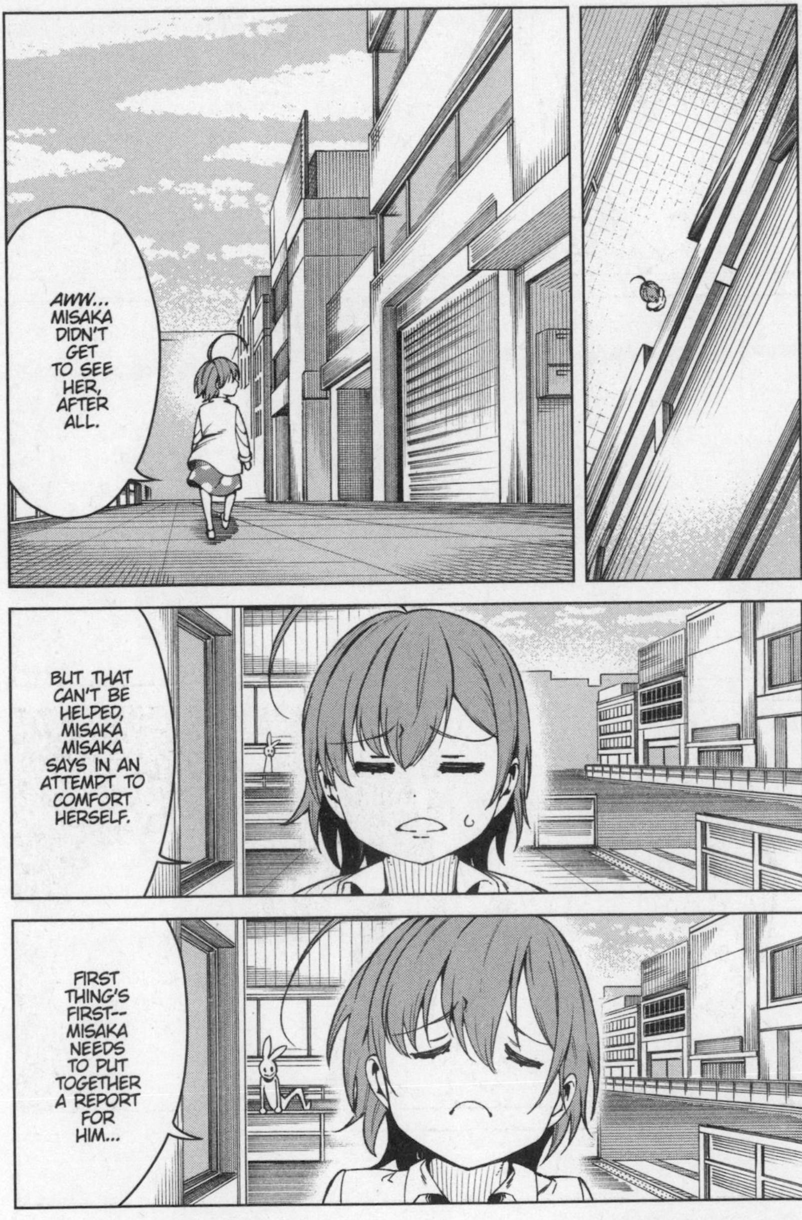
AWW... MISAKA DIDN'T GET TO SEE HER, AFTER ALL.
BUT THAT CAN'T BE HELPED, MISAKA MISAKA SAYS IN AN ATTEMPT TO COMFORT HERSELF.
FIRST THING'S FIRST-- MISAKA NEEDS TO PUT TOGETHER A REPORT FOR HIM...

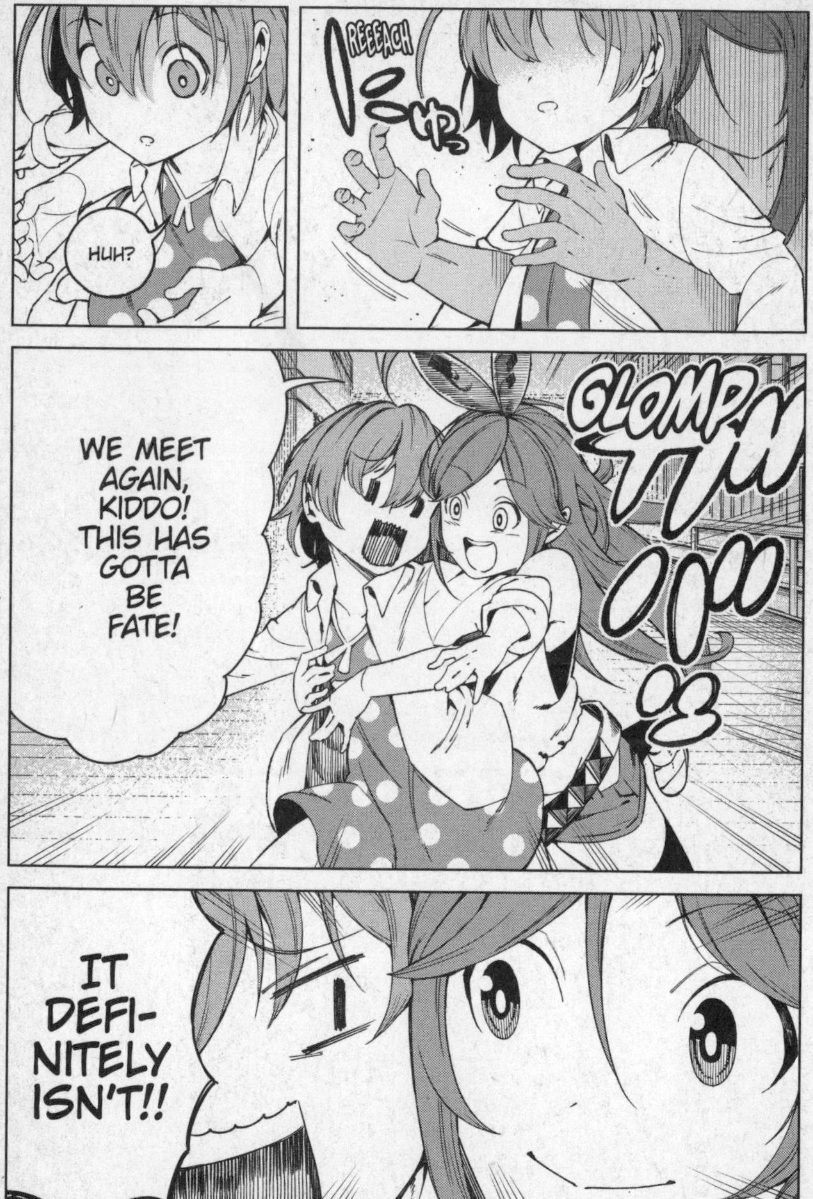
REEEACH
WE MEET AGAIN, KIDDO! THIS HAS GOTTA BE FATE!
HUH?
GLOMP
IT DEFINITELY ISN'T!!

To be continued...

SEVEN SEAS ENTERTAINMENT PRESENTS

a certain SCIENTIFIC ACCELERATOR
volume 8

story by KAZUMA KAMACHI / art by ARATA YAMAJI

TRANSLATION
Nan Rymer

ADAPTATION
Maggie Danger

LETTERING AND RETOUCH
Roland Amago
Bambi Eloriaga-Amago

COVER DESIGN
Nicky Lim

PROOFREADER
Shanti Whitesides
Janet Houck

ASSISTANT EDITOR
Jenn Grunigen

PRODUCTION ASSISTANT
CK Russell

PRODUCTION MANAGER
Lissa Pattillo

EDITOR-IN-CHIEF
Adam Arnold

PUBLISHER
Jason DeAngelis

A CERTAIN SCIENTIFIC ACCELERATOR VOL. 8
© KAZUMA KAMACHI/ARATA YAMAJI 2018
First published in 2018 by KADOKAWA CORPORATION, Tokyo.
English translation rights arranged with KADOKAWA CORPORATION, Tokyo.

Seven Seas books may be purchased in bulk for promotional, educational, or business use. Please contact your local bookseller or the Macmillan Corporate and Premium Sales Department at 1-800-221-7945, extension 5442, or by e-mail at MacmillanSpecialMarkets@macmillan.com.

Seven Seas and the Seven Seas logo are trademarks of Seven Seas Entertainment, LLC. All rights reserved.

ISBN: 978-1-626928-22-0

Printed in Canada

First Printing: December 2018

10 9 8 7 6 5 4 3 2 1

FOLLOW US ONLINE: *www.sevenseasentertainment.com*

READING DIRECTIONS

This book reads from *right to left*, Japanese style. If this is your first time reading manga, you start reading from the top right panel on each page and take it from there. If you get lost, just follow the numbered diagram here. It may seem backwards at first, but you'll get the hang of it! Have fun!!

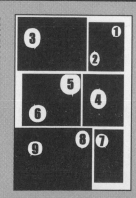

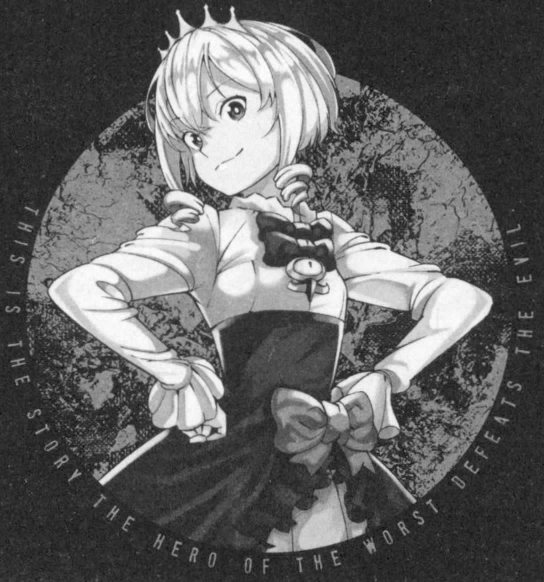
THIS IS THE STORY THE HERO OF THE WORST DEFEATS THE EVIL

A Certain Scientific ACCELERATOR

Story by Kazuma Kamachi
Art by Arata Yamaji
Character Design by
Kiyotaka Haimura & Arata Yamaji